I0114890

THE

PRINCIPLES

OF

POLITIC LAW:

BEING

A SEQUEL

TO THE

Principles of NATURAL LAW.

By *J. J. BURLAMAQUI*,
Counsellor of State, and late Professor of NATURAL and CIVIL LAW at GENEVA.

Translated into ENGLISH by Mr. NUGENT.

THE LAWBOOK EXCHANGE, LTD.
Clark, New Jersey

ISBN 978-1-58477-380-1

Lawbook Exchange edition 2004, 2019

The quality of this reprint is equivalent to the quality of the original work.

The Lawbook Exchange, Ltd.
33 Terminal Avenue
Clark, New Jersey 07066-1321

Please see our website for a selection of our other publications and fine facsimile reprints of classic works of legal history:
www.lawbookexchange.com

Library of Congress Cataloging-in-Publication Data

Burlamaqui, J. J. (Jean Jacques), 1694-1748.
[Principes du droit politique. English]
The principles of politic law: being a sequel to The principles of natural law / by J.J. Burlamaqui ; translated into English by Mr. Nugent.
p. cm.
Originally published: London: J. Nourse, 1752.
Includes bibliographical references.
ISBN 1-58477-380-4 (cloth: alk. paper)
1. Constitutional law—Early works to 1800. 2. Sovereignty—Early works to 1800. 3. Law and politics.—Early works to 1800. 4. Political science—Early works to 1800. I. Burlamaqui, J. J. (Jean Jacques), 1694-1748. Principes du droit naturel. English. II. Title.

K3165.B86513 2003
342—dc22 2003065670

Printed in the United States of America on acid-free paper

THE PRINCIPLES OF POLITIC LAW:

BEING

A SEQUEL

TO THE

Principles of NATURAL LAW.

By *J. J. BURLAMAQUI*,

Counſellor of State, and late Profeſſor of NATURAL and CIVIL LAW at GENEVA.

Tranſlated into ENGLISH by Mr. NUGENT.

LONDON,

Printed for J. NOURSE, oppoſite *Katherine Street* in the *Strand*. M.DCC.LII.

THE

CONTENTS.

PART I.

PART

CONTENTS.

PART II.

CHAP.

CONTENTS.

CHAP.

CONTENTS.

CONTENTS.

THE

THE

PRINCIPLES OF POLITIC LAW;

Being a SEQUEL to the

PRINCIPLES of the LAW of NATURE.

PART I.

Which treats of the original and nature of civil ſociety, of ſovereignty in general, of its peculiar character, limitations, and eſſential parts.

CHAP. I.

Containing ſome general and preliminary reflections, which ſerve as an introduction to this and the following parts.

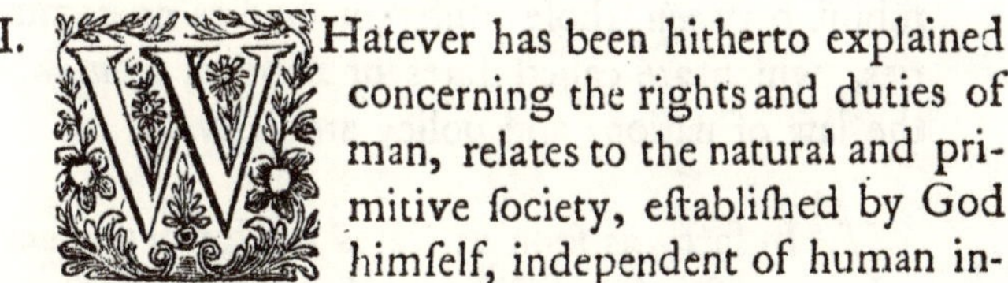

I. WHatever has been hitherto explained concerning the rights and duties of man, relates to the natural and primitive ſociety, eſtabliſhed by God himſelf, independent of human inſtitution: We muſt now treat of civil ſociety, or the body politic, which is deſervedly eſteemed the completeſt of ſocieties, and to which the name of *State* has been given by way of preference.

II. For this purpoſe we ſhall repeat here the ſubſtance of ſome principles eſtabliſhed in the preceding volume, and we ſhall give a further explication of others relative to this ſubject.

1°. Human ſociety is originally and in itſelf a ſtate of equality and independence.

2°. The inſtitution of ſovereignty deſtroys this independence.

3°. This inſtitution does not ſubvert natural ſociety.

4°. On the contrary, it contributes to ſtrengthen and cement it.

III. To form therefore a juſt idea of civil ſociety, we muſt call it natural ſociety itſelf, modified in ſuch a manner, that there is a ſovereign preſiding over it, on whoſe will whatever relates to the welfare of the ſociety ultimately depends, to the end that, by this means, mankind may attain, with greater certainty, that happineſs to which they all do naturally aſpire.

IV. The inſtitution of civil ſocieties produces ſome new relations amongſt mankind; I mean ſuch as ſubſiſt between thoſe different bodies or communities, which are called ſtates or nations, from whence the law of nations and policy are derived.

V. In fact, as ſoon as ſtates are formed, they acquire, in ſome meaſure, perſonal properties; and conſe-

consequently we may attribute the same rights and obligations to them, as are attributed to individuals, considered as members of human society. And indeed it is evident, that if reason imposes certain duties on individuals towards each other, it prescribes likewise those very same rules of conduct to nations, (which are composed only of men) in affairs relating to the intercourse which they may have with each other.

VI. We may therefore apply to kingdoms and nations the several maxims of natural law hitherto explained; and the same law, which is called natural, when speaking of individuals, is distinguished by the name of the law of nations, when applied to men, considered as members forming those different bodies, known by the name of states or nations.

VII. In order to enter into some particulars concerning this subject, we must observe, that the natural state of nations, with respect to each other, is that of society and peace. This society is likewise a state of equality and independence, which establishes between them an equality of right, by which they are obliged to have an equal regard for each other. The general principle therefore of the law of nations, is nothing more than the general law of sociability, which obliges nations to the same duties as are prescribed to individuals.

VIII. Thus the law of natural equality, that which prohibits our injuring any person, and commands the reparation of damage done, the law likewise of beneficence, of fidelity to our engagements, &c.

are ſo many laws in regard to nations, which impoſe both on the people and on their ſovereigns the ſame duties as they are productive of in regard to individuals.

IX. It is a point of ſome importance to attend to the nature and original of the law of nations, ſuch as has been here explained; for it follows from thence, that the maxims of the law of nations are of equal authority with the laws of nature itſelf, of which they conſtitute a part, and that they are equally ſacred and venerable, ſince both have God alike for their author.

X. There cannot even be any other law of nations really obligatory, and of itſelf inveſted with the force of a law. For ſince all nations are in reſpect to each other in a ſtate of perfect equality, it is beyond contradiction, that if there be any common law betwixt them, it muſt neceſſarily have God, their common ſovereign, for its author.

XI. As to what concerns the tacit conſent or cuſtoms of nations, on which ſome doctors eſtabliſh a law of nations, they cannot of themſelves produce a real obligation. For from this only, that ſeveral nations have behaved towards each other during a certain time after a certain manner, with regard to a particular affair, it does not follow that they have laid themſelves under a neceſſity of acting conſtantly ſo for the future, and much leſs that every other nation is obliged to conform to this cuſtom.

XII.

XII. All that can be ſaid is, that when once a particular uſage or cuſtom is introduced between nations that have a frequent intercourſe with each other, theſe nations are, and may reaſonably be, ſuppoſed to ſubmit to this uſage, unleſs they have, in expreſs terms, declared that they will not conform at preſent; and this is all the effect that can be attributed to the received uſages between nations.

XIII. This being premiſed, we may diſtinguiſh two ſorts of laws of nations, one of neceſſity, which is obligatory of itſelf, and no way differs from the law of nature; the other arbitrary and free, which is founded only on a kind of tacit convention; a convention that derives all its force from the law of nature, which commands us to be faithful to our engagements.

XIV. What we have been ſaying concerning the law of nations, furniſhes princes, by whom they are governed, with ſeveral important reflections; among others, that ſince the law of nations is, in reality, nothing elſe but the law of nature itſelf, there is but one and the ſame rule of juſtice for all mankind, inſomuch that thoſe princes who violate them are as guilty of as great a crime as private people, eſpecially as their bad actions are generally attended with more unhappy conſequences than thoſe of private people.

XV. Another conſequence that may be drawn from the principles we have eſtabliſhed relating to the law of nature and nations, is to form a juſt idea of that art ſo neceſſary to the directors of nations, which is called *Policy:* By policy therefore is meant that art, or ability by which a ſovereign provides for the preſervation, ſecurity, proſperity, and glory of the nation he governs, without doing any hurt to other people, but rather conſulting their advantage as much as poſſible.

XVI. In ſhort, that which is called prudence, in reſpect to private people, is diſtinguiſhed by the name of policy when applied to ſovereigns; and as that bad ability, by which a perſon ſeeks his own advantage to the prejudice of others, and which is called artifice or cunning, is deſerving of cenſure in individuals, it is equally ſo in thoſe princes, whoſe policy aims at procuring the advantage of their own nation, to the prejudice of what they owe to other people, in virtue of the laws of humanity and juſtice.

XVII. From what has been ſaid of the nature of civil ſociety in general, it is eaſy to comprehend that among all human inſtitutions, there is none more conſiderable than this; and that as it embraces whatever is intereſting to the happineſs of human ſociety, it is a very extenſive ſubject, and conſequently that it is important alike both to princes and people to have proper inſtructions upon this head.

XVIII. That we may reduce the ſeveral articles relative to this ſubject into ſome order, we ſhall divide our work into four parts.

The firſt will treat of the original and nature of civil ſocieties, of the manner in which ſtates are formed,

formed, of ſovereignty in general, of its proper characters, its limitations and eſſential parts.

In the ſecond we ſhall explain the different forms of government, the various ways of acquiring or loſing ſovereignty, and the reciprocal duties of ſovereigns and ſubjects.

The third will contain a more particular inquiry into the eſſential parts of ſovereignty which are relative to the internal adminiſtration of the ſtate, ſuch as the legiſlative power, the ſupreme power in reſpect to religion, the right of inflicting puniſhments, and that which the ſovereign has over the eſtates and effects contained in his dominions *&c.*

In the fourth, in fine, we ſhall explain the rights of ſovereigns with regard to foreigners, where we ſhall treat of the right of war, and of whatever is relative thereto, of alliances and other public treaties, and likewiſe of the rights of ambaſſadors.

CHAP. II.

Of the original of civil ſocieties in fact.

I. CIVIL ſociety is nothing more than the union of a multitude of people, who agree to live in ſubjection to a ſovereign, in order to find, thro' his protection and care, the happineſs to which they naturally aſpire.

II. Whenever the queſtion concerning the original of civil ſociety is ſtarted, it may be conſidered two different ways; for either I am aſked my opinion

 concern-

concerning the firſt original of governments in reality and fact; or elſe in regard to the right of conveniency in this reſpect, that is, what are the reaſons which ſhould induce mankind to renounce their natural liberty, and to prefer a civil ſtate to that of nature? Let us ſee firſt what can be ſaid in regard to the fact.

III. As the eſtabliſhment of ſociety and civil government is almoſt coeval with the world, and there are but very few records extant of thoſe firſt ages; nothing can be advanced with certainty concerning the firſt original of civil ſocieties. All that political writers ſay upon this ſubject, is reduced to conjectures that have more or leſs probability.

IV. Some attribute the original of civil ſocieties to paternal authority. Theſe obſerve that all the ancient traditions inform us, that the firſt men lived a long time; by this longevity, joined to the multiplicity of wives, which was then permitted, a great number of families ſaw themſelves united under the authority of one grand father; and as it is difficult that a ſociety, any thing numerous, can maintain itſelf without a ſupreme authority, it is natural to imagine that their children, accuſtomed from their infancy to reſpect and obey their fathers, voluntarily reſigned the ſupreme authority into their hands, as ſoon as they arrived to a full maturity of reaſon.

V. Others ſuppoſe that the fear and diffidence which mankind had of one another, was their inducement to unite together more particularly under a chief, in order to ſhelter themſelves from thoſe miſchiefs

miſchiefs which they apprehended. From the iniquity of the firſt men, ſay they, proceeded war, as alſo the neceſſity to which they were reduced of ſubmitting to maſters, by whom their rights and privileges might be determined.

VI. Some there are, in fine, who pretend that the firſt beginnings of civil ſocieties are to be attributed to ambition ſupported by force or abilities. The moſt dexterous, the ſtrongeſt and the moſt ambitious reduced at firſt the ſimpleſt and weakeſt into ſubjection; and theſe infant ſtates were afterwards inſenſibly ſtrengthened by conqueſts, and by the concurrence of ſuch as became voluntary members of thoſe primitive ſocieties.

VII. Such are the principal conjectures of political writers in regard to the original of ſocieties; to which let us add a few reflections.

The firſt is, that in the inſtitution of ſocieties, mankind in all probability thought rather of redreſſing the evils which they had experienced, than of procuring the ſeveral advantages reſulting from laws, from commerce, from the arts and ſciences, and from all thoſe other things in which the beauty of hiſtory conſiſts.

2°. The natural diſpoſition of mankind, and their general manner of acting, do not by any means permit us to refer the inſtitution of all goverments to a general and uniform principle. More natural it is to think that different circumſtances gave riſe to different ſtates.

3°. We

3°. We behold without doubt the first image of governments in democratic society, or in families; but there is all the probability in the world, that it was ambition supported by force or abilities which first subjected the several fathers of families under the dominion of a chief. This appears very agreeable to the natural disposition of mankind, and seems further supported by the manner in which the scripture speaks of Nimrod, * the first king mentioned in history.

4°. When such a body politic was once framed, several others joined themselves to it afterwards, thro' different motives; and other fathers of families being afraid of insults or oppression from those growing states, determined to form themselves into like societies, and to chuse to themselves a chief.

5°. Be this as it will, we must not imagine that those first states were such as exist in our days. Human institutions are always weak and imperfect in their beginnings, there is nothing but time and experience that can gradually bring them to perfection.

The first states were in all probability very small; Kings in those days were only a kind of chieftains, or particular magistrates, appointed for deciding disputes, or for the command of armies. Hence we find by the most ancient histories that there were sometimes several kings in one and the same nation.

VIII. But to conclude, whatever can be said in regard to the original of the first governments, is reducible, according to what we have already observed, to meer conjectures that have only more or

* See Genesis, c. x. ỷ. 8. & seq.

lefs probability. Befides, this is a queftion rather curious than ufeful or neceffary; the point of importance, and that which is particularly interefting to mankind, is to know whether the eftablifhment of a government, and of a fupreme authority, was really neceffary, and whether mankind derive from thence any confiderable advantages: This is what we call the right of conveniency, and what we are going now to examine.

CHAP. III.

Of the right of convenience with regard to the inftitution of civil fociety, and the neceffity of a fupreme authority; of civil liberty, that it is far preferable to natural liberty, and that the civil ftate is of all human ftates the moft perfect, the moft reafonable, and confequently the natural ftate of man.

I. WE are here to inquire, whether the eftablifhment of a civil fociety, and of a fupreme authority, was abfolutely neceffary to mankind, or whether they could not live happy without it? And whether fovereignty, whofe original is owing perhaps to ufurpation, ambition, and violence, does not include an attempt againft the natural equality and independency of man? Thefe are without doubt queftions of importance, and which merit to be examined with the utmoft attention.

II. I grant, at firſt ſetting out, that the primitive and original ſociety, which nature has eſtabliſhed amongſt mankind, is a ſtate of equality and independence; it is likewiſe true that the law of nature is that to which all men are obliged to conform their actions, and in fine it is certain, that this law is in itſelf moſt perfect, and the beſt adapted for the preſervation and happineſs of mankind.

III. It muſt likewiſe be granted, that if mankind, during the time they lived in natural ſociety, had exactly conformed to nature's laws, nothing would have been wanting to complete their happineſs, nor would there have been any occaſion to eſtabliſh a ſupreme authority upon earth. They would have lived in a mutual intercourſe of love and beneficence, in a ſimplicity without ſtate or pomp, in an equality without jealouſy, ſtrangers to all ſuperiority but that of virtue, and to every other ambition, than that of being diſintereſted and generous.

IV. But mankind were not long directed by ſo perfect a rule; the vivacity of their paſſions ſoon weakened the force of nature's law, which ceaſed now to be a bridle ſufficient for man, ſo that he could no longer be left to himſelf thus weaken'd and blinded by his paſſions. Let us explain this a little more particularly.

V. Laws are incapable of contributing to the happineſs of ſociety, unleſs they are ſufficiently known. The laws of nature cannot be known to man but inaſmuch as he makes a right uſe of his reaſon; but as the greateſt part of mankind, abandoned to themſelves, liſten rather to the prejudices of paſſion than to reaſon and truth, it thence follows, that in the ſtate of natural ſociety, the laws of nature were known but very imperfectly, and conſequently that in this ſtate of things man could not live happily.

VI. Beſides, the ſtate of nature wanted another thing neceſſary for the happineſs and tranquillity of ſociety, I mean a common judge acknowledged as ſuch, whoſe buſineſs it would be to decide the differences that might every day ariſe betwixt individuals.

VII. In this ſtate as every one would be ſupreme arbiter of his own actions, and would have a right of being judge himſelf, both of the laws of nature and of the manner in which he ought to apply them, this independence and exceſſive liberty could not but be productive of diſorder and confuſion, eſpecially in caſes where there happened to be any claſhing of intereſts or paſſions.

VIII. In fine, as in the ſtate of nature no one had a power of enforcing the execution of the laws, nor an authority to puniſh the violation of them, this was a third inconveniency of the ſtate of primitive ſociety, by which the virtue of natural laws was almoſt intirely deſtroyed. For as men are framed, the laws derive their greateſt force from the coercive power, which, by exemplary puniſhments, intimidates the wicked, and balances the ſuperior force of pleaſure and paſſion.

IX. Such were the inconveniences that attended the ſtate of nature. By the exceſſive liberty and independence

pendence which mankind enjoyed, they were hurried into perpetual troubles; for which reaſon they were under an abſolute neceſſity of quitting this ſtate of independence, and of ſeeking a remedy againſt the evils of which it was productive, and this remedy they found in the eſtabliſhment of civil ſociety and a ſovereign authority.

X. But this could not be effected without doing two things equally neceſſary; the firſt was to unite together by means of a more particular ſociety; the ſecond to form this ſociety under the dependence of a perſon who was to be inveſted with an uncontrolable power, to the end that he might maintain order and peace.

XI. By this means they remedied the inconveniences abovementioned. The ſovereign, by publiſhing his laws, acquaints private people with the rules which they ought to follow. Each man is no longer independent judge in his own cauſe, our whims and paſſions are checked, and we are obliged to contain ourſelves within the limits of that regard and reſpect which we owe to each other.

XII. This might be ſufficient to prove the neceſſity of a government, and of a ſupreme authority in ſociety, and to eſtabliſh the right of convenience in this reſpect. But as it is a queſtion of the utmoſt importance, as mankind have a particular intereſt in being well acquainted with their ſtate, as they have a natural paſſion for independence, and as they generally frame falſe notions of liberty; it will not be improper

to

to carry our reflections on this ſubject ſomewhat further.

XIII. Let us therefore ſee what is natural, and what is civil, liberty; let us afterwards endeavour to ſhew, that civil liberty is far preferable to that of nature, and conſequently that the civil ſtate which it produces, is of all human ſtates the moſt perfect, and, to ſpeak with exactneſs, the true natural ſtate of man.

XIV. The reflections we have to make upon this ſubject are of the laſt importance, affording uſeful leſſons both to princes who govern, and to the people who are governed. The greateſt part of mankind are ſtrangers to the advantages of civil ſociety, or at leaſt they live in ſuch a manner, as to give no attention to the beauty or excellence of this ſalutary inſtitution. On the other hand, princes often loſe ſight of the end for which they were appointed, and inſtead of thinking that the ſupreme authority was eſtabliſhed for no other purpoſe than for the maintenance and ſecurity of the liberty of mankind, that is, to make them enjoy a ſolid happineſs, they frequently direct it to quite contrary ends, and to their own private advantage. Nothing therefore is more neceſſary than to remove the prejudices both of ſovereigns and ſubjects in this reſpect.

XV. Natural liberty is the right which nature gives to all mankind, of diſpoſing of their perſons and property, after the manner they judge moſt convenient to their happineſs, on condition of their acting

ing within the limits of the law of nature, and that they do not any way abuſe it to the prejudice of other men. To this right of liberty there is a reciprocal obligation correſponding, by which the law of nature binds all mankind to reſpect the liberty of other men, and not to diſturb them in the uſe they make of it, as long as they do not abuſe it.

XVI. The laws of nature are therefore the rule and meaſure of liberty; and in the primitive and natural ſtate, mankind have no liberty but what the laws of nature give them; for which reaſon it is proper to obſerve here, that the ſtate of natural liberty is not that of an intire independence. In this ſtate, men are indeed independent with regard to one another, but they are all in a ſtate of dependence on God and his laws. Independence, generally ſpeaking, is a ſtate unſuitable to man, becauſe by his very nature he holds of a ſuperior.

XVII. Liberty and independence of any ſuperior, are two very diſtinct things, which muſt not be confounded. The firſt belongs eſſentially to man, the other cannot ſuit him. And ſo far is it from being true, that human liberty is of itſelf inconſiſtent with dependence on a ſovereign and ſubmiſſion to his laws, that on the contrary 'tis this power of the ſovereign, and the protection which men derive from thence, that forms the greateſt ſecurity of their liberty.

XVIII. This will be ſtill better underſtood by recollecting what we have already ſettled, when ſpeak-

ſpeaking of natural liberty. We have ſhewn that the reſtrictions which the law of nature makes to the liberty of man, far from diminiſhing or ſubverting it, on the contrary conſtitutes its perfection and ſecurity. The end of natural laws is not ſo much to reſtrain the liberty of man, as to make him act agreeably to his real intereſts; and moreover as theſe very laws are a check to human liberty, in whatever may be of pernicious conſequence to others, it ſecures, by this means, to all mankind, the higheſt, and the moſt advantageous degree of liberty they can reaſonably deſire.

XIX. We may therefore conclude, that in the ſtate of nature, man could not enjoy all the advantages of liberty, but inaſmuch as this liberty was made ſubject to reaſon, and the laws of nature were the rule and meaſure of the exerciſe of it. But if it be true in fact, that the ſtate of nature was attended with all the inconveniences already mentioned, inconveniences which almoſt effaced the impreſſion and force of natural laws, it muſt be granted, that natural liberty muſt have greatly ſuffered thereby, and that by not being reſtrained within the limits of the law of nature, it could not but degenerate into licentiouſneſs, and reduce mankind to the moſt frightful, the moſt melancholy of ſituations.

XX. As they were perpetually divided by contentions, the ſtrongeſt oppreſſed the weakeſt; they poſſeſſed nothing with tranquillity; they enjoyed no repoſe: and what we ought particularly to obſerve, is, that all theſe evils were owing chiefly to that very

inde-

independence which mankind were poſſeſſed of in regard to each other, which deprived them of all ſecurity of the exerciſe of their liberty; inſomuch that by being too free, they enjoyed no freedom at all, for freedom there can be none, when it is not ſubject to the direction of laws.

XXI. If it be therefore true, that the civil ſtate gives a new force to the laws of nature, if it be true, that the eſtabliſhment of a ſovereign in ſociety ſecures, in a more effectual manner, the obſervance of thoſe laws, we muſt conclude, that the liberty, which man enjoys in this ſtate, is far more perfect, more ſecure, and better adapted to procure his happineſs, than that which he was poſſeſſed of in the ſtate of nature.

XXII. True it is that the inſtitution of government and ſovereignty is a conſiderable limitation to natural liberty, for man muſt renounce that arbitrary diſpoſal which he had of his own perſon and actions, in a word, his independence. But what better uſe could mankind make of their liberty, than to renounce every dangerous tendency it had in regard to themſelves, and to preſerve no more of it than was neceſſary to procure their own real and ſolid happineſs.

XXIII. Civil liberty is therefore, in the main, nothing more than natural liberty, diveſted of that part of it which formed the independence of individuals, by the authority which they have conferred on their ſovereign.

XXIV. This liberty is ſtill attended with two conſiderable advantages, which natural liberty had not. The firſt is, the right of inſiſting that their ſovereign ſhall make a good uſe of his authority, agreeably to the purpoſes for which he was intruſted with it. The ſecond is, the ſecurity which prudence requires that the people ſhould reſerve to themſelves for the execution of the former right, a ſecurity abſolutely neceſſary, and without which the people can never enjoy any ſolid liberty.

XXV. Let us therefore conclude, that to give an adequate definition of civil liberty, we muſt ſay, that it is natural liberty itſelf, diveſted of that part, which conſtituted the independence of individuals, by the authority which it confers on ſovereigns, attended with a right of inſiſting on his making a good uſe of his authority, and with a moral ſecurity that this right will have its effect.

XXVI. Since civil liberty therefore is far preferable to that of nature, we have a right to conclude, that the civil ſtate, which procures this liberty to mankind, is of all human ſtates the moſt perfect, the moſt reaſonable, and of courſe the true natural ſtate of man.

XXVII. In effect, ſince man, by his nature, is a free and intelligent being, capable of diſcovering his ſtate by himſelf, as well as its ultimate end, and of taking the neceſſary meaſures to attain it, it is properly in this point of view that we muſt take his natural ſtate; that is, the natural ſtate of man muſt be that, which is moſt agreeable to his nature, to his conſtitution, to reaſon, to the good uſe of his faculties, and to his laſt end; all which circumſtances perfectly agree with the civil ſtate. In ſhort, as the inſtitution of a government and ſupreme authority brings men back to the obſervance of the laws of nature, and conſequently to the road of happineſs, it makes them return to their natural ſtate, from whence they had ſtrayed by the bad uſe which they made of their liberty.

XXVIII. The reflections we have here made on the advantages which men derive from government, deſerve very great attention.

1°. They are extremely proper for removing the falſe notions which men generally have upon this ſubject; as if the civil ſtate could not be eſtabliſhed but in prejudice to their natural liberty, and as if government had been invented only to ſatisfy the moſt conſiderable and leading men amongſt them, contrary to the intereſt of the reſt of the community.

2°. They inſpire mankind with a love and reſpect for ſo ſalutary an inſtitution, diſpoſing them thus to ſubmit voluntarily to whatever the civil ſociety requires of them, from a conviction that the advantages from thence derived are very conſiderable.

3°. They may likewiſe contribute greatly to the increaſe of the love of one's country, the firſt ſeeds of which nature herſelf has implanted, as it were, in the hearts of all mankind, in order to promote, as it moſt effectually does, the happineſs of ſociety. *Sextus Empiricus* relates, "that it was a cuſtom among "the ancient *Perſians*, upon the death of a king, "to "to paſs five days in a ſtate of anarchy, as an inducement to be more faithful to his ſucceſſor, "from the experience they themſelves had had of "the inconveniences of anarchy, of the many murders, robberies, and every other miſchief, with "which it is attended *.

XXIX. If theſe reflections are proper for removing the prejudices of private people, they likewiſe contain moſt excellent inſtructions even for ſovereigns. For is there any thing better adapted for making princes ſenſible of the full extent of their duty, than to reflect ſeriouſly on the ends which the people propoſed to themſelves when they intruſted them with their liberty, that is, with whatever is moſt valuable to them; and on the engagements into which they entered, by charging themſelves with ſo ſacred a depoſit? If mankind renounced their independence and natural liberty, by giving maſters to themſelves, it was in order to be ſheltered from the evils with which they were afflicted, and in hopes, that under the protection and care of their ſovereign, they ſhould meet with ſolid happineſs. Thus we have ſeen, that by civil liberty mankind acquired a right of inſiſting upon their ſovereign's uſing his authority agreeably to the views with which he was entruſted with it, that is, to render their ſubjects wiſe and virtuous, and to promote, by this means, their real felicity. In a word, whatever has been ſaid concerning the advantages of the civil ſtate preferably to that of nature, ſuppoſes that

* Adverſ. Mathemat. lib. 2. §. 33. Vid. Herodot. lib. 1. cap. 96, & ſeq.

this ſtate is ſuch as it may, and ought to be; and that both ſubjects and ſovereign diſcharge their reciprocal duties towards each other.

CHAP. IV.

Of the eſſential conſtitution of ſtates, and of the manner in which they are formed.

I. AFTER treating of the original of civil ſocieties, the natural order of our ſubject leads us to examine into the eſſential conſtitution of ſtates, that is, into the manner in which they are formed, and the conſtruction of thoſe ſurprizing edifices.

II. From what has been ſaid in the preceding chapter it follows, that the only effectual method which mankind could employ in order to ſhelter themſelves from the evils with which they were afflicted in the ſtate of nature, and to procure to themſelves all the advantages that were wanting to their ſecurity and happineſs, muſt be drawn from man himſelf, and from the aſſiſtance of ſociety.

III. For this purpoſe, it was neceſſary that a multitude of people ſhould unite in ſo particular a manner, that their preſervation muſt depend on each other, to the end that they ſhould be under a neceſſity of a mutual aſſiſtance, and by this junction of ſtrength and intereſts, they might be able to repel, with eaſe, the inſults againſt which each individual could

could not be guarded, to contain thoſe within duty who ſhould attempt to deviate from it, and to promote, more effectually, their common advantage. Let us explain more particularly how this could be effected.

IV. Two things were neceſſary for this purpoſe.

1°. It was neceſſary to unite for ever the wills of all the members of the ſociety, in ſuch a manner that from that time forward they ſhould never deſire but one and the ſame thing in whatever relates to the end and purpoſe of ſociety. It was neceſſary afterwards to eſtabliſh a ſupreme power ſupported by the ſtrength of the whole body, by which means they might intimidate thoſe who ſhould be inclinable to diſturb the peace, and to inflict a preſent and ſenſible evil on ſuch as ſhould attempt to act contrary to the common utility.

V. 'Tis from this union of wills and of ſtrength, that the body politic or ſtate reſults, and without it we could never conceive a civil ſociety. For let the number of confederates be ever ſo great, if each man was to follow his own private judgment in things relating to the public good, they would only embarraſs one another, and the diverſity of inclinations and judgments, ariſing from the levity and natural inconſtancy of man, would ſoon demoliſh all concord, and mankind would thus relapſe into the inconveniences of the ſtate of nature. Beſides, a ſociety of that kind could never act a long time in concert, and for the ſame end, nor maintain itſelf in that harmony which conſtitutes its whole ſtrength, without a ſuperior power who is to ſerve as a check to the inconſtancy and malice of man, and to oblige each individual to direct all his actions to the public utility.

VI. All this is performed by means of covenants; for this union of wills in one and the ſame perſon could never be ſo effected as to actually deſtroy the natural diverſity of inclinations and ſentiments; but it is done by an engagement which every man enters into, of ſubmitting his private will to that of a ſingle perſon, or of an aſſembly; inſomuch that every reſolution of this perſon or aſſembly, concerning things relative to the public ſecurity or advantage, muſt be conſidered as the poſitive will of all in general, and of each in particular.

VII. With regard to the union of ſtrength, which produces the ſovereign power, it is not formed by each man's communicating phyſically his ſtrength to a ſingle perſon, ſo as to remain utterly weak and impotent; but by a covenant or engagement, whereby all in general, and each in particular, oblige themſelves to make no uſe of their ſtrength, but in ſuch a manner as ſhall be preſcribed to them by the perſon on whom they have, with one common accord, conferred the ſupreme authority.

VIII. By this union of the body politic, under one and the ſame chief, each individual acquires, in ſome meaſure, as much ſtrength as the whole ſociety united. Suppoſe, for inſtance, there are a million of men in the commonwealth, each man is able to reſiſt this million, by means of their ſubjection to the ſovereign

reign power, who keeps them all in awe, and hinders them from hurting one another. This multiplication of ſtrength in the body politic reſembles that of each member in the human body; take them aſunder, and their vigor is no more, but by their mutual union the ſtrength of each increaſes, and they form, all together, a robuſt and animated body.

IX. The ſtate may be defined, a ſociety by which a multitude of people unite together, under the dependence of a ſovereign, in order to find, thro' his protection and care, the happineſs to which they naturally aſpire. The definition which *Tully* gives, amounts pretty near to the ſame. *Multitudo juris conſenſu, & utilitatis communione ſociata.* A multitude of people united together by a communion of intereſt, and by common laws, to which they ſubmit with one accord.

X. The ſtate is therefore conſidered as a body, or as a moral perſon, of which the ſovereign is the chief or head, and the ſubjects are the members; in conſequence of which we attribute to this perſon certain actions peculiar to him, certain rights, privileges, and poſſeſſions, diſtinct from thoſe of each citizen, and to which neither each citizen, nor many, nor even all together can pretend, but only the ſovereign.

XI. 'Tis moreover this union of ſeveral perſons in one body, produced by the concurrence of the wills and the ſtrength of every individual in one and the ſame perſon, that diſtinguiſhes the ſtate from a multitude. For a multitude is only an aſſemblage of ſeveral perſons, each

each of whom has his own private will, with the liberty of judging according to his own notions of whatever is proposed to him, and of determining as he pleases; for which reason they cannot be said to have only one will. Whereas the state is a body, or a society, animated by one only soul, which directs all its motions, and makes all its members act after a constant and uniform manner, with a view to one and the same end, namely, the public utility.

XII. But it will be here objected, that if the union of the will and of the strength of each member of the society, in the person of the sovereign, destroys neither the will, nor the natural force of each individual, if they always continue in possession of it, and if they are able, in fact, to employ it against the sovereign himself, what does the force of the state consist in, and what is it that constitutes the security of this society? I answer, that two things contribute chiefly to maintain the state, and the sovereign, who is the soul of it.

The first is, the engagement itself, by which individuals have subjected themselves to the command of a sovereign, an engagement which derives a considerable force both from divine authority, and from the religion of an oath. But as to vicious and ill disposed minds, on whom these motives make no impression, the strength of the government consists chiefly in the fear of those punishments which the sovereign may inflict upon them, by virtue of the power with which he is invested.

XIII. Now ſince the means, by which the ſovereign is enabled to compel rebellious and refractory ſpirits to their duty, conſiſts in this, that the reſt of the ſubjects join their ſtrength with him for this end (for, were it not for this, he would have no more power than the loweſt of his ſubjects) it follows from thence, that 'tis the ready ſubmiſſion of good ſubjects that furniſhes the ſovereign with the means of repreſſing the inſolent, and of maintaining his authority.

XIV. But provided a ſovereign ſhews never ſo ſmall an attachment to his duty, he will always find it eaſy to fix the better part of his ſubjects in his intereſt, and of courſe to have the greateſt part of the ſtrength of the ſtate in his hands, and to maintain the authority of the government. Experience has always ſhewn that princes need only to have a common ſhare of virtue to be adored by their ſubjects. We may therefore affirm, that the ſovereign is capable of deriving from himſelf the means neceſſary for the ſupport of his authority, and that a prudent exerciſe of the ſovereignty purſuant to the end for which it was deſigned, conſtitutes at the ſame time the happineſs of the people, and by a neceſſary conſequence the greateſt ſecurity of the government in the perſon of the ſovereign.

XV. By following the principles here eſtabliſhed concerning the manner in which ſtates are formed, &c. if we ſuppoſe that a multitude of people, who had lived hitherto independent of each other, wanted to eſtabliſh a civil ſociety, there is a neceſſity for different covenants, and for a general decree.

1°. The firſt covenant is that by which each individual engages with all the reſt to join for ever in one body, and to regulate, with one common conſent, whatever regards their preſervation and their common ſecurity. Thoſe who do not enter into this firſt engagement, remain excluded from the new ſociety.

2°. There muſt afterwards be a decree made for ſettling the form of government; otherwiſe they could never take any fixt meaſures for promoting, effectually and in concert, the public ſecurity and welfare.

3°. In fine, when once the form of government is ſettled, there muſt be another covenant, whereby after having pitched upon one or more perſons to be inveſted with the power of governing, thoſe on whom this ſupreme authority is conferred, engage to conſult moſt carefully the common ſecurity and advantage, and the others promiſe fidelity and allegiance to the ſovereign. This laſt covenant includes a ſubmiſſion of the ſtrength and will of each individual to the will of the head of the ſociety, as far as the public good requires; and thus it is that a regular ſtate and perfect government is formed.

XVI. What we have hitherto delivered may be further illuſtrated by the account we have in hiſtory concerning the foundation of the *Roman* ſtate. At firſt we behold a multitude of people, who flock together with a view of ſettling on the banks of the *Tiber*; afterwards they conſult about what form of government they ſhall eſtabliſh, and the party for monarchy prevailing, they confer the ſupreme authority on *Romulus* *.

XVII. And tho' we are ſtrangers to the original of moſt ſtates, yet we muſt not imagine that what has been here ſaid, concerning the manner in which civil ſocieties are formed, is an arbitrary fiction. For ſince it is certain, that all civil ſocieties had a beginning, it is impoſſible to conceive, how the members, of which they are compoſed, could unite to live together dependent on a ſupreme authority, without ſuppoſing the covenants abovementioned.

XVIII. And yet all political writers do not explain the generation of ſtates after our manner. Some there are † who pretend, that ſtates are formed merely by the covenant of the ſubjects with one another, by which each man enters into an engagement with all the reſt not to reſiſt the will of the ſovereign, upon condition that the reſt on their ſide ſubmit to the ſame engagement; but they pretend that there is no original compact between the ſovereign and the ſubjects.

XIX. The reaſon why theſe writers give this explication of the matter, is obvious. Their deſign is to give an arbitrary and unlimited authority to ſovereigns, and to deprive the ſubjects of every means of withdrawing their allegiance upon any pretext whatever, notwithſtanding any uſe the ſovereign may

* See Dionyſius Halicarn. lib. 2. in the beginning.

† A. Hobbes, de Cive, cap. v. §. 7.

make

make of his authority. For this purpose it was absolutely necessary to free kings from all restraint of compact or covenant between them and their subjects, which, without doubt, is the chief instrument of limiting their power.

XX. But notwithstanding it is of the utmost importance to mankind, to support the authority of kings, and to defend it against the attempts of restless or mutinous spirits, yet we must not deny evident truths, or refuse to acknowledge a covenant, in which there is manifestly a mutual promise, of performing things to which they were not before obliged.

XXI. When I submit voluntarily to a prince, I promise him allegiance, on condition that he will protect me; the prince on his side promises me his protection, on condition that I will obey him. Before this promise, I was not obliged to obey him, nor was he obliged to protect me, at least by any *perfect* obligation; it is therefore evident, that there must be a mutual engagement.

XXII. But there is still something more; for so far is the system we are here refuting, from strengthening the supreme authority, and from screening it from the capricious invasions of the subject, that, on the contrary, nothing is of a more dangerous consequence to sovereigns, than to fix their right on such a foundation. For if the obligation of the subjects towards their princes is founded merely on the mutual covenant between the subjects, by which each

man

man engages for the ſake of the reſt to obey the ſovereign, on condition that the reſt do the ſame for his ſake; it is evident, that at this rate every ſubject makes the force of his engagement depend on the execution of that of every other fellow-ſubject; and conſequently if any one refuſes to obey the ſovereign, all the reſt ſtand releaſed from their allegiance. Thus by endeavouring to puſh the rights of ſovereigns beyond their juſt limits, inſtead of ſtrengthening, they rather inadvertently weaken them.

CHAP. V.

Of the ſovereign, ſovereignty, and the ſubjects.

I. THE ſovereign in a ſtate, is that perſon who has a right of commanding finally.

II. As to the ſovereignty we muſt define it, the right of commanding finally in civil ſociety, which right the members of this ſociety have conferred on one and the ſame perſon, to preſerve order and ſecurity in the commonwealth, and, in general, to procure, under his protection and thro' his care, real felicity, and eſpecially the ſure exerciſe of their liberty.

III. I ſay, in the firſt place, that ſovereignty is the right of commanding finally in ſociety, to ſhew that the nature of ſovereignty conſiſts chiefly in two things.

The

The firſt is, the right of commanding the members of the ſociety, that is, of directing their actions with authority, or with a power of compelling.

The ſecond is, that this right ought to be that of commanding finally in ſuch a manner, that every private perſon be obliged to ſubmit to it, without a power left to any man of reſiſting it. Otherwiſe, if this authority was not ſuperior to every other upon earth, it could eſtabliſh no order or ſecurity in the commonwealth, tho' theſe are the ends for which it was eſtabliſhed.

IV. In the ſecond place, I ſay, that it is a right conferred upon a perſon, and not upon a man, to give to underſtand that this perſon may be, not only a ſingle man, but likewiſe, and intirely as well, a multitude of men, united in council, and forming only one will, by means of a plurality of ſuffrages, as we ſhall more particularly explain hereafter.

V. Thirdly, I ſay, to one and the ſame perſon, to ſhew that ſovereignty can admit of no ſhare or partition, that there is no ſovereign at all when there are many, becauſe there is no one who commands finally, and none of them being obliged to give way to the other, their competition muſt neceſſarily throw every thing into diſorder and confuſion.

VI. I add, in fine, to procure real felicity *&c.* in order to point out the end of ſovereignty, that is, the happineſs of the people. When ſovereigns once loſe

lose sight of this end, when they pervert it to their private interests, or caprices, sovereignty then degenerates into tyranny, and ceases to be a legitimate authority. Such is the idea we ought to form of a sovereign and of sovereignty.

VII. All the other members of the state, are called subjects, that is, they are under an obligation of obeying the sovereign.

VIII. Now a person becomes a member or subject of a state, two ways, either by an express, or by a tacit, covenant.

IX. If, by an express covenant, the thing admits of no difficulty. But with regard to a tacit covenant, we must observe that the first founders of states, and all those who afterwards became members thereof, are supposed to have stipulated, that their children and descendants should, at their coming into the world, have the right of enjoying those advantages which are common to all the members of the state, provided nevertheless that these descendants, when they attain to the use of reason, be on their side willing to submit to the government, and to acknowledge the authority of the sovereign.

X. I said, provided the descendants acknowledged the authority of the sovereign; for the stipulation of the parents cannot, of itself, have the force of subjecting the children against their will to an authority, to which they would not of themselves chuse to submit: Hence the authority of the sovereign over the

 children

children of the members of the ſtate, and the right on the other hand which theſe children have to the protection of the ſovereign, and to the advantages of the government, are founded on mutual conſent.

XI. Now if the children of members of the ſtate, upon attaining to the years of diſcretion, are willing to live in the place of their parentage, or in their native country, they are by this very act ſuppoſed to ſubmit themſelves to the power that governs the ſtate, and conſequently they ought to enjoy, as members of the ſtate, the advantages naturally ariſing from it. This is the reaſon likewiſe, that when once the ſovereign is acknowledged, he has no occaſion to tender the oath of allegiance to the children, who are afterwards born in his dominions.

XII. Beſides, it is a maxim which has been always conſidered as a general law of governments, that whoſoever merely enters upon the territories of a ſtate, and by a much ſtronger reaſon, thoſe who are deſirous of enjoying the advantages which are to be found there, are ſuppoſed to renounce their natural liberty, and to ſubmit to the eſtabliſhed laws and government, as far at leaſt as the public and private ſafety requires. And if they refuſe to do this, they may be conſidered as enemies, ſo far at leaſt as that the government has a right to expel them the country; and this is likewiſe a tacit covenant, by which they make a temporary ſubmiſſion to the government.

XIII. Subjects are ſometimes called *cives*, or members

bers of the civil ſtate; ſome indeed make no diſtinction between theſe two terms, but I think it is better to diſtinguiſh them. The appellation of *civis* ought to be underſtood only of thoſe who ſhare in all the advantages, and privileges of the aſſociation, and who are properly members of the ſtate, either by birth, or in ſome other manner. All the reſt are rather inmates, ſtrangers, or temporary inhabitants, than members. As to women and ſervants, the title of member is applicable to them only inaſmuch as they enjoy certain rights, in virtue of their dependence on their domeſtical governor, who is properly a member of the ſtate; and all this depends in general on the laws and particular cuſtoms of each government.

XIV. To proceed; members, beſides the general relation of being united in the ſame civil ſociety, have likewiſe many other particular relations, which are all reducible to two principal ones.

The firſt is, when private people compoſe particular bodies or corporations.

The ſecond is, when ſovereigns entruſt particular perſons with ſome part of the government.

XV. Thoſe particular bodies are called, *Companies*, *Chambers*, *Colléges*, *Societies*, *Communities*. But it is to be obſerved, that all theſe particular ſocieties are finally ſubordinate to the ſovereign.

XVI. Beſides, we may conſider ſome as more ancient than the eſtabliſhment of civil ſtates, and others as formed ſince.

 XVII,

XVII. The latter are likewiſe either public, ſuch as are eſtabliſhed by the authority of the ſovereign, and then they generally enjoy ſome particular privileges, agreeably to their patents: or private, ſuch as are formed by private people.

XVIII. In fine, theſe private bodies are either lawful or unlawful. The former are thoſe, which, having nothing in their nature, contrary to good order, good manners, or to the authority of the ſovereign, are ſuppoſed to be approved of by the ſtate, tho' they have not received any formal ſanction. With reſpect to unlawful bodies, we mean not only thoſe whoſe members unite for the open commiſſion of any crime, ſuch as gangs of robbers, thieves, pirates, banditti, but likewiſe all other kinds of confederacy, which the ſubjects enter into, without the conſent of the ſovereign, and are contrary to the end of civil ſociety. Theſe engagements are called cabals, factions, conſpiracies.

XIX. Thoſe members whom the ſovereign entruſts with ſome part of the government, which they exerciſe in his name and by his authority, have in conſequence thereof particular relations to the reſt of the members, and are under ſtronger engagements to the ſovereign; theſe are called miniſters, public officers, or magiſtrates.

XX. Such are the regents of a kingdom, during a minority, the governours of provinces and towns, the commanders of armies, the directors of the treaſury, the preſidents of courts of juſtice, ambaſſa-

dors,

dors, or envoys to foreign powers, &c. As all theſe perſons are entruſted with a part of the government, they repreſent the ſovereign, and 'tis they that have properly the name of public miniſters.

XXI. Others there are, who aſſiſt merely in the execution of public buſineſs, ſuch as counſellors, who only give their opinion, ſecretaries, receivers of the public revenue, ſoldiers, ſubaltern officers, &c.

CHAP. VI.

Of the immediate ſource, and foundation of ſovereignty.

I. THO' what has been ſaid in the fourth chapter concerning the ſtructure of ſtates, is ſufficient to ſhew the original and ſource of ſovereignty, as well as its real foundation; yet as this is one of thoſe queſtions on which political writers are greatly divided, it will not be amiſs to examine it ſomewhat more particularly, and what remains ſtill to be ſaid upon this ſubject, will help to give us a more complete idea of the nature and end of ſovereignty.

II. When we inquire here into the ſource of ſovereignty, our intent is to know the neareſt and immediate ſource of it; now it is certain, that the ſupreme authority, as well as the title on which this power is eſtabliſhed, and which conſtitutes its right, is is derived immediately from the very covenants which conſtitute civil ſociety, and give birth to government.

III. And in fact, upon conſidering the primitive ſtate of man, it appears moſt certain, that the appellations of ſovereigns and ſubjects, maſters and ſlaves, are unknown to nature. Nature has made us all of the ſame ſpecies, all equal, all free and independent of each other; and was willing that thoſe, on whom ſhe has beſtowed the ſame faculties, ſhould have all the ſame rights. It is therefore beyond all doubt that in this primitive ſtate of nature, no man has of himſelf an original right of commanding others, or any title to ſovereignty.

IV. There is none but God alone that has of himſelf, and in conſequence of his nature and perfections, a natural, eſſential, and inherent right of giving laws to mankind, and of exerciſing an abſolute ſovereignty over them. The caſe is otherwiſe between man and man, they are of their own nature as independent of one another, as they are dependent of God. This liberty and independence is therefore a right naturally belonging to man, of which it would be unjuſt to deprive him againſt his will.

V. But if this be the caſe, and there is yet a ſupreme authority ſubſiſting amongſt mankind, whence can this authority ariſe, unleſs it be from the compacts or covenants, which men have made amongſt themſelves upon this ſubject? For as we have a right of transferring our property to another by a covenant, ſo, ſo, by a voluntary ſubmiſſion, a perſon may convey to another, who accepts of the renunciation, the natural right he had of diſpoſing intirely of his liberty and natural ſtrength.

VI. It muſt therefore be agreed, that ſovereignty reſides originally in the people, and in each individual with regard to himſelf; and that it is the transferring and uniting the ſeveral rights of individuals in the perſon of the ſovereign, that conſtitutes him ſuch, and really produces ſovereignty. It is beyond all diſpute, for example, that when the *Romans* choſe *Romulus* and *Numa* for their kings, they muſt have conferred upon them, by this very act, the ſovereignty, which thoſe princes were not poſſeſſed of before, and to which they had certainly no other right but what was derived from the election of the people.

VII. Nevertheleſs, tho' it be evident to the laſt degree, that the immediate original of ſovereignty is owing to human covenants, yet nothing can hinder us from ſaying, with good grounds, that it is of divine as well as human right.

VIII. In fact, right reaſon having made it plainly appear, after the multiplication of mankind, that the eſtabliſhment of civil ſocieties and of a ſupreme authority, was abſolutely neceſſary for the order, tranquillity, and preſervation of the ſpecies, it is as convincing a proof that this eſtabliſhment is agreeable to the deſigns of Providence, as if God himſelf had declared it to mankind by a poſitive revelation. And ſince God is eſſentially fond of order, he is doubtleſs willing that there ſhould be a ſupreme authority upon earth, which alone is capable of procuring and ſupporting it amongſt mankind, by enforcing the obſervance of the laws of nature.

IX. There is a beautiful paſſage of *Cicero*'s to this purpoſe *. *Nothing is more agreeable to the ſupreme Deity, that governs this univerſe, than civil ſocieties lawfully eſtabliſhed.*

X. When therefore we give to ſovereigns the title of God's vicegerents upon earth, this does not imply that they derive their authority immediately from God, but it ſignifies only, that by means of the power lodged in their hands, and with which the people have inveſted them, they maintain, agreeably to the views of the Deity, both order and peace, and thus procure the happineſs of mankind.

XI. But if theſe magnificent titles add a conſiderable luſtre to ſovereignty, and render it more reſpectable, they afford likewiſe, at the ſame time, an excellent leſſon to princes. For they cannot deſerve the title of God's vicegerents upon earth, but inaſmuch as they make uſe of their authority, purſuant to the views and purpoſes for which they were intruſted with it, and agreeably to the intention of the Deity, that is for the happineſs of the people, by uſing all their endeavours to inſpire them with virtuous principles.

* *Nihil eſt illi principi Deo, qui omnem hunc mundum regit, quod quidem in terris fiat acceptius, quam conſilia cœtuſque hominum jure ſociati, quæ civitates appellantur. Somn. Scip. c.* 3.

XII.

XII. This, without doubt, is ſufficient to make us look upon the original of government as ſacred, and to induce ſubjects to ſhew ſubmiſſion and reſpect to the perſon of the ſovereign. But there are political writers who carry the thing further, and maintain that 'tis God who confers immediately the ſupreme power on princes, without any intervention or concurrence of man.

XIII. For this purpoſe, they make a diſtinction betwixt the cauſe of the ſtate, and the cauſe of the ſovereignty. They confeſs indeed that ſtates are formed by covenants, but they inſiſt that God himſelf is the immediate cauſe of the ſovereignty. According to their notions, the people, who chuſe to themſelves a king, do not, by this act, confer the ſupreme authority upon him, they only point out the perſon whom heaven is to entruſt with it. The conſent of the people to the dominion of one or more perſons, may be conſidered indeed as a channel, thro' which the ſupreme authority flows, but is not its real ſource.

XIV. The principal argument which theſe writers adopt, in order to eſtabliſh their opinion, is, that as neither each individual amongſt a great number of free and independent people, nor the whole collective multitude, are in any wiſe poſſeſſed of the ſupreme authority, they cannot confer it on the prince. But this argument proves nothing: 'tis true that neither each member of the ſociety, nor the whole multitude collected, are formally inveſted with the ſupreme authority, ſuch as we behold it in the ſove-

ſovereign, but it is ſufficient that they poſſeſs it virtually, that is, that they have within themſelves all that is neceſſary to enable them, by the concurrence of their free will and conſent, to produce it in the ſovereign.

XV. Since every individual has a natural right of diſpoſing of his perſon and actions according as he thinks proper, why ſhould he not have a power of transferring to another that right which he has of directing himſelf? Now is it not manifeſt, that if all the members of a ſociety agree to transfer this right to one of their fellow-members, this ceſſion will be the neareſt and immediate cauſe of ſovereignty? It is therefore evident, that there are, in each individual, the ſeeds, as it were, of the ſupreme power. The caſe is here very near the ſame as in that of ſeveral voices, collected together, which, by their union, produce a harmony, that was not to be found ſeparately in each.

XVI. But it will be here objected, that the ſcripture itſelf ſays, that every man ought to be ſubject to the ſupreme powers, becauſe they are eſtabliſhed by God *. I anſwer, with *Grotius*, that men have eſtabliſhed civil ſocieties, not in conſequence of a divine ordinance, but of their voluntary motion, induced to it by the experience they had had of the incapacity which ſeparate families were under, of defending themſelves againſt the inſults and attacks of human violence. From thence (he adds) ariſes the civil power, which St. *Peter*, for

* Rom. xiii.

this reaſon, calls *a human* power *, tho' in other parts of ſcripture it bears the name of a divine inſtitution †, becauſe God has approved of it as an eſtabliſhment uſeful to mankind §.

XVII. All the other arguments, in favour of the opinion we have been here refuting, do not even deſerve our notice. In general, it may be obſerved, that never were more wretched reaſons produced upon this ſubject, as the reader may be eaſily convinced by reading *Puffendorf* on the Law of Nature and Nations, who, in the chapter correſponding to this, gives theſe arguments at length, and completely refutes them ||.

XVIII. Let us therefore conclude, that the opinion of thoſe, who pretend that God is the immediate cauſe of ſovereignty, has no other foundation than that of adulation and flattery, by which, in order to render the authority of ſovereigns more abſolute, they have attempted to render it independent of all human compact, and dependent only on God. But were we even to grant that princes hold their authority immediately of God, yet the conſequences, which ſome political writers want to infer, could not be drawn from this principle.

XIX. For ſince it is moſt certain that God could never entruſt princes with this ſupreme authority,

* Ep. i. c. 2. v. 13. † Rom. xiii. 1.

§ Grotius of the right of war and peace, book I. c. 4 §. 7, 12. No. 3. See above, No. 7, and following.

|| See the Law of Nature and Nations, book VII. c. 3.

but

but for the good of ſociety in general, as well as of individuals, the exerciſe of this power muſt neceſſarily be limited, by the very intention which the Deity had in conferring it on the ſovereign, inſomuch that the people would ſtill have the ſame right of refuſing to obey a prince, who, inſtead of concurring with the views of the Deity, would, on the contrary, endeavour to croſs and defeat them, by rendering his people miſerable, as we ſhall prove more particularly hereafter.

CHAP. VII.

Of the eſſential characters of ſovereignty, its modifications, extent, and limits.

1°. *Of the characters of ſovereignty.*

I. SOvereignty we have defined, to be a right of commanding finally in civil ſociety, which the members of this ſociety have conferred upon ſome perſon, with a view of maintaining order and ſecurity in the commonwealth. This definition ſhews us the principal characters of the power that governs the ſtate, and this is what it will be proper to explain here in a more particular manner.

II. The firſt character, and that from which all the others flow, is its being a ſupreme and independent power, that is, a power that judges finally of whatever is ſuſceptible of human direction, and relates to the welfare and advantage of ſociety; inſomuch

much that this power acknowledges no ſuperior upon earth.

III. It muſt be obſerved however, that when we ſay the civil power is, of its nature, ſupreme and independent, we do not mean thereby, that it does not depend, in regard to its original, on the human will *: all that we would have underſtood is, that, when once this power is eſtabliſhed, it acknowledges no other upon earth, ſuperior or equal to it, and conſequently that whatever it ordains in the plenitude of its power, cannot be reverſed by any other human will, as ſuperior to it.

IV. That in every government there ſhould be ſuch a ſupreme power, is a point abſolutely neceſſary; the very nature of the thing requires it, otherwiſe it is impoſſible for it to ſubſiſt. For ſince powers cannot be multiplied to infinity, we muſt neceſſarily ſtop at ſome degree of authority ſuperior to all other; and let the form of government be what it will, monarchical, ariſtocratical, democratical, or mixt, we muſt always ſubmit to a ſupreme deciſion, ſince it implies a contradiction to ſay, that there is any perſon above him, who holds the higheſt rank in the ſame order of beings.

V. A ſecond character, which is a conſequence of the firſt, is that the ſovereign as ſuch, is not accountable to any perſon upon earth for his conduct, nor liable to any puniſhment from man; for both ſuppoſe a ſuperior.

* See above, c. 4 *&c.* where we have proved the contrary.

VI. There are two ways of being accountable.

One as to a ſuperior, who has a right of reverſing what has been done, if he does not find it to his liking, and even of inflicting ſome puniſhment, and this is inconſiſtent with the idea of a ſovereign.

The other as to an equal, whoſe approbation we are deſirous of having; and in this ſenſe a ſovereign may be accountable, without any abſurdity. And even thoſe who have a ſenſibility of honour, endeavour by this means to acquire the approbation and eſteem of mankind, by letting all the world ſee, that they act with prudence and integrity: but this does not imply any dependance.

VII. I ſaid that the ſovereign as ſuch was neither accountable nor puniſhable; that is, as long as he continues really a ſovereign, and has not forfeited his right. For it is paſt all doubt, that if the ſovereign, utterly forgetful of the end for which he was entruſted with the ſovereignty, applied it to a quite contrary purpoſe, and is thus become an enemy to the ſtate; the ſovereignty returns *(ipſo facto)* to the nation, who, in that caſe, can act towards the perſon, who was their ſovereign, in the manner they think moſt agreeable to their ſecurity and intereſts. For whatever notion we may entertain of ſovereignty, no man, in his ſenſes, will pretend to ſay, that it is a right and undoubted title to follow the impulſe of our irregular paſſions with impunity, and thus to become an enemy to ſociety.

VIII. A third character eſſential to ſovereignty, conſidered in itſelf, is, that the ſovereign as ſuch, be be above all human or civil law. I ſay, all human law; for there is no doubt but the ſovereign himſelf is ſubject to the divine laws, whether natural, or poſitive.

Regum timendorum in proprios greges,
Reges in ipſos imperium eſt Jovis.

HOR. l. 3. Od. 1.

IX. But with regard to laws merely human, as their whole force and obligation ultimately depends on the will of the ſovereign, they cannot, with any propriety of ſpeech, be ſaid to be obligatory in reſpect to him: for obligation neceſſarily ſuppoſeth two perſons, a ſuperior and an inferior.

X. And yet natural equity requires ſometimes, that the prince ſhould conform to his own laws, to the end that his ſubjects may be more effectually induced to obſerve them. This is extremely well expreſſed in theſe verſes of *Claudian* *.

In commune jubes ſi quid, cenſeſve tenendum,
Primus juſſa jubi? tunc obſervantior æqui
Fit populus, nec ferre negat, cum viderit ipſum
Auctorem parêre ſibi, componitur orbis
Regis ad exemplum, nec ſic inflectere ſenſus
Humanos edicta valent, ut vita regentis.

XI. To proceed; we ſuppoſe the ſovereignty ſuch as it really is in itſelf, and that the eſtabliſhment of civil laws ultimately depends on the ſole will of

* De IV. Conſul. Honor. v. 296 & ſeq.

the

the person who enjoys the honours and title of sovereign, insomuch that his authority, in this respect, cannot be limited: otherwise this superiority of the prince above the laws is not applicable to him in the full extent in which we have given it him.

XII. This sovereignty, such as we have now represented it, resided originally in the people. But when once the people have transferred their right to a sovereign, they cannot, without contradiction, be supposed to continue still masters of it.

XIII. Hence the distinction which some political writers make between *real sovereignty*, which always resides in the people, and *actual sovereignty*, which belongs to the king, is equally absurd and dangerous. For it is ridiculous to pretend, that after the people have conferred the supreme authority on the king, they should still continue in possession of that very authority, superior to the king himself.

XIV. We must therefore observe here a just medium, and establish principles that neither favour tyranny, nor the spirit of mutiny and rebellion.

1°. It is certain, that as soon as a people submit to a king, really such, they have no longer the supreme power.

2°. But it does not follow, from the people's having conferred the supreme power in such a manner, that they have reserved to themselves in no case the right of resuming it.

3°. This reservation is sometimes explicit; but there is always a tacit one, the effect of which discloses

closes itself, when the person, entrusted with the supreme authority, perverts it to a use directly and intirely contrary to the end for which it was conferred upon him, as will better appear hereafter.

XV. But tho' it be absolutely necessary, that there should be a supreme and independent authority in the state, there is nevertheless some difference, especially in monarchies and aristocracies, with regard to the manner in which those who are intrusted with this power, exercise it. In some states the prince governs as he thinks proper; in others, he is obliged to follow some fixt and constant rules, from which he is not allowed to deviate; this is what I call the modifications of sovereignty, and from thence arises the distinction of absolute and limited sovereignty.

2°. *Of absolute sovereignty.*

XVI. Absolute sovereignty is therefore nothing else but the right of governing the state as the prince thinks proper, according as the present situation of affairs seems to require, and without being obliged to consult any person whatever, or to follow any fixt or determinate and perpetual rules.

XVII. Upon this head we have several important reflections to make.

1°. The word *absolute power* is generally very odious to republicans; and I must confess, that when it is misunderstood, it is apt to make the most dangerous impressions on the minds of princes, especially in the mouths of flatterers.

2°. In order to form a juſt idea of it, we muſt trace it to its principle. In the ſtate of nature, every man has an abſolute right to diſpoſe of his perſon and actions, after what manner he thinks moſt conducive to his happineſs, and without being obliged to conſult any body, provided however that he does nothing contrary to the laws of nature: conſequently when a multitude of men unite together, in order to form a ſtate, this body hath the ſame liberty in regard to matters in which the public good is concerned.

3°. When therefore the whole body of the people confer the ſovereignty upon a prince, with this extent and abſolute power, which originally reſided in themſelves, and without adding any particular limitation to it, we call that ſovereignty abſolute.

4°. This being ſo, we muſt not confound an abſolute power with an arbitrary, deſpotic, and unlimited authority. For, from what we have now ſaid concerning the original and nature of abſolute ſovereignty, it manifeſtly follows, that it is limited, from its very nature, by the intention of thoſe who conferred it on the ſovereign, and by the very laws of God. This is what we muſt explain more at large.

XVIII. The end which mankind propoſed to themſelves in renouncing their natural independence, and eſtabliſhing government and ſovereignty, was doubtleſs to redreſs the evils which they laboured under, and to ſecure their happineſs. If ſo, how is it poſſible to conceive, that thoſe, who, with this view, granted an abſolute power to the ſovereign, ſhould

have

have intended to give him an arbitrary and unlimited power, ſo as to intitle him to gratify his caprice and paſſions, to the prejudice of the life, property, and liberty of the ſubjects? on the contrary, we have ſhewn above, that the civil ſtate muſt neceſſarily empower the ſubjects to inſiſt upon the ſovereign's uſing his authority for their advantage, and according to the purpoſes for which he was entruſted with it.

XIX. It muſt therefore be acknowledged, that it never was the intention of the people to confer abſolute ſovereignty upon a prince, but with this expreſs condition, that the public good ſhould be the ſupreme law to direct him; conſequently as long as the prince acts with this view, he is authorized by the people; but, on the contrary, if he makes uſe of his power merely to ruin and deſtroy his ſubjects, he acts intirely of his own head, and not in virtue of the power with which he was entruſted by the people.

XX. Still further, the very nature of the thing does not allow abſolute power to be extended beyond the bounds of public utility; for abſolute ſovereignty cannot confer a right upon the ſovereign, which the people had not originally in themſelves. Now before the eſtabliſhment of civil ſociety, ſurely no man had a power of injuring either himſelf or others; conſequently abſolute power cannot give the ſovereign a right to hurt and abuſe his ſubjects.

XXI. In the ſtate of nature every man was abſolute maſter of his own perſon and actions, provided he confined himſelf within the limits of the law of nature. Abſolute power is formed only by the union of all the rights of individuals in the perſon of the ſovereign; of courſe the abſolute power of the ſovereign is confined within the ſame bounds, as thoſe by which the abſolute power of individuals was originally limited.

XXII. But I go ſtill further, and affirm that, ſuppoſing even a nation had been really willing to grant their ſovereign an arbitrary and unlimited power, this conceſſion would of itſelf be void and of no effect.

XXIII. No man can diveſt himſelf ſo far of his liberty as to ſubmit to an arbitrary power, who is to treat him abſolutely according to his fancy. This would be renouncing his own life, which he is not maſter of; it would be renouncing his duty, which is never permitted: and if thus it be with regard to an individual who ſhould make himſelf a ſlave, much leſs hath an intire nation that power, which is not to be found in any of its members.

XXIV. By this it appears moſt evident, that all ſovereignty, how abſolute ſoever we ſuppoſe it, hath its limits; and that it can never imply an arbitrary power in the prince of doing whatever he pleaſes without any other rule or reaſon than his own deſpotic will.

XXV. For how indeed ſhould we attribute any ſuch power to the creature, when it is not to be found

in

in the ſupreme Being himſelf? His abſolute dominion is not founded on a blind will; his ſovereign will is always determined by the immutable rules of wiſdom, juſtice, and beneficence.

XXVI. In ſhort, the right of commanding, or ſovereignty, ought always to be eſtabliſhed ultimately on a power of doing good, otherwiſe it cannot be productive of a real obligation; for reaſon cannot approve or ſubmit to it, and this is what diſtinguiſhes empire and ſovereignty from violence and tyranny. Such are the ideas we ought to form of abſolute ſovereignty.

3°. *Of limited ſovereignty.*

XXVII. But notwithſtanding abſolute power, conſidered in itſelf, and ſuch as we have now repreſented it, implies nothing odious or unlawful, and, in that ſenſe, people may confer it upon the ſovereign; yet we muſt allow, that the experience of all ages has informed mankind, that this is not the form of government which ſuits them beſt, nor the fitteſt for procuring them a ſtate of tranquillity and happineſs.

XXVIII. Whatever diſtance there may be between the ſubjects and the ſovereign, in whatſoever degree of elevation the latter may be placed above the reſt, ſtill he is man like themſelves; their ſouls are all caſt, as it were, in the ſame mould, they are all ſubject to the ſame prejudices, ſuſceptible all of the ſame paſſions.

XXIX. Again, the very ſtation, which ſovereigns occupy, expoſes them to temptations, unknown to private people. The generality of princes have neither virtue nor courage ſufficient to moderate their paſſions, when they find they may do whatever they pleaſe. The people have therefore great reaſon to fear, that an unlimited authority will turn out to their prejudice, and that if they do not reſerve ſome ſecurity to themſelves, againſt the ſovereign's abuſing it, he will actually abuſe it.

XXX. 'Tis theſe reflections, juſtified by experience, that have induced moſt, and thoſe the wiſeſt, nations, to ſet bounds to the power of their ſovereigns, and to preſcribe the manner in which they are to govern; and this has produced what is called limited ſovereignty.

XXXI. But tho' this limitation of the ſupreme power is advantageous to the people, yet it does no wrong to the princes themſelves; nay it may rather be ſaid, that it turns out to their advantage, and forms the greateſt ſecurity to their authority.

XXXII. It does no wrong to princes; for if they could not be ſatisfied with a limited authority, their buſineſs was to refuſe the crown; and when once they have accepted of it upon theſe conditions, they are no longer at liberty to endeavour afterwards to break thro' them, or to ſtrive to render themſelves abſolute.

XXXIII. It is rather advantageous to princes, becauſe thoſe

thofe who are invefted with abfolute power, and are defirous of difcharging their duty, are obliged to a far greater vigilance and circumfpection, and expofed to more fatigue, than thofe who have their tafk, as it were, marked out to them, and are not allowed to deviate from certain rules.

XXXIV. In fine, this limitation of fovereignty forms the greateft fecurity to the authority of princes; for as they are lefs expofed hereby to temptation, they avoid that popular fury, which is fometimes difcharged on thofe, who, having been invefted with abfolute authority, abufe it to excefs. Abfolute power eafily degenerates into defpotifm, and defpotifm paves the way for the greateft and moft fatal revolutions that can befall to fovereigns. This is what the experience of all ages has verified: it is therefore a happy incapacity in kings not to be able to act contrary to the laws of their country.

XXXV. Let us therefore conclude, that it intirely depends upon a free people, to inveft the fovereigns, whom they place over their heads, with an authority either abfolute or limited by certain laws, provided thefe laws contain nothing contrary to juftice, nor to the end of government. Thefe regulations, by which the fupreme authority is kept within bounds, are called, *The fundamental laws of the ftate.*

4°. *Of fundamental laws.*

XXXVI. The fundamental laws of a ftate, taken in their full extent, are not only the decrees by which the entire body of the nation determine the form of government, and the manner of ſucceeding to the crown; but are likewiſe the covenants betwixt the people and the perſon on whom they confer the ſovereignty, which regulate the manner of governing, and by which the ſupreme authority is limited.

XXXVII. Theſe regulations are called fundamental laws, becauſe they are the baſis, as it were, and foundation of the ſtate, on which the ſtructure of the government is raiſed, and becauſe the people look upon them as their principal ſtrength and ſupport.

XXXVIII. The name of laws however has been given to theſe regulations in an improper and figurative manner; for, properly ſpeaking, they are real covenants. But as theſe covenants are obligatory between the contracting parties, they have the force of laws themſelves. Let us explain this more at large.

XXXIX. 1°. I obſerve in the firſt place, that there is a kind of fundamental law of right and of neceſſity, eſſential to all governments, even in thoſe ſtates where the moſt abſolute ſovereignty prevails. This law is that of the public good, from which the ſovereign can never depart, without being wanting in his duty; but this alone is not ſufficient to limit the ſovereignty.

XL. Hence thoſe promiſes, either tacit or expreſs, by which princes bind themſelves even by oath, when they come to the crown, of governing according to the laws of juſtice and equity, of conſulting the

the public good, of oppreſſing nobody, of protecting the virtuous, and of puniſhing evil doers, and the like, do not imply any limitation to their authority, nor any diminution of their abſolute power. It is ſufficient that the choice of the means for procuring the advantage of the ſtate, and the method of putting them in practiſe, be left to the judgment and diſpoſal of the ſovereign; otherwiſe the diſtinction of abſolute and limited power would be utterly aboliſhed.

XLI. 2°. But with regard to fundamental laws, properly ſo called, they are only more particular precautions taken by the people, to oblige ſovereigns more ſtrongly to employ their authority, agreeably to the general rule of the public good. This may be done ſeveral ways; but ſtill theſe limitations of the ſovereignty have more or leſs force, according as the nation has taken more or leſs precautions, that they ſhall have their due effect.

XLII. Hence 1°. a nation may require of a ſovereign, that he will engage, by a particular promiſe, not to make any new laws, nor to levy new impoſts, to tax only ſome particular things, to give places and employments only to a certain ſet of people, and not to take any foreign troops into his pay, *&c.* Then indeed the ſupreme authority is limited in theſe different reſpects, inſomuch that whatever the king attempts afterwards contrary to the formal engagement he entered into ſhall be void and of no effect. But if there ſhould happen to be an extraordinary caſe, in which the ſovereign thought it conducive

ducive to the public good, to deviate from the fundamental laws, he is not allowed to do it of his own head, in contempt of his ſolemn engagement, but in that caſe he ought to conſult the people themſelves or their repreſentatives. Otherwiſe, under pretence of ſome neceſſity or utility, the ſovereign might eaſily break his word, and fruſtrate the effect of the precautions taken by the nation to limit his power. And yet *Puffendorff* thinks otherwiſe *. But for a ſtill greater ſecurity of the performance of the engagements into which the ſovereign entered, and which limit his power, it is proper to require explicitly of him, that he ſhall convene a general aſſembly of the people, or of their repreſentatives, or of the nobility of the country, when any matters happen to fall under debate, which it was thought improper to leave to his deciſion. Or elſe the nation may previouſly eſtabliſh a council, a ſenate, or parliament, without whoſe conſent the prince ſhall be rendered incapable of acting in regard to things which the nation did not think fit to ſubmit to his will.

XLIII. 2°. Hiſtory informs us, that ſome nations have carried their precautions ſtill further, by inſerting, in plain terms, in their fundamental laws, a condition or clauſe, by which the king was declared to have forfeited his crown, if he broke thro' thoſe laws. *Puffendorff* gives an example of this, taken from the oath of allegiance, which the people of *Arragon* formerly made to their kings. *We, who have as much power as you, make you our king, upon condition you maintain inviolably our rights and liberties, and not otherwiſe.*

* See the Law of Nature and Nations, book VII. c. 6. §. 10.

XLIV.

XLIV. 'Tis by ſuch precautions as theſe, that a nation really limits the authority ſhe confers on the ſovereign, and ſecures her liberty. For as we have already obſerved, civil liberty ought to be accompanied not only with a right of inſiſting on the ſovereign's making a due uſe of his authority, but moreover with a moral certainty that this right ſhall have its effect. And the only way to render the people thus certain, is to uſe proper precautions againſt the abuſe of the ſovereign power, in ſuch a manner as theſe precautions ſhall not be eaſily eluded.

XLV. Beſides, we muſt obſerve here, that theſe limitations of the ſovereign power do not render it defective, nor make any diminution in the ſupreme authority; for a prince, or a ſenate, who has been inveſted with the ſupreme power upon this footing, may exerciſe every act of it as well as in an abſolute monarchy. All the difference is, that in the latter the prince alone determines ultimately according to his private judgment; but in a limited monarchy, there is a certain aſſembly, who, in conjunction with the king, take cognizance of particular affairs, and whoſe conſent is a neceſſary condition, without which the king can determine nothing. But the wiſdom and virtue of good princes, are always ſtrengthened by the concurring aſſiſtance of thoſe who have a ſhare in the authority. They always do what they incline to, when they incline to nothing but what is juſt and good; and they ought to eſteem themſelves happy in having it put out of their power to do otherwiſe.

XLVI. 3°. In a word, as the fundamental laws, which

which limit the ſovereign authority, are nothing elſe but the means which the people uſe to aſſure themſelves that the prince will not recede from the general law of the public good in the moſt important circumſtances, it cannot be ſaid that they render the ſovereignty imperfect or defective. For if we ſuppoſe a prince inveſted with abſolute authority, but at the ſame time bleſſed with ſo much wiſdom and virtue, that he will never, even in the moſt trifling caſe, deviate from the laws which the public good requires, and that all his determinations ſhall be ſubjected to this ſuperior rule, can we, for that reaſon, ſay, that his power is in the leaſt weakened or diminiſhed? No to be ſure; ſo that the precautions, which the people take againſt the weakneſs or the wickedneſs inſeparable from human nature, in limiting the power of their ſovereigns to hinder them from abuſing it, do not in the leaſt weaken or diminiſh the ſovereignty; but, on the contrary, render it perfect, by reducing the ſovereign to a neceſſity of doing good, and conſequently putting him, as it were, out of a capacity of miſbehaving.

XLVII. Neither are we to believe that there are two diſtinct wills in a ſtate, whoſe ſovereignty is limited in the manner we have explained; for the ſtate wills or determines nothing but by the will of the king. Only 'tis to be obſerved, that when a certain condition ſtipulated happens to be broken, the king cannot decree at all, or at leaſt muſt do ſo in vain in certain points; but he is not, for this reaſon, leſs the ſovereign than he was before. Becauſe a prince cannot do every thing according to his humour, it

does

does not follow from this, that he is not the sovereign. Sovereign power and absolute power ought not to be confounded; and, from what has been said, it is evident, that the one may subsist without the other.

XLVIII. 4°. Lastly, there is still another manner of limiting the power of those to whom the sovereignty is committed, which is not to trust all the different rights included in the sovereignty to one single person, but to lodge them in separate hands, or in different bodies, that they may modify or restrain the sovereignty.

XLIX. For example, if we suppose that the body of the nation reserves to itself the legislative power, and that of creating the principal magistrates; that it gives the king the military and executive powers *&c.* and that it trusts to a senate composed of the principal men, the judiciary power, that of laying taxes *&c.* it is easily conceived, that this may be executed in different manners, in the choice of which prudence must determine us.

L. If the government is established on this footing, then, by the original compact of association, there is a kind of sharing the rights of the sovereignty, by a reciprocal contract or stipulation between the different bodies of the state. This sharing produces a balance of power, which places the different bodies of the state in such a mutual dependance, as retains every one, who has a share in the sovereign authority, within the bounds which the law prescribes to them, by which means liberty is secured; for example, the regal authority is balanced by the power of the people, and a third order ſerves as a counter-balance to the two firſt, to keep them always in an æquilibrium, and hinder the one from riſing above the other. But what has been ſaid is ſufficient, concerning the diſtinction between abſolute and limited ſovereignty.

5°. *Of patrimonial, and uſufructuary kingdoms.*

LI. In order to finiſh this chapter let us obſerve, that there is ſtill another accidental difference in the manner of poſſeſſing the ſovereignty, eſpecially with reſpect to kings. Some are maſters of their crown in the way of patrimony, which they are permitted to ſhare, transfer, or alienate to whom they have a mind; in a word, of which they can diſpoſe as they think proper: others hold the ſovereignty in the way of *uſe* only, not of property, and this either for themſelves only, or with the power of tranſmitting it to their deſcendants according to the laws eſtabliſhed for the ſucceſſion. 'Tis upon this foundation that the doctors diſtinguiſh kingdoms into patrimonial, and uſufructuary or not patrimonial.

LII. We ſhall here add, that thoſe kings poſſeſs the crown in full propriety, who have acquired the ſovereignty by right of conqueſt; or thoſe to whom a people have delivered themſelves up without reſerve in order to avoid a greater evil; but that, on the contrary, thoſe kings, who have been eſtabliſhed by a free conſent of the people, poſſeſs the crown in the way of *uſe* only. This is the manner in which

which *Grotius* explains this diſtinction, in which he has been followed by *Puffendorff*, and moſt of the other commentators or writers *.

LIII. On this we may make the following remarks.

1°. Nothing in reality hinders the ſovereign power, as well as every other right, from being alienated or transferred. In this there is nothing contrary to the nature of the thing; and if the agreement between the prince and the people bears that the prince ſhall have full right to diſpoſe of the crown as he ſhall think proper, this will be what we call a patrimonial kingdom.

2°. But examples of ſuch agreements are very rare; and we hardly find any other except that of the *Egyptians* with their king, mentioned in *Geneſis* †.

3°. The ſovereign power, however abſolute, is not, of itſelf, inveſted with the right of property, nor conſequently with the power of alienation. Theſe two ideas are intirely diſtinct, and have no neceſſary connection with each other.

4°. 'Tis true, ſome alledge a great many examples of alienations made in all ages by ſovereigns; but either theſe alienations had no effect, or they were made by an expreſs or tacit conſent of the people, or laſtly they were founded on no other titles but force.

* See *Grotius* on the Right of War and Peace, lib. I. ch. 3. §. 11 & 12 *&c.* *Puffendorff*, on the *Law of Nature and Nations*, lib. VII. ch. 6. §. 14, 15.

† Ch. 47. ℣. 18 *&c.*

5°. Let us therefore take it for an inconteſtable principle, that, in dubious caſes, every kingdom ought to be judged not patrimonial, ſo long as it cannot be proved in any manner, that a people ſubmitted themſelves on that footing to a ſovereign.

CHAP. VIII.

Of the parts of ſovereignty, or of the different eſſential rights which it includes.

I. IN order to finiſh this firſt part, nothing remains but to treat of the parts of ſovereignty in general. We may conſider ſovereignty as an aſſemblage of various rights and different powers, which, tho' diſtinct, are nevertheleſs conferred for the ſame end, that is to ſay, for the good of the ſociety, and which are all eſſentially neceſſary for this ſame end; theſe different rights and powers are called the eſſential parts of ſovereignty.

II. To know that theſe are the parts of ſovereignty, we need only attend to its nature and end.

The end of ſovereignty is the preſervation, the tranquillity, and the happineſs of the ſtate, as well within itſelf, as with reſpect to its intereſts abroad; ſo that ſovereignty muſt include every thing that is eſſentially neceſſary to it for procuring this double end.

III. 1°. As this is the caſe, the firſt part of ſovereignty, and that which is, as it were, the foundation

tion of all the reſt, is the legiſlative power, by virtue of which the ſovereign finally eſtabliſhes general and perpetual rules, which are called *laws*. By this means every one knows what he ought to do, or not to do, for the preſervation of peace and good order, what ſhare he retains of his natural liberty, and how he ought to uſe his rights ſo as not to diſturb the public repoſe.

'Tis by means of the laws that we reduce to a noble unity that prodigious diverſity of ſentiments and inclinations obſervable among men, and that we eſtabliſh between them that concert and harmony which are eſſentially neceſſary to ſociety, and which direct all the actions of the members that compoſe it, to the common good and advantage; but it muſt be ſuppoſed that the laws of the ſovereign ought to contain nothing oppoſite to the divine laws, whether natural or revealed.

IV. 2°. To the legiſlative we muſt join the coercive power, that is to ſay, the right of eſtabliſhing puniſhments againſt thoſe who moleſt the ſociety by their enormities; and the power of actually inflicting them. Without this the eſtabliſhment of civil ſociety and of laws, would be abſolutely uſeleſs, and we could not propoſe to live in peace and ſafety. But that the dread of puniſhments may make a ſufficient impreſſion on the minds of the people, the right of puniſhing muſt extend to the power of inflicting the greateſt of natural evils, I mean death; otherwiſe the dread of puniſhment would not be always capable of counter-balancing the force of pleaſure and paſſion. In a word, the people muſt have more intereſt to obſerve, than to violate the law; thus the right of the ſword is certainly the greateſt power which one man can exerciſe over another.

V. 3°. After this, 'tis neceſſary for the preſervation of peace in a ſtate, that the ſovereign ſhould have a right to take cognizance of the different quarrels between the ſubjects, and to decide them finally, as alſo to examine the accuſations laid againſt any perſon, in order to abſolve or puniſh him by his ſentence, conformably to the laws: this is what we call *juriſdiction*, or the *judiciary power*. To this we muſt alſo refer the right of pardoning criminals when any reaſon of public uſe requires it.

VI. 4°. Beſides, as the ways of thinking, or opinions embraced by the ſubjects, may have a very great influence on the good or ill of the commonwealth, 'tis neceſſary that the ſovereignty ſhould include a right of examining the doctrines taught in the ſtate, ſo that nothing may be advanced publicly but what is conformable to truth, and conducive to the advantage and tranquillity of the ſociety: hence it is that it belongs to the ſovereign to eſtabliſh public doctors, academies, and ſchools; and that the ſovereign power, in matters of religion, belongs to him of right, at leaſt as much as the nature of the thing will permit. After having ſecured the public repoſe at home, 'tis neceſſary to guard it from abroad, and to procure to it, from foreign ſtates, all the aids and advantages which are neceſſary to it, whether in time of peace or war. VII.

VII. 5°. In consequence of this, the sovereign ought to be invested with the power of assembling and arming his subjects, or of raising other troops in as great a number as is necessary for the safety and defence of the state, and of making peace afterwards when he shall think proper.

VIII. 6°. Hence also arises the right of contracting public engagements, of making treaties and alliances with foreign states, and of obliging all the subjects to observe them.

IX. 7°. But as the public affairs, both at home and abroad, cannot be managed and carried on by a single person, and as the sovereign cannot of himself discharge all these duties, he must necessarily have a right to create ministers and subordinate magistrates, whose business it is to take care of the public good, and transact the affairs of the state in his name, and under his authority. The sovereign, who has entrusted them with these employments, may and ought to compel them to discharge them, and make them give an exact account of their administration.

X. 8°. Lastly, the affairs of the state necessarily demand, both in times of peace and war, considerable expences, which the sovereign himself neither can, nor ought to furnish. He must therefore have a right of reserving to himself a part of the wealth of the subjects, or of the revenues of the country, or of obliging the subjects to contribute either by their money, or by their labour and personal service, as much as the public neceſſities demand, and this is called the *Right of ſubſidies or taxes.*

To this part of the ſovereignty we may refer the right of coining money, the right of hunting, that of fiſhing *&c.* Theſe are the principal parts eſſential to ſovereignty.

The End of the Firſt Part.

THE

THE PRINCIPLES OF POLITIC LAW.

PART II.

In which are explained the different forms of government, the ways of acquiring or losing sovereignty, and the reciprocal duties of sovereigns and subjects.

CHAP. I.

Of the various forms of government.

I. ALL nations have been sensible, that it was essential to their happiness and safety, to establish a government. They have all agreed in this point, that a sovereign power was necessary, to whose will every thing should be finally submitted.

II. But, the more the establishment of a sovereign is necessary, the more the choice of him alſo is important. For this reaſon, in ſuch a choice, nations are extremely divided, and have entruſted the ſovereign power in different hands according as they thought it moſt conducive to their ſafety and happineſs; neither have they even done this without combinations and modifications, which may vary very greatly. This is the origin of the different forms of government.

III. There are therefore various forms of government, according to the different ſubjects in whom the ſovereignty reſides immediately, and according as it belongs either to a ſingle perſon, or to a ſingle aſſembly, more or leſs compounded; and this is what forms the conſtitution of the ſtate.

IV. All theſe different forms of government may be reduced to two general claſſes, namely, to the ſimple forms, or to thoſe which are compounded or mixed, and which are produced by the mixture or aſſemblage of the ſimple forms.

V. There are three ſimple forms of government; Democracy, Ariſtocracy, and Monarchy.

VI. Some nations, more diffident than others, have placed the ſovereign power in the multitude itſelf, that is to ſay, in all the heads of families aſſembled and met in council, and ſuch governments are called popular or Democratic.

VII. Other nations of a bolder turn, paſſing to the oppoſite extremity, have eſtabliſhed Monarchy, or the

the government of one ſingle man. Thus Monarchy is a ſtate, in which the ſovereign power, and all the rights eſſential to it, reſide preciſely in a ſingle man, who is called *King*, *Monarch*, or *Emperor*.

VIII. Others have kept a due medium between theſe two extremes, and lodged the whole ſovereign authority in a council compoſed of ſome ſelect members, and this is the government of the Nobles, or the Ariſtocratic government.

IX. Laſtly, other nations have been perſuaded, that it was neceſſary, by a mixture of the ſimple forms, to eſtabliſh a mixed or compound government, and by making a diviſion of the ſovereignty, to entruſt the different parts of it to different hands; to temper, for example, Monarchy with Ariſtocracy; and at the ſame time to give the people ſome ſhare in the ſovereignty; and this may be executed different ways.

X. In order to have a more particular knowledge of the nature of theſe different forms of government, we muſt obſerve, that as in Democracies the ſovereign is a moral perſon, compoſed and formed by the reunion of all the heads of families into a ſingle will, ſo there are three things abſolutely neceſſary for the conſtitution of a Democracy.

1°. That there be a certain place, and certain regulated times for deliberating in common on the public affairs; without this the members of the ſovereign council might aſſemble at different times, or in different places, whence factions would ariſe,

 which

which would break the unity essential to the state.

2°. It must be established for a rule, that the plurality of suffrages shall pass for the will of the whole; otherwise no affair can be determined, it being impossible that a great number of people should be always of the same opinion. We must therefore esteem it the essential quality of a moral body, that the sentiment of the greatest number of those who compose it pass for the will of the whole.

3°. Lastly, it is essential to the establishment of a Democracy, that magistrates should be appointed to call the assembly of the people in extraordinary cases, to dispatch ordinary affairs, in their name, and to see that the decrees of the sovereign assembly be executed; for since the sovereign council cannot always sit, it is evident that it cannot take care of every thing of itself.

XI. As for Aristocracies, since the sovereignty resides in a council or senate, composed of the principal men of the nation, it is absolutely necessary that the same conditions which are essential to the constitution of a Democracy, and which we have now mentioned, should also concur to establish an Aristocracy.

XII. Besides, an Aristocracy may be of two kinds, either by birth and hereditary, or elective. The Aristocracy by birth, or hereditary, is that which is confined to a certain number of families, to which birth alone gives right, and which passes from parents to their children, without any choice, and

and to the exclusion of all others. On the contrary, the elective Aristocracy is that in which a person arrives at the government by election only, and without receiving any right from birth.

XIII. In a word, it may be equally observed of Aristocracies and Democracies, that in a popular state, or in a government of the nobles, every citizen, or every member of the supreme council, has not the supreme power, nor even a part of it; but this power resides either in the general assembly of the people convened according to the laws, or in the council of the nobles; for it is one thing to have a share in the sovereignty, and another to have the right of suffrage in an assembly invested with the sovereign power.

XIV. As for Monarchy, it is established when the whole body of the people confer the sovereign power on a single man, which is done by an agreement betwixt the king and his subjects, as we have before explained.

XV. There is therefore this essential difference betwixt Monarchy and the two other forms of government, that, in Democracies and Aristocracies, the actual exercise of the sovereign authority, the decrees and deliberations depend on the concurrence of certain circumstances, times and places; whereas in a Monarchy, at least when it is simple and absolute, the Monarch can give his orders at all times, and in all places: *Rome is wherever the Emperor is.*

XVI.

XVI. Another remark, which very naturally occurs on this occaſion, is, that in a Monarchy, when the king orders any thing contrary to juſtice and equity, he is certainly to blame, becauſe in him the civil and phyſical wills are the ſame thing. But when the aſſembly of the people or a ſenate form any unjuſt reſolution, only thoſe citizens or ſenators, whoſe opinions carried the point, render themſelves truly culpable, and not thoſe who were of the oppoſite opinion. Let this ſuffice for the ſimple forms of government.

XVII. As for mixed or compound governments, they are eſtabliſhed, as we have obſerved, by the concurrence of the three ſimple forms, or only of two; when, for example, the king, the nobles, and the people, or only the two laſt, ſhare the different parts of the ſovereignty between them, ſo that the one adminiſters ſome parts of it, and the others the reſt. This combination may be made in various manners, as we ſee in moſt republics.

XVIII. 'Tis true, to conſider ſovereignty in itſelf, and in the height of plenitude and perfection, all the rights, which it includes, ought to belong to one ſingle perſon, or to one body without diviſion or ſharing; ſo that there be but one ſupreme will to govern the ſtate. There cannot, properly ſpeaking, be ſeveral ſovereigns in a ſtate, ſo as to act as they pleaſe, independently of, and even in a manner oppoſite to each other. This is morally impoſſible, and would tend manifeſtly to the ruin and deſtruction of the ſociety.

XIX. But this unity of the supreme power does not hinder the whole body of the nation, in whom this power originally resides, from regulating the government by the fundamental law, in such a manner as to commit the exercise of the different parts of the sovereign power to different persons or different bodies, who may act independently of each other, in the extent of the rights committed to them, but always in a manner subordinate to the laws from which they hold these rights.

XX. And provided the fundamental laws, which establish this species of division of the sovereignty, regulate the respective limits of the power of those to whom they commit them, so that we may easily see the extent of the jurisdiction of each of these collateral powers; this division produces neither a plurality of sovereigns, nor an opposition between them, nor any irregularity in the government.

XXI. In a word, there is never here, properly speaking, but one sovereign, who has the plenitude of sovereignty in himself. There is but one supreme will. This sovereign is the body of the people, formed by the union of all the orders of the state; and this supreme will is the very law, by which the whole body of the nation makes its will known.

XXII. Those, who thus share the sovereignty among them, are properly no more than the executors of the law, since it is from the law itself that they hold their power. And as these fundamental laws are real covenants, or what the civilians call

pacta

pacta conventa between the different orders of the republic *; by which they mutually ſtipulate, that each ſhall have ſuch or ſuch a part of the ſovereignty, and that this ſhall eſtabliſh the form of government, it is evident that, by this means, each of the contracting parties acquires a primitive right not only of exerciſing the power granted to it, but alſo of retaining that right.

XXIII. Such party cannot even be diveſted of its right in ſpite of itſelf, and by the ſingle will of others, ſo long at leaſt as it uſes its right in a manner conformable to the laws, and not manifeſtly or totally oppoſite to the public good.

XXIV. In a word, the conſtitution of theſe governments can be changed only in the ſame manner, and by the ſame methods, by which it is eſtabliſhed, that is to ſay, by the unanimous concurrence of all the contracting parties who have fixed the form of government by the primitive contract of aſſociation.

XXV. This œconomy of the government, this conſtitution of the ſtate, by no means deſtroys the unity proper for a moral body compoſed of ſeveral perſons, or of ſeveral bodies, really diſtinct and ſeparate in themſelves, but joined together in a reciprocal engagement by a fundamental law, which makes but one of them.

XXVI. From what has been ſaid on the nature of mixed or compound governments it follows, that in all ſuch, the ſovereignty is always limited; for

* See part I. chap. 7. No. 35 &c.

for as the different branches are not entrusted to a single person, but lodged in different hands, the power of those, who have a share in the government, is, by this very means, restrained; and the power of the one keeps the other in awe, which produces such a balance of power and authority as secures the public good, and the liberty of individuals.

XXVII. But with respect to simple governments; in these the sovereignty may be either absolute or limited. Those who are possessed of the sovereignty exercise it sometimes in an absolute, and sometimes in a limited manner, by fundamental laws, which fix bounds to the sovereign, with respect to the manner in which he ought to govern.

XXVIII. On this occasion it is expedient to observe, that all the accidental circumstances, which can modify simple Monarchies or Aristocracies, and which, in some measure, limit sovereignty, do not, for that reason, change the form of government, which still continues the same. One government may partake somewhat of another, when the manner, in which the sovereign governs, seems to be borrowed from the form of the latter, but it does not, for that reason, change its nature.

XXIX. For example, in a Democratic state, the people may entrust the care of several affairs either to a principal member, or to a senate. In an Aristocratical state, there may be a principal magistrate invested with a particular authority, or an assembly of the people to be consulted on some occasions. Or lastly, in a Monarchic

Monarchic state, important affairs may be laid before a senate *&c.* But all these accidental circumstances do by no means change the form of the government; there is not a division of the sovereignty on this account; and the state still continues purely either Democratic, Aristocratic, or Monarchic.

XXX. In a word, there is a great difference between exercising a proper power, and acting by a foreign and precarious power, which may every minute be taken away by him who gave it. Thus what constitutes the essential characteristic of mixed or compound commonwealths, and distinguishes them from simple governments, is, that the different orders of the state, who have a share in the sovereignty, possess the rights which they exercise by an equal title, that is to say, by virtue of the fundamental law, and not by the title of simple commission, as if the one was only the minister or executor of the will of the other. We must therefore carefully distinguish between the form of government, and the manner of governing.

XXXI. These are the principal observations which occur with respect to the various forms of government. *Puffendorff* explains himself in a somewhat different manner, and calls those governments irregular; which we have called mixed and regular, the simple governments *

XXXII. But this regularity is only a regularity in idea; the true rule of practice ought to be that

* See Law of Nature and Nations, book VII. chap. 5.

which

which is most conformable to the end of civil societies, supposing men to be such as they ordinarily are, and taking the common state of the world into the account, according to the experience of all places and all ages. Now on this footing, the states, in which the whole depends on a single will, are so far from being happy, that 'tis certain their subjects have the most frequent reasons for lamenting the loss of their natural independency.

XXXIII. Besides it is with the body politic, as with the human body; there is a difference between a sound and a cathectic state.

XXXIV. These disorders arise either from the abuse of the sovereign power, or from the bad constitution of the state, and the causes of them are to be sought for either in the failings of those who govern, or in the defects of the government itself.

XXXV. In Monarchies, the faults of the person are, when the king has not the qualities necessary for reigning, when he has little or no attachment to the public good, and when he delivers his subjects up as a prey, either to the avarice or ambition of his ministers *&c.*

XXXVI. As for Aristocracies, the faults of the persons are when, by intrigue and other sinister methods, they bring into the council, either wicked men, or such as are incapable of business, while men of merit are excluded; when factions and cabals are formed; and when the nobles treat the populace as slaves *&c.*

XXXVII.

XXXVII. In fine, we ſometimes ſee alſo in Democracies, that their aſſemblies are diſturbed with broils, and merit is oppreſſed by envy *&c.*

XXXVIII. As for the defects of the government, there may be various kinds of them. For example, if the laws of the ſtate are not conformable to the natural genius of the people, as if they tended to engage in war a people, that is not naturally warlike, but proper for the arts of peace; if theſe laws are not agreeable to the ſituation and the qualities of the country: it is bad conduct, for inſtance, not to promote commerce and manufactures, in a country which is well ſituated for that purpoſe, and produces commodities with which a trade can be carried on. If the conſtitution of the ſtate renders the diſpatch of affairs very ſlow or difficult, as in *Poland*, where the oppoſition of one member of the aſſembly diſſolves the diet.

XXXIX. We generally give particular names to theſe defects in government. Thus the corruption of Monarchy is called Tyranny. Oligarchy is the abuſe of Ariſtocracy; and the abuſe of Democracy is called Ochlocracy. But it often happens that theſe words, in their appellation, denote leſs a defect or diſorder in the ſtate, than ſome particular paſſion or diſguſt in thoſe who uſe them.

XL. To finiſh this chapter, nothing remains, but to ſay ſomething of thoſe compound forms of government which are formed by the union of ſeveral particular ſtates. Theſe may be defined an aſſemblage of perfect ſtates ſtrictly united by ſome particular bond, ſo that they ſeem to make but one ſingle body with reſpect to the affairs which intereſt them in common, tho' each of them alſo preſerves the ſovereignty full and entire, independently of the others.

XLI. This aſſemblage of ſtates is formed either by the union of two or more diſtinct ſtates, under one and the ſame king; as for inſtance, *England*, *Scotland*, and *Ireland*, before the union lately made between *England* and *Scotland*; or when ſeveral independent ſtates agree among themſelves to form but one ſingle body: Such are the united provinces of the *Netherlands*, and the *Swiſs* cantons.

XLII. The firſt kind of union may happen, either on account of a marriage, or by virtue of a ſucceſſion, or when a people chooſes for a king, a prince who was already ſovereign of another kingdom; ſo that theſe different ſtates come to be united under a prince who governs each of them in particular by their reſpective fundamental laws.

XLIII. As for the compound governments, which are formed by the perpetual confederacy of ſeveral ſtates, it is to be obſerved, that this confederacy is the only means by which ſeveral ſmall ſtates, too weak to maintain themſelves ſeparately againſt their enemies, can preſerve their liberties.

XLIV. Theſe confederate ſtates engage to each other only to exerciſe, with common conſent, certain parts of the ſovereignty, eſpecially thoſe which relate to their mutual defence against foreign enemies: But each of the confederate parties retains an entire liberty of exercising as it thinks proper, those parts of the sovereignty which are not mentioned in the act of confederacy, as parts that ought to be exercised in common.

XLV. Lastly, it is absolutely necessary, in confederate states, to ascertain some time and place for assembling when occasion requires, and to invest some member with a power of calling the assembly for extraordinary affairs, and such as will not admit of delay. Or, by going another way to work, they may establish an assembly which always sits, composed of the deputies of each state, for dispatching common affairs according to the orders of their superiors.

CHAP. II.

An essay on this question, Which is the best form of government?

I. 'TIS certainly one of the finest questions in politics, and that which has most divided the men of genius, to determine, *Which is the best form of government?*

II. Every form of government has its advantages and inconveniencies, which are inseparable from it. It would be in vain to seek for a government perfect in every respect, and however perfect it might appear in speculation, yet 'tis certain, that in practice, and under

under the adminiſtration of men, it will always be accompanied with ſome defects ſo long as men govern men.

III. But if we cannot arrive at the height of perfection in this point, 'tis nevertheleſs certain, that there is a greater and a leſs, or different degrees between which prudence muſt determine. That government ought to be accounted the moſt perfect, which beſt anſwers its end, and is accompanied with the feweſt inconveniencies. Be this as it will, the examination of this queſtion furniſhes very uſeful inſtructions both to ſubjects and ſovereigns.

IV. 'Tis long ſince diſputes have been made on this ſubject; and there is nothing more intereſting upon the topic, than what we read in the father of hiſtory, *Herodotus*, who relates what paſſed in the council of the ſeven chiefs of *Perſia*, when the government was to be re-eſtabliſhed after the death of *Cambyſes*, and the puniſhment of the *Magus*, who had uſurped the throne under a pretext of being *Smerdis* the ſon of *Cyrus*.

V. *Otanes* was of opinion, that *Perſia* ſhould be made a republic, and ſpoke nearly in the following ſtrain. "I am not of opinion that we ſhould lodge the government in the hands of a ſingle perſon. Ye know to what exceſs *Cambyſes* went, and to what degree of inſolence we have ſeen the *Magus* arrive: how can the ſtate be well governed in a monarchy, where a ſingle perſon is permitted to do every thing according to his pleaſure? An au-

" thority, without a check, corrupts the moſt virtu-" ous man, and deprives him of his beſt qualities. " Envy and inſolence ariſe from preſent riches and " proſperity; and all other vices flow from theſe " two, when a man is poſſeſſed of every thing. " Kings hate virtuous men who oppoſe their unjuſt " deſigns, but careſs the wicked who favour them. " A ſingle man cannot ſee every thing with his own " eyes; he often lends a favourable ear to bad " reports and falſe accuſations; he ſubverts the laws " and cuſtoms of the country; he attacks the ho-" nour of women, and puts the innocent to death " by his caprice and his power. When the people " have the government in their hands, the equality " among the members prevents all theſe evils. The " magiſtrates are, in this caſe, choſen by lot; they " render an account of their adminiſtration, and " they form all their reſolutions in common with " the people. I am therefore of opinion, that we " ought to reject Monarchy and introduce a popular " government, becauſe we rather find theſe advan-" tages in many, than in a ſingle perſon." This was the opinion of *Otanes*.

VI. But *Megabyſes* ſpoke in favour of Ariſtocracy. " I approve (ſaid he) of the opinion of *Otanes* with " reſpect to exterminating Monarchy, but I believe " he is wrong in endeavouring to perſuade us to truſt " the government to the diſcretion of the people, " for it's certain, that nothing can be imagined more " fooliſh and inſolent than the populace. Why " ſhould we reject the power of a ſingle man, to deli-" ver up ourſelves to the tyranny of a blind and diſ-

" orderly multitude? If a king ſets about any en-" terprize, he is at leaſt capable of liſtening to " others; but the people is a blind monſter, equally " deſtitute of reaſon and capacity. They are un-" acquainted both with decency, virtue, and their " own intereſts. They do every thing with preci-" pitation, without judgment, and without order, " and reſemble a rapid torrent, which can have no " bounds ſet to it. If therefore ye wiſh the ruin of " the *Perſians*, eſtabliſh a popular government " among them. As for myſelf, I am of opinion, that " we ſhould make choice of ſome virtuous men, " and lodge the government and the power in their " hands." Such was the ſentiment of *Megabyſes*.

VII. After him, *Darius* ſpoke in the following terms. " I am of opinion, that there is a great " deal of juſtice in the ſpeech which *Megabyſes* has " made againſt a popular ſtate; but I alſo think, " that he is not intirely in the right, when he prefers " the government of a ſmall number to Monarchy. " 'Tis certain, that nothing can be imagined better, " or more perfect, than the government of a virtu-" ous man. Beſides, when a ſingle man is the " maſter, it is more difficult for enemies to diſco-" ver ſecret counſels and enterprizes. When the " government is in the hands of many, it is im-" poſſible but enmity and hatred muſt ariſe among " them; for as every one wants that his opinion " ſhould be followed, they gradually become ene-" mies. Emulation and jealouſy divide them, and " then their hatreds run to exceſs. Hence ariſe ſe-" ditions; from ſeditions, murders; and from "murders and blood, we ſee a monarch become "inſenſibly neceſſary. Thus the government al- "ways falls into the hands of a ſingle perſon. In "a popular ſtate, there muſt neceſſarily be a great "deal of malice and corruption. It is true, equa- "lity generates no hatred, but it foments friendſhip "among the wicked, who ſupport each other, till "ſome man, who has rendered himſelf agreeable to "the people, and acquired an authority over the "multitude, diſcovers their frauds, and expoſes "their perfidy. Then ſuch a man ſhews himſelf "truly a monarch; and hence we may know that "Monarchy is the moſt natural government, ſince "the ſeditions of Ariſtocracy, and the corruption of "Democracy, have an equal tendency to make us "have recourſe to the unity of a ſupreme power."

The opinion of *Darius* was approved, and the government of *Perſia* continued monarchic. We thought this paſſage of hiſtory ſufficiently intereſting to be related on this occaſion.

VIII. To determine ſurely, with reſpect to this queſtion, we muſt trace matters from their principles. Liberty, under which we muſt comprehend all the moſt precious goods, has two enemies to be afraid of in civil ſociety. The firſt is licentiouſneſs, diſorder and confuſion; and the ſecond is the oppreſſion ariſing from tyranny.

IX. The firſt of theſe evils ariſes from liberty itſelf, when it is not kept in due order.

The ſecond, from the remedy which mankind have contrived againſt this firſt evil, that is, from ſovereignty.

X.

X. The height of happineſs and human prudence is to know how to guard againſt theſe two enemies: the only method of doing ſo is to have a well concerted ſovereignty, a government formed with ſuch precautions, as, by baniſhing licentiouſneſs, not to introduce tyranny.

XI. 'Tis therefore in this happy temperament that we can find the general idea of a good government. It is evident, that the government which avoids the extremes, is ſo well adapted for the preſerving of good order, and for providing againſt the wants of the people both at home and abroad, that it leaves, at the ſame time, ſufficient ſureties to the public, that this end ſhall never be varied from.

XII. But among all governments, Which approaches moſt to this perfection? Before we anſwer this queſtion, 'tis proper to obſerve, that it is very different from this, Which is the moſt lawful government?

XIII. As for this laſt queſtion, 'tis certain, that governments of every kind, which are founded on the free acquieſcence of the people, whether expreſs or juſtified by a long and peaceable poſſeſſion, are all equally lawful, ſo long at leaſt as, by the intention of the ſovereign, they tend to promote the happineſs of the people: thus no other cauſe can degrade a government, but an open and actual violence, either in its eſtabliſhment, or in its exerciſe; I mean uſurpation, or tyranny.

XIV. To return to the principal queſtion, I affirm, that the beſt government is neither abſolute Monarchy, nor that which is entirely popular: the firſt is too ſtrong, encroaches too much on liberty, and inclines too much to tyranny; the ſecond is too weak, delivers the people too much to themſelves, and tends to confuſion and licentiouſneſs.

XV. It were to be wiſhed, for the glory of ſovereigns and for the happineſs of the people, that we could conteſt the fact with reſpect to abſolute governments. I venture to affirm, that nothing can be compared to an abſolute government, in the hands of a wiſe and virtuous prince. Order, diligence, ſecrecy, quickneſs in execution, the greateſt enterprizes, and the moſt happy executions, are the certain effects of it. Dignities, honours, rewards and puniſhments, are all diſpenſed under it with juſtice and diſcernment. So beautiful a reign is the golden age.

XVI. But to reign in this manner, a ſuperior genius, a perfect virtue, great experience, and an uninterrupted application, are neceſſary. Man, in ſo high an elevation, is rarely capable of ſo many things. The multitude of objects diſtracts him, pride ſeduces him, pleaſure tempts him, and flattery, which is the bane of the great, does him more injury than all the reſt. It is difficult to reſiſt ſo many ſnares; and what generally happens is, that a prince, maſter of all, eaſily becomes a prey to his paſſions, and conſequently renders his ſubjects miſerable.

XVII.

XVII. Hence proceeds the disgust of people to absolute governments, and this disgust sometimes rises to aversion and hatred. This has also given occasion to politicians to make two important reflections.

The first is, that, in an absolute government, it is rare to see the people interest themselves in its preservation. Wearied with the burdens they bear, they long for a revolution, which cannot render their situation worse.

The second is, that it is the interest of princes to engage the people in the maintenance of their government, and for that purpose to give them a share in it, by privileges which secure their liberty. Nothing is more proper to promote the safety of princes at home, their power abroad, and their glory in all respects.

XVIII. It has been said of the *Roman* people, that, so long as they fought for their own interests, they were invincible; but, as soon as they became slaves to absolute masters, they grew cowardly and dastardly, and asked for no more than bread and public diversions, *Panem & Circenses*.

XIX. On the contrary, in states where the people have some share in the government, all the individuals interest themselves in the public good, because each, according to his quality or merit, partakes of the good success, or feels the loss. This is what renders men dexterous and generous, what inspires them with an ardent love of their country, and with an invincible courage, which is proof against the greatest misfortunes.

XX.

XX. When *Hannibal* had gained four victories over the *Romans*, and killed more than two hundred thousand of them, when, much about the same time, the two brave *Scipios* had been cut in pieces in *Spain*, besides several considerable losses at sea, and in *Sicily*, who could have thought that *Rome* could have resisted her enemies? However the virtue of her citizens, the love they bore their country, and the interest they had in the government, augmented the strength of that republic in the midst of her calamities, and at last she surmounted every thing. Among the *Lacedæmonians* and *Athenians* we find several examples which prove this truth.

XXI. All these advantages are not found in absolute governments. We may justly affirm, that it is an essential fault in them not to interest the people in their preservation, that they are too violent, tend too much to oppression, and not enough to the good of the subjects.

XXII. Such are absolute governments: the popular are no better, and we may say they have nothing good but liberty, and that they leave the people to choose a better.

XXIII. Absolute governments have at least two advantages: the first is, that now and then they have happy intervals when they are in the hands of good princes: the second is, that they have more force, activity, and quickness of execution.

XXIV. But a popular government has none of these advantages;

advantages; formed by the multitude, it aſſumes all the characters of it. The multitude is a mixture of all kinds of people, a few men of parts, ſome who have good ſenſe and honeſt intentions; but a far greater number who cannot be depended upon, who have nothing to loſe, and who conſequently cannot be ſafely truſted. Beſides, a multitude always produces ſlowneſs and diſorder. Secrecy and foreſight are advantages unknown to it.

XXV. Liberty is not wanting in popular ſtates; they have rather too much of it, and ſince it degenerates into licentiouſneſs. Hence it is that they are weak and ſtaggering. Commotions at home, or attacks from abroad, often throw them into conſternation: 'tis their ordinary fate to be the prey of the ambition of ſome citizens or ſome ſtrangers, and thus to paſs from the greateſt liberty to the greateſt ſlavery.

XXVI This is proved by the experience of a hundred different nations. Even at preſent, *Poland* is a ſtriking example of the defects of popular government from the anarchy and diſorder which reigns there. It is the ſport of its own inhabitants and of foreigners, and often a field of blood; becauſe, under the appearance of a Monarchy, it is in reality too popular a government.

XXVII. We need only read the hiſtories of *Florence* and *Genoa*, to ſee a lively picture of the misfortunes which republics ſuffer from the multitude when it wants to govern. The antient republics, eſpecially *Athens*,

Athens, the moſt conſiderable of thoſe in *Greece*, place this truth in a ſtill clearer light.

XXVIII. In a word, *Rome* periſhed in the hands of the people; and royalty gave birth to it. The Patricians, who compoſed the ſenate, by freeing it from royalty, had rendered it miſtreſs of *Italy*. The people, by means of the Tribunes, gradually uſurped the authority of the ſenate. From that time diſcipline was relaxed, and gave place to licentiouſneſs. At laſt the republic was, by the hands of the people, reduced to the greateſt ſlavery.

XXIX. 'Tis not therefore to be doubted, after ſo many proofs, but popular governments are the weakeſt and worſt of all others. Certainly if we conſider the education of the vulgar, their application to labour, their ignorance and brutality, we muſt readily perceive, that they are made to be governed, and not at all to govern others; and that good order, and their own advantage, forbid them to interfere with that charge.

XXX. If therefore neither the government of the multitude, nor the abſolute government of a ſingle perſon, are proper to procure the happineſs of a people, it follows, that the beſt governments are thoſe which are ſo tempered, that, by equally avoiding tyranny and licentiouſneſs, they ſecure the happineſs of the ſubjects.

XXXI. There are, in general, two ways of finding this temperament.

The firſt conſiſts in lodging the ſovereignty in a council ſo compoſed, both as to the number and choice of perſons, as that there may be a moral certainty that they ſhall have no other intereſts than thoſe of the community, and that they ſhall always give a faithful account of their conduct to it. This is what we ſee happily practiſed in moſt republics.

XXXII. The ſecond is, by fundamental laws, to limit the ſovereignty of the prince in monarchic ſtates, or to give the perſon, who enjoys the honours and title of the ſovereignty, only a part of the ſovereign authority, and to lodge the other in different hands, for example, in a council or parliament. This is what produces limited monarchies *.

XXXIII. As for Monarchies, it is proper, for example, that the military power, the legiſlative power, and that of raiſing taxes, ſhould be lodged in different hands, to the end that they may not be eaſily abuſed. 'Tis eaſy to conceive, that theſe modifications can be made in different manners. The general rule, which prudence directs to follow, is to limit the power of the prince, ſo that nothing may be dreaded from it; but at the ſame time not to go to exceſs, for fear of weakening and enervating the government altogether.

XXXIV. By following this juſt medium the people will enjoy the moſt perfect liberty, ſince they have all the moral ſureties that the prince will not abuſe his power. The prince, on the other hand,

* See part I. chap. 7. §. 26, &c.

being,

being, as it were, under a neceſſity of doing his duty, conſiderably ſtrengthens his authority, and enjoys the greateſt happineſs and the moſt ſolid glory: for as the felicity of the people is the end of government, it is alſo the ſureſt foundation of the throne. See what has been already ſaid on this ſubject.

XXXV. This ſpecies of Monarchy, limited by a mixed government, unites the principal advantages of abſolute Monarchy, and of the Ariſtocratic and popular governments; and at the ſame time avoids the dangers and inconveniencies which are peculiar to each. This then is the happy temperament which we ſeek for.

XXXVI. This is alſo what has been proved by the experience of all ages. Such was the government of *Sparta*; *Lycurgus*, knowing that the three ſorts of ſimple governments had each very great inconveniencies; that Royalty eaſily degenerated into arbitrary power and tyranny; that Ariſtocracy degenerated into an unjuſt government of ſome particulars, and Democracy into a wild dominion without rule, thought it expedient to combine thoſe three governments in that of *Sparta*, and mix them, as it were, into one, ſo that they might ſerve as a remedy and counterpoiſe to each other. This wiſe legiſlator was not deceived, and no republic has longer preſerved its laws, cuſtoms, and liberty, than that of *Sparta*.

XXXVII. It may be ſaid, that the government of the *Romans* under the republic, united in ſome meaſure, as that of *Sparta*, the three kinds of authority. The consuls held the place of kings, the senate formed the public council, and the people had also some share in the administration of affairs.

XXXVIII. If more modern examples are wanted, is not *England* at present a proof of the goodness of mixed governments and temperate monarchies? Is there a nation, every thing considered, which enjoys more prosperity at home, or more renown abroad?

XXXIX. The northern nations, who took possession of the *Roman* empire, had carried into the countries, where they established themselves, that species of government which was then called *Gothic*. They had kings, lords, and commons; and experience proves, that the states, who have retained that form of government, have prospered much better than those who have reduced all to the absolute government of a single man.

XL. As for Aristocratic governments, we must first distinguish Aristocracy by birth, from that which is elective. Aristocracy, by birth, has several advantages, but it has also very great inconveniencies. It inspires the nobility, who govern, with pride, and it entertains, between the grandees and the people, a separation, a contempt, and a jealousy, which produces great evils.

XLI. But elective Aristocracy has all the advantages of the former, without its defects. As there is no privilege of exclusion, and as the door

to

to employments is open to all the citizens, we find neither pride nor ſeparation among them. On the contrary, there is a general emulation among all the members, which turns every thing to the public good, and contributes infinitely to the preſervation of liberty.

XLII. Thus if we ſuppoſe that, in an elective Ariſtocracy, the ſovereignty is in the hands of a council ſo numerous, as to include in its boſom the moſt important intereſts of the ſtate, and never to have any oppoſite to them: If beſides, this council is ſo ſmall, as to maintain order, concord and ſecrecy; if it is choſen from among the wiſeſt, and moſt virtuous of the citizens; and laſtly if the authority of this council is limited and kept within rule; it cannot be doubted but ſuch a government is very proper of itſelf to promote the happineſs of a nation.

XLIII. What is moſt delicate in theſe governments, is to temper them in ſuch a manner, as that, at the ſame time, that the people are aſſured of their liberty, by giving them ſome ſhare in the government, not to puſh theſe aſſurances too far, and make the government approach too much to Democracy: for the reflections we have made before ſufficiently evince the inconveniencies which would reſult from this.

XLIV. Let us therefore conclude, from this examination of the different forms of government, that the beſt are either a limited Monarchy, or an Ariſtocracy tempered with Democracy, by ſome privileges in favour of the body of the people.

XLV.

XLV. 'Tis true, in reality, there are always ſome deductions to be made from the advantages which we have aſcribed to theſe governments; but this is the fault of men, and not of the eſtabliſhments. The conſtitution is the moſt perfect that can be imagined, and if men ſpoil it by their vices and follies, this is the nature of all human affairs; and ſince a choice muſt be made, the beſt is always that which is attended with the feweſt inconveniencies.

XLVI. In a word, if it ſhould ſtill be aſked, which government is beſt? I would anſwer, that all good governments are not equally proper for all nations, and that, in this point, we muſt have a regard to the humour and character of the people, and to the extent of the ſtates.

XLVII. Great ſtates can hardly admit of republican governments; hence a monarchy, wiſely limited, ſuits them better. But as to ſtates, of an ordinary extent, the moſt advantageous government for them, is an elective ariſtocracy, tempered with ſome reſerves in favour of the body of the people.

CHAP. III.

Of the different ways of acquiring ſovereignty.

I. THE only lawful foundation of all acquiſition of ſovereignty, is the conſent, or the will of the people *. But as this conſent may be

* On this ſubject, ſee part I. chap. 6.

given different ways, according to the different circumstances which accompany it; hence it is that we distinguish the different ways of acquiring sovereignty.

II. Sometimes a people are constrained, by force of arms, to submit to the dominion of a conqueror; sometimes also, the people, of their own accord, give the sovereign authority to some person, with a full and entire liberty. Sovereignty may therefore be acquired either in a forced manner and by violence, or in a free and voluntary manner.

III. These different acquisitions of sovereignty may agree in some measure to all sorts of governments; but as they disclose themselves most visibly in monarchies, so it shall be principally with respect to these, that we shall examine this point.

1°. *Of Conquest.*

IV. Sovereignty is sometimes acquired by force, or rather it is seized by conquest or by usurpation.

V. Conquest is the acquisition of sovereignty, by the superiority of a foreign prince's arms, which at last reduces the vanquished to submit to his government. Usurpation is properly made by a person naturally submitted to him from whom he wrests the sovereignty; but custom often confounds these two terms.

VI. There are several remarks to be made on conquest,

conqueſt, conſidered as a means of acquiring the ſovereignty.

1°. Conqueſt, conſidered in itſelf, is rather the occaſion of acquiring the ſovereignty, than the immediate cauſe of this acquiſition. The immediate cauſe of the acquiſition of ſovereignty, is the conſent of the people, either tacit or expreſſed. Without this conſent the ſtate of war always ſubſiſts between two enemies, and the one is not obliged to obey the other. All that can be ſaid is, that the conſent of the vanquiſhed is extorted by the ſuperiority of the conqueror.

VII. 2°. All lawful conqueſt ſuppoſes, that the conqueror has had juſt reaſon to wage war againſt the vanquiſhed. Without this, conqueſt is by no means, of itſelf, a juſt title; for a man cannot acquire a ſovereignty over a nation, by bare ſeizure, as over a thing which belongs to no body. Thus when *Alexander* waged war againſt diſtant people, who had never heard of his name, certainly ſuch a conqueſt was no more a lawful title to the ſovereignty, than robbery is a lawful means of becoming rich. The quality and number of the perſons do not change the nature of the action, the injury is the ſame, and the crime equal.

VIII. But if the war is juſt, the conqueſt is alſo the ſame: for firſt it is a natural conſequence of the victory; and the vanquiſhed, who deliver themſelves to the conqueror, only purchaſe their lives by the loſs of their liberties. Beſides, the vanquiſhed having, thro' their own fault, engaged in an unjuſt war, rather

ther than grant the juſt ſatisfaction they owed, they are deemed to have tacitly conſented beforehand to the conditions which the conqueror ſhould impoſe on them, provided they were neither unjuſt, nor inhuman.

IX. 3°. What muſt we think of unjuſt conqueſts, and of ſubmiſſion extorted by unjuſt violence? Can it give a lawful right? I anſwer, we muſt diſtinguiſh whether an uſurper has changed a republic into a monarchy, or diſpoſſeſſed the lawful monarch. In the laſt caſe, he is indiſpenſably obliged to reſtore the crown to him from whom he has taken it, or to his heirs, 'till it can be reaſonably preſumed that they have renounced their pretenſions; and this is always preſumed, when a conſiderable time is elapſed without their being willing or able to make any effort to recover the crown.

X. The law of nations therefore admits of a kind of preſcription with reſpect to the ſovereignty. This is requiſite for the intereſt and tranquillity of ſocieties; a long and peaceable poſſeſſion of the ſovereignty, muſt eſtabliſh the legality of it, otherwiſe there would never be an end of the diſputes about kingdoms and their limits, which would be a ſource of perpetual quarrels, and there would at preſent hardly be a ſovereign lawfully poſſeſſed of the authority.

XI. It is, indeed, the duty of the people, in the beginning, to reſiſt the uſurper with all their power, and to continue faithful to their ſovereign; but if, in ſpite of all their efforts, their ſovereign is baffled,

baffled, and can no longer aſſert his right, they are obliged to no more, and they may lawfully take care of their own preſervation.

XII. The people cannot do without a government, and as they are not obliged to expoſe themſelves to perpetual wars, in defence of the rights of their firſt ſovereign, they may, by their conſent, render the right of the uſurper lawful; and in this caſe the ſovereign, who is ſtripped, ought to reſt contented with the loſs of his dominions, and look upon it as a misfortune.

XIII. As for the firſt caſe, when the uſurper has changed a republic into a monarchy; if he governs with moderation and equity, it is ſufficient that he has reigned peaceably for ſome time, to afford reaſon to believe, that the people conſent to his dominion, and to efface what was faulty in the manner of his acquiring it. This may be very well applied to the reign of *Auguſtus*. But if, on the contrary, the prince, who has made himſelf maſter of a republic, exerciſes his power tyrannically, and oppreſſes his ſubjects, they are not then obliged to obey him. In theſe circumſtances the longeſt poſſeſſion imports no more than a long continuation of injuſtice.

2°. *Of the election of ſovereigns.*

XIV. But the moſt lawful way of acquiring ſovereignty, is certainly that founded on the free conſent of the people. This is done either by the way of election, or by the right of ſucceſſion; for which reaſon kingdoms are diſtinguiſhed into elective and hereditary.

XV. Election is that act, by which the people design or nominate a certain person, whom they judge capable of succeeding the deceased king, to govern the state; and so soon as this person has accepted the offer of the people, he is invested with the sovereignty.

XVI. We may distinguish two sorts of elections, the one entirely free, and the other limited in certain respects; the first when the people can choose whom they think proper, and the second when they are obliged for example to choose a person of a certain nation, a certain family, a certain religion *&c.* Among the antient *Persians*, no man could be king unless he had been instructed by the Magi *.

XVII. The time, between the death of the king and the election of his successor, is called an *Interregnum*.

XVIII. During the *Interregnum* the state is, as it were, an imperfect body without a head, but yet the civil society is not dissolved. The sovereignty then returns to the people, who, till they choose a new king to exercise it as he thinks proper, have it even in their power to change the form of the government.

XIX. But it is a wise precaution, to prevent the troubles of an *Interregnum*, to nominate beforehand those, who, during that time, are to hold the reins of government. Thus in *Poland* it is the archbishop

* See Cicer. de divinat. lib. I. cap. 4.

of

of *Gnesna*, with the deputies of great and little *Poland*, who are established for that purpose.

XX. The persons, invested with this employment, are called *Regents of the kingdom*; and the *Romans* called them *Interreges*. They are temporary, and, as it were, provisional magistrates, who, in the name, and by the authority of the people, exercise, till the election, the acts of the sovereignty, so that they are obliged to give an account of their administration. This may suffice for the way of election.

3°. *Of the succession to the crown.*

XXI. The other manner of acquiring the sovereignty, is the right of succession, by which princes, who have once acquired the crown, transmit it to their successors.

XXII. It may seem at first that elective kingdoms have the advantage over those which are hereditary, because, in the former, the subjects may always choose a prince of merit and capable of governing. However experience shews, that, taking all things into the account, the way of succession is more for the good of the state.

XXIII. For, 1°. by this means we avoid the great inconveniencies, both at home and abroad, which arise from frequent elections. 2°. There is less contention and uncertainty, with respect to those who ought to succeed. 3°. A prince, whose crown is hereditary, all other circumſtances being equal, will take more care of his kingdom, and ſpare his ſubjects more, in hopes to leave the crown to his children, than if he only poſſeſſed it for himſelf. 4°. A kingdom, where the ſucceſſion is regulated, has much more ſtability and force. It can form greater projects, and purſue the execution of them more vigorouſly than if it was elective. 5°. In a word, the perſon of the prince appears more venerable to the people by the ſplendor of his birth, and they have reaſon to hope that he will have the qualities proper for the throne, by the impreſſions of the noble blood from whence he deſcends, and by the education he is to receive.

XXIV. The order of the ſucceſſion to the crown is regulated either by the will of the laſt king, or by that of the people.

XXV. In kingdoms, truly patrimonial, every king has a right to regulate the ſucceſſion, and to diſpoſe of the kingdom as he has a mind; provided the choice he makes of his ſucceſſor, and the manner in which he ſettles the ſtate, are not manifeſtly and remarkably oppoſite to the public good, which, even in patrimonial kingdoms, is always the ſovereign law.

XXVI. But if ſuch a king, prevented perhaps by death, has not named his ſucceſſor, then it ſeems natural to follow, with reſpect to the crown, the laws or cuſtoms eſtabliſhed in the country, concerning private inheritances, ſo far at leaſt as the ſafety and

and preſervation of the ſtate will permit *. But it is certain that, in theſe caſes, the moſt approved and powerful candidate will always carry it.

XXVII. In kingdoms, which are not patrimonial, the people regulate the order of the ſucceſſion: and tho', to ſpeak in general, they may eſtabliſh the ſucceſſion as they pleaſe, yet prudence requires that, in this reſpect, they follow the method moſt advantageous to the ſtate, moſt proper to maintain order and peace, and moſt expedient to promote the the public ſafety.

XXVIII. The moſt uſual methods are, a ſucceſſion, ſimply hereditary, which follows nearly the rules of common inheritances; and the lineal ſucceſſion which receives more particular limitations.

XXIX. The good of the ſtate therefore requires that a ſucceſſion, ſimply hereditary, ſhould vary in ſeveral things from private inheritances.

1°. The kingdom ought to remain indiviſible, and not be ſhared among ſeveral heirs, in the ſame degree; for firſt, this would weaken the ſtate conſiderably, and render it leſs proper to reſiſt the attacks it may be expoſed to. Beſides, the ſubjects having different maſters, would no longer be ſo cloſely united among themſelves: and laſtly, this might lay a foundation for inteſtine wars, as experience has too often proved.

XXX. 2°. The crown ought to remain in the

* See the Law of Nature and Nations, book VII. chap. 7. §. 11.

posterity

posterity of the first possessor, and not to pass to his relations in a collateral line, and much less to those who have only connections of affinity with him. This is, no doubt, the intention of a people who have rendered the crown hereditary in the family of a prince. Thus, unless it is otherwise determined, in default of the descendants of the first possessor, the right of disposing of the kingdom returns to the nation.

XXXI. 3°. Those only ought to be admitted to the succession, who are born of a marriage conformable to the laws of the nation. For this there are several reasons. 1°. This was, no doubt, the intention of the people, when they gave the crown to the descendants of the king. 2°. The people have not the same respect for the king's natural or base sons, as for his lawful children. 3°. The father of natural children is not known for certain, there being no sure method of ascertaining the father of a child born out of wedlock; and yet it is of the last importance that there should be no doubt about the birth of those who are to reign, in order to avoid the disputes which might arise thereon, and embroil the kingdom. Hence it is, that, in several countries, the queen is brought to bed in public, or in the presence of several persons.

XXXII. 4°. Adopted children, not being of the royal blood, are also excluded from the crown, which ought to return to the disposal of the people, as soon as the royal line fails.

XXXIII. 5°. Among those who are in the same degree,

degree, whether really or by reprefentation, the males are to be preferred to the females, becaufe they are prefumed more proper for the command of armies, and for exercifing the other functions of government.

XXXIV. 6°. Among feveral males, or feveral females in the fame degree, the eldeft ought to fucceed. 'Tis birth which gives this right; for the crown being at the fame time indivifible and hereditary, the eldeft, in confequence of his birth, has a right of preference, which the younger cannot take from him. But it is juft that the eldeft fhould give his brothers a fufficiency to fupport themfelves decently, and in a manner fuitable to their rank. What is allotted them for this purpofe is called by the name of *Appennage*.

XXXV. 7°. Laftly, we muft obferve, that the crown does not pafs to the fucceffor in confequence of the pleafure of the deceafed king, but by the will of the people, who have fettled it in the royal family. Hence it follows, that the inheritance of the particular eftate of the king, and that of the crown, are of a quite different nature, and have no connection with each other; fo that, ftrictly fpeaking, the fucceffor may accept of the crown, and refufe the inheritance of the particular eftate; and, in this cafe, he is not obliged to pay the debts due upon this particular eftate.

XXXVI. But it is certain, that honour and equity hardly permit a prince, who afcends the throne, to to uſe this rigorous right, and that, if he has the glory of his Royal houſe at heart, he will, by good œconomy and frugality, find wherewithal to pay the debts of his predeceſſor. But this ought not to be done at the expence of the public treaſure. Theſe are the rules of ſucceſſion ſimply hereditary.

XXXVII. But ſince in this hereditary ſucceſſion, where the next to the deceaſed king is called to the crown, very terrible diſputes may happen concerning the degree of proximity, when thoſe who remain, are a little diſtant from the common ſtem; ſeveral nations have eſtabliſhed the lineal ſucceſſion from branch to branch, the rules of which are theſe following.

1°. All thoſe deſcended from the Royal founder are accounted ſo many lines or branches, each of which has a right to the crown according to the degree of its proximity.

2°. Among thoſe of this line, who are in the ſame degree, firſt ſex, and then age, gives the preference.

3°. We muſt not paſs from one line to another, ſo long as there remains one of the preceding, even tho' there ſhould be another line of relations nearer to the deceaſed king. For example:

A king

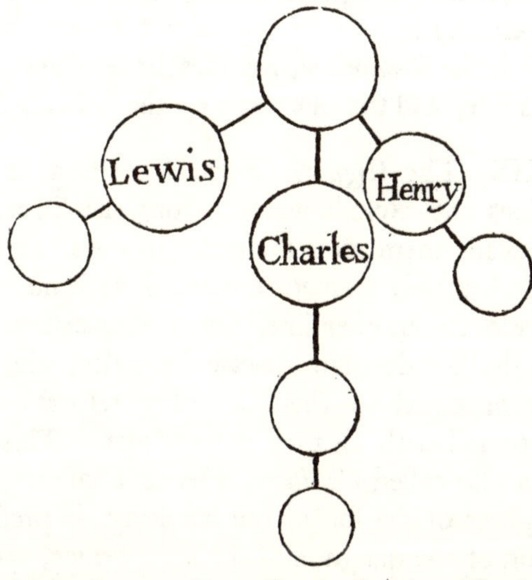

A king leaves three ſons, *Lewis*, *Charles*, and *Henry*. The ſon of *Lewis*, who ſucceeds him, dies without children; *Charles* leaves a grandſon; *Henry* is ſtill living, and is the uncle of the deceaſed king; the grand-child of *Charles* is only his couſin-german: and yet this grand-child will have the crown as being tranſmitted to him by his grand-father, whoſe line has excluded *Henry* and his deſcendants, till it is quite extinct.

4°. Every one has therefore a right to ſucceed in his rank, and tranſmits this right to his deſcendants, with the ſame order of ſucceſſion, tho' he has never reigned himſelf; that is to ſay, the right of the dead paſſes to the living, and that of the living to the dead.

5°. If the laſt king has died without iſſue, we make choice of the neareſt line to his, and ſo on.

XXXVIII. There are two principal kinds of lineal ſucceſſion,

ſucceſſion, namely, *Cognatic* and *Agnatic*. Theſe names come from the Latin words *Cognati* and *Agnati*, the firſt of which, in the *Roman* law, ſignifies the relations on the mother's ſide, and the laſt thoſe on the father's ſide.

XXXIX. The *Cognatic* lineal ſucceſſion is that which does not exclude women from the ſucceſſion, but only calls them after the males in the ſame line; ſo that, when only women remain, there is no tranſition made to another line, but the ſucceſſion runs back to the female again, in caſe the males, who were ſuperior or equal to them in other reſpects, ſhall happen to fail with all their deſcendants. This ſucceſſion is alſo called *Caſtilian*. Hence it follows, that the daughter of the ſon of the laſt king, is preferred to the ſon of the daughter of the ſame prince, and the daughter of one of his brothers to the ſon of one of his ſiſters.

XL. The *Agnatic* lineal ſucceſſion is that in which only the male iſſue of males ſucceeds, ſo that women, and all thoſe deſcending from them, are perpetually excluded. It is alſo called the *French* ſucceſſion. This excluſion of women and their deſcendants is principally eſtabliſhed to hinder the crown from coming to a foreign race, by the marriages of princeſſes of the blood royal.

XLI. Theſe are the principal kinds of ſucceſſion in uſe, and may be tempered in different manners by the people; but prudence directs us to prefer thoſe which are ſubject to the leaſt difficulty; and in this reſpect the lineal ſucceſſion has the advantage over that which is ſimply hereditary.

XLII.

XLII. Several queſtions, equally curious and important, may be ſtarted with regard to the ſucceſſion of kingdoms. On this ſubject the reader may conſult *Grotius* *. We ſhall only here examine who has a right to decide the diſputes which may ariſe between two or more pretenders to a crown.

1°. If the kingdom is patrimonial, and ſome diſputes ariſe after the death of the king, between the pretenders, the beſt method is to refer the cauſe to arbitrators who are of the royal family. The good and peace of the kingdom require this conduct.

2°. But in kingdoms eſtabliſhed by the voluntary act of the people, if the diſpute ariſes even when the king is alive, he is not for that reaſon a competent judge of it; for then the people muſt have given him the power of regulating the ſucceſſion according to his own pleaſure, which is not to be ſuppoſed. It therefore belongs to the people to decide the diſpute, either by themſelves or by their repreſentatives.

3°. The ſame holds true, if the diſpute does not ariſe till after the death of the king: in this caſe it is either neceſſary to determine which of the pretenders is neareſt to the deceaſed king; and this is a point of fact which the people only ought to determine, becauſe they are principally intereſted in it.

4°. Or the diſpute is to know, what degree, or what line, ought to have the preference according to the order of the ſucceſſion which the people have eſtabliſhed; and then it is a point of right. Now who can better determine this point than the people themſelves, who have eſtabliſhed the order of ſucceſſion? otherwiſe there would be no method of de-

* The Right of War and Peace, book II. chap. 7. §. 25, *&c.*

termining the dispute but by force of arms, which would be entirely contrary to the good of the society.

XLIII. But to avoid every perplexity of this kind, it would be proper that the people should, by a fundamental law, formally reserve to themselves the right of judging in similar cases. What has been said is sufficient on the different ways of acquiring sovereignty.

CHAP. IV.

Of the different ways of losing sovereignty.

I. LET us now enquire how sovereignty can be lost; and in this there is no great difficulty, after the principles we have established on the ways of acquiring it.

II. Sovereignty may be lost by abdication, that is, by an act by which the reigning prince renounces the sovereignty, so far as it regards himself. Of this the history even of late ages furnishes us with several remarkable examples.

III. As sovereignty derives its origin from a covenant founded on a free consent between the king and his subjects; if, for some plausible reasons, the king thinks proper to renounce the sovereignty, the people have not properly a right to constrain him to keep it.

IV. But ſuch an abdication muſt not be made at an unſeaſonable juncture: as for inſtance, when the kingdom is like to ſink into a minority, eſpecially if it is threatened with a war; or when the prince, by his bad conduct, has thrown the ſtate into a dangerous ſituation, in which he cannot abandon it without betraying or deſtroying it.

V. But we may ſafely ſay, that a prince very rarely finds himſelf in ſuch circumſtances, as can engage him voluntarily to renounce the crown. In whatever ſituation he is, he may get rid of the drudgery of government, and ſtill retain the ſuperiority of command. A king ought to die upon the throne, and it is always a weakneſs unworthy of him, to ſtrip himſelf voluntarily of his authority. Beſides, experience has frequently ſhewn, that abdication has been attended with a melancholy and miſerable end.

VI. 'Tis therefore certain, that a prince may, for himſelf, renounce the crown, or the right of ſucceſſion. But there is a great difficulty in determining whether he can do it for his children.

VII. To judge rightly of this point, which has ſo much divided politicians, we muſt eſtabliſh the following principles.

1°. Every acquiſition of a right over another, and conſequently of ſovereignty, ſuppoſes the conſent of him over whom this right is to be acquired, and the acceptance of him who is to acquire it. So long as this acceptance is not given, the intention of the former does not produce, in favour of the other, an absolute and irrevocable right: It is only a simple designation, which he is at liberty to accept of or not.

VIII. 2°. Let us apply these principles. The princes of the blood Royal, who have accepted the will of the people, by which the crown has been conferred on them, have certainly, by that means, acquired an absolute and irrevocable right, of which they cannot be stripped without their own consent.

IX. As for those who are not yet born, as they have not accepted of the designation of the people, so they have not as yet any right. Hence it follows, that, with regard to them, this designation is only an imperfect act, a kind of expectancy, the completion of which intirely depends on the will of the people.

X. 4°. But it may be said, the ancestors of those, who are not yet born, have consented and stipulated for them, and consequently received the engagement of the people in their behalf. But this is rather an argument in favour of renunciation, which it effectually establishes; for as the right of those, who are not yet born, has no other foundation but the concurrence of the will of the people and of their ancestors, it is evident that this right may be taken from them without injustice, by those very persons, from the single will of whom they hold it.

XI. The single will of a prince, without the consent of the nation, cannot effectually exclude his children from the crown to which the people have called them. In like manner, the single will of the people,

people, without the consent of the prince, cannot deprive his children of an expectancy which their father has stipulated with the people in their favour. But if these two wills unite, they may, without doubt, change what they have established.

XII. 6°. 'Tis true this renunciation ought not to be made without a cause, and thro' a motive of inconstancy and levity. In these circumstances, reason cannot authorize them, and the good of the state does not permit, that, without a necessity, an alteration should be made in the order of the succession.

XIII. 7°. If, on the contrary, the nation is in such circumstances, that the renunciation of a prince or a princess, is absolutely necessary to its tranquillity and happiness, then the supreme law of the public good, which has established the order of the succession, requires it should be set aside.

XIV. 8°. Let us add, that it is for the common good of nations, that such renunciations should be valid, and that the parties interested should not attempt to disannul them. For there are times and conjunctures in which they are necessary for the good of the state; and if those, who are concerned in the affair, imagine that the renunciation will afterwards be despised, it is not likely that they will be satisfied with it. It is evident that bloody and cruel wars must always arise from this source. *Grotius* decides this question nearly in the same manner. The reader may see what he says of it *.

* Book II. chap. 7. §. 26. and book II. chap. 4. §. 10.

XV. 9°. As war or conqueſt is a means of acquiring ſovereignty, as we have ſeen in the preceding chapter, ſo 'tis evident that it is alſo a means of loſing it. But what we have already ſaid is, at preſent, ſufficient on this ſubject.

XVI. With regard to tyranny and the depoſing of ſovereigns, both which are alſo ways of loſing the ſovereignty, as theſe two things have a relation to the duties of ſubjects towards their ſovereigns, we ſhall treat of them, after we have, in the next chapter, conſidered theſe duties.

CHAP. V.
Of the duties of ſubjects in general.

I. According to the plan we have laid down, we muſt here treat of the duties of ſubjects. *Puffendorff* has given us a clear and diſtinct idea of them, in the laſt chapter of his *Duties of a Man and a Citizen.* We ſhall follow him ſtep by ſtep.

II. The duties of ſubjects are either general or particular; and both flow from their ſtate and condition.

III. All ſubjects have this in common, that they live under the ſame ſovereign and the ſame government, and that they are members of the ſame ſtate. From theſe relations the general duties ariſe.

IV.

IV. But as they have different employments, enjoy different poſts in the ſtate, and follow different profeſſions; hence alſo ariſe their particular duties.

V. It is alſo to be obſerved, that the duties of ſubjects, ſuppoſe and include thoſe of man, conſidered ſimply as ſuch, and as a member of human ſociety in general.

VI. The general duties of ſubjects have, for their object, either the governors of the ſtate, or the whole body of the people, *viz.* their country, or the individuals among their fellow-ſubjects.

VII. As for ſovereigns and governors of the ſtate, every ſubject owes them that reſpect, fidelity, and obedience, which their character demands. Hence it follows, that we ought to be contented with the preſent government, and to form no cabals nor ſeditions, but to be attached to the intereſt of our prince, more than to that of any other perſon, to honour him, to think favourably of him, and to ſpeak with reſpect of him and his actions. We ought even to have a veneration for the memory of good princes *&c.*

VIII. With reſpect to the whole body of the ſtate, a good ſubject makes it his rule to prefer the public good to every thing elſe, bravely to ſacrifice his fortune, and all his private intereſts, and even his life, for the preſervation and the good of the ſtate; and to employ all his talents and his induſtry to advance the honour, and to procure the advantage of his native country.

IX. Laſtly, the duty of a ſubject to his fellow-ſubjects conſiſts in living with them, as much as he poſſibly can, in peace and ſtrict union, in being mild, complaiſant, affable, and obliging to each of them, in creating no trouble by a rude or litigious humour, and in bearing no envy or prejudice againſt the happineſs of others *&c.*

X. As for the particular duties of ſubjects, they are connected with the particular employments which they follow in ſociety. We ſhall here lay down ſome general rules on this matter.

1°. A ſubject ought not to aſpire after any public employment, nor even to accept of it when he is ſenſible that he is not duly qualified for it. 2°. He ought not to accept of more employments than he can diſcharge. 3°. He muſt not uſe bad means to obtain offices. 4°. It is even ſometimes a kind of juſtice not to ſeek after certain employments, which are not neceſſary to us, and which may be as well filled by others, for whom they are perhaps more proper. 5°. He ought to diſcharge the ſeveral functions of the employments he has obtained, with all the application, exactneſs, and fidelity he is capable of.

XI. Nothing is more eaſy than to apply theſe general maxims to the particular employments of ſociety, and to draw conſequences proper to each of them; as for inſtance, with reſpect to miniſters and counſellors of ſtate, miniſters of religion, public profeſſors, magiſtrates and officers of juſtice, officers in the army and ſoldiers, receivers of taxes, ambaſſadors, *&c.*

XII.

XII. The particular duties of ſubjects ceaſe with the public charges from whence they ariſe. But as for the general duties, they ſubſiſt as long as a man is a ſubject of the ſtate, and till he has loſt that quality. Now a man ceaſes to be a ſubject, principally three ways. 1°. When he goes to ſettle elſewhere. 2°. When he is baniſhed from a country for ſome crime, and deprived of the rights of a ſubject. 3°. And laſtly, when he is reduced to a neceſſity of ſubmitting to the dominion of a conqueror.

XIII. It is a right natural to all free people, that every one ſhould have the liberty of removing out of the commonwealth, if he thinks proper. In a word, when a man becomes a member of a ſtate, he does not for that reaſon entirely renounce the care of himſelf and his own affairs. On the contrary, he ſeeks a powerful protection, under the ſhelter of which he may procure to himſelf both the neceſſaries and conveniences of life. Thus the ſubjects of a ſtate cannot be denied the liberty of ſettling elſewhere, in order to procure the advantages which they do not find in their native country.

XIV. On this occaſion there are however certain maxims of duty and decency, which cannot be diſpenſed with.

1°. In general, a man ought not to quit his native country without the permiſſion of his ſovereign: But his ſovereign ought not to refuſe it him, without very important reaſons.

2°. It would be contrary to the duty of a good subject to abandon his native country at an unseasonable juncture, and when the state has a particular interest that he should stay at home *.

3°. If the laws of the country have determined any thing in this point, we must be determined by them; for we have consented to those laws in becoming members of the state.

XV. The *Romans* forced no person to continue under their government, and *Cicero* † highly commends this maxim, calling it the surest foundation of liberty, "which consists in being able to preserve "or renounce our right as we think proper."

XVI. Some make a question, whether subjects can go out of the state in great companies? In this point *Grotius* and *Puffendorff* are of opposite sentiments §. As for my own part, I am of opinion that it can hardly happen, that subjects should go out of the state in large companies, except in one or other of these two cases; either when the government is tyrannical, or when a multitude of people cannot subsist in the country; as when manufacturers, for

* See *Grotius* of the Right of War and Peace, book II. chap. 5. §. 24.

† O excellent and divine laws, enacted by our ancestors in the beginning of the *Roman* empire——Let no man change his city against his will, nor let him be compelled to stay in it. These are the surest foundations of our liberty, that every one should have it in his power either to preserve or relinquish his right. *Orat.* pro L. Corn. Balb. cap. 13. adde Leg. 12. §. 9. Digest. de cap. diminut. & postlim. lib. XLIX. tit. 15.

§. See *Grotius*, ubi supra, and *Puffendorff* of the Law of Nature and Nations, lib. VIII. cap. 11. §. 4.

example,

example, or other tradesmen, cannot find the means of making or distributing their commodities. In these circumstances, the subjects may retire if they will, and they are authorized so to do by virtue of a tacit exception. If the government is tyrannical, it is the duty of the sovereign to change his conduct; for no subject is obliged to live under tyranny. If misery forces them to remove, this is also a reasonable exception against the most express engagements, unless the sovereign furnishes them with the means of subsistence. But, except in these cases, if the subjects were to remove in great companies, without a cause, and by a kind of general desertion, the sovereign may certainly oppose their remove, if he finds that the state suffers great prejudice by it.

XVII. A man ceases to be a subject of the state when he is for ever banished, in punishment for some crime: for the moment that the state will not acknowledge a man for one of its members, but drives him from its territories, he is released from his engagements as a subject. The Civilians call this punishment a civil death. But it is evident that the state, or sovereign, cannot expel a subject from their territories when they please, unless he has deserved it by the commission of some crime.

XVIII. Lastly, a man may cease to be a subject by the superior force of an enemy, by which he is reduced to a necessity of submitting to his dominion: and this necessity is founded on the right which every man has to take care of his own preservation.

CHAP.

CHAP. VI.

Of the inviolable rights of ſovereignty, of the depoſing of ſovereigns, of the abuſe of ſovereignty, and of tyranny.

I. WHAT we have ſaid in the preceding chapter, of the duties of ſubjects to their ſovereigns, admits of no difficulty. We are agreed in general upon the rule, that the ſovereign is a ſacred and inviolable perſon. But the queſtion is, whether this prerogative of the ſovereign be ſuch, that it is never lawful for the people to riſe againſt him, to diſpoſſeſs him, or to change the form of government?

II. To anſwer this queſtion, I obſerve at firſt, that the nature and end of government lay an indiſpenſable obligation on all ſubjects not to reſiſt their ſovereign, but to reſpect and obey him, ſo long as he uſes his power with juſtice and moderation, and does not paſs the bounds of his authority.

III. 'Tis this obligation to obedience in the ſubjects, which conſtitutes the whole force of civil ſociety and government, and conſequently the whole happineſs of the ſtate. Whoever therefore riſes againſt the ſovereign, or makes an attack upon his perſon or authority, renders himſelf manifeſtly guilty of the greateſt crime which a man can commit, ſince, by ſo doing, he endeavours to ſubvert the firſt foundations of the public happineſs, in which that of every individual is included.

IV.

IV. But if this maxim is true with respect to individuals, may we also apply it to the whole body of the nation, of whom the sovereign originally holds his authority? If the people think fit to resume, or to change the form of government, why should they not be at liberty to do it? Cannot he, who makes a king, depose him?

V. Let us try to clear up this difficulty. I therefore affirm, that the people themselves, that is, the whole body of the nation, have not a right to depose the sovereign, or to change the form of government, without any other reason than their own pleasure, and purely thro' inconstancy or levity.

VI. In general, the same reasons which establish the necessity of government and sovereign authority in society, also prove that the government ought to be stable, and that the people should not have the power of deposing their sovereigns, whenever, thro' caprice or levity, they are inclined so to do, and when they have no good reason to change the form of government.

VII. In fact, it would be abolishing government, to make it depend on the caprice or inconstancy of the people. It would be impossible for the state to be ever settled amidst these continual revolutions, which would expose it so often to destruction; for we must either grant that the people cannot dispossess their sovereigns, and change the form of government; or we must give them, in this respect, a liberty without bounds.

VIII. 'Tis certainly an inconteſtable maxim, that an opinion which ſaps the foundations of all authority, which deſtroys all power, and conſequently all ſociety, cannot be admitted as a principle of reaſoning, or of conduct in politics.

IX. The law of conveniency is in this caſe of the utmoſt force. What ſhould we ſay of a minor, who, without any other reaſon than his caprice, ſhould withdraw from his guardian, or change him at his pleaſure? In this caſe 'tis all the ſame. 'Tis with reaſon that politicians compare the people to minors; neither one nor other of them are capable of governing themſelves. They muſt have maſters, and this neceſſity forbids them, without a reaſon, to withdraw from their authority, or to alter the form of government.

X. 'Tis not only the law of conveniency, which does not permit the people, without a reaſon, to riſe againſt their ſovereign or the government; but the law of juſtice alſo forbids the ſame thing.

XI. Government and ſovereignty are eſtabliſhed by reciprocal agreement betwixt thoſe who govern, and thoſe who are governed; and the natural law of juſtice requires that perſons ſhould be faithful to their engagements. 'Tis therefore the duty of the people to keep their word which they have given their ſovereign, and religiouſly to obſerve their contract, ſo long as the ſovereign performs his engagements.

XII. Otherwiſe the people would do a manifeſt injuſtice

injuſtice to the ſovereign, in depriving him of a right which he has lawfully acquired, which he has not abuſed to their prejudice, and for the loſs of which they cannot indemnify him.

XIII. But what muſt we think of a ſovereign, who, far from uſing his authority well, injures his ſubjects, neglects the intereſts of the ſtate, ſubverts the fundamental laws, drains the people by exceſſive taxes, which he ſquanders away in fooliſh and uſeleſs expences *&c.* Ought the perſon of ſuch a king to be ſacred to the ſubjects? Ought they patiently to ſuffer all his injuſtices? Or, can they withdraw from his authority.

XIV. To anſwer this queſtion, which is one of the moſt delicate in politics, I obſerve, that diſaffected, mutinous, or ſeditious ſubjects, often make things, highly innocent, paſs for acts of injuſtice in the ſovereign. The people often murmur at the moſt neceſſary taxes; others ſeek to deſtroy the government, becauſe they have not a ſhare in the adminiſtration. In a word, the complaints of ſubjects oftener denote the bad humour and ſeditious ſpirit of thoſe who make them, than real diſorders in the government, or injuſtice in thoſe who govern.

XV. It were indeed to be wiſhed, for the glory of ſovereigns, that the complaints of ſubjects never had juſter foundations. But hiſtory and experience teach us that they are too often very well founded. In theſe circumſtances, what is then the duty of ſubjects? Ought

Ought they patiently to ſuffer? Or, may they reſiſt their ſovereign?

XVI. We muſt diſtinguiſh between the extreme abuſe of ſovereignty, which degenerates manifeſtly and openly into tyranny, and tends to the entire ruin of the ſubjects; and a moderate abuſe of it, which may be attributed to human weakneſs, rather than to a determined intention of ruining the liberty and happineſs of the people.

XVII. In the firſt caſe, I think the people have always a right to reſiſt their ſovereign, and even to reſume the ſovereignty which they have given him, and which he has abuſed to exceſs. But if the abuſe is only moderate, 'tis the duty of the people to ſuffer ſomething, rather than to riſe in arms againſt their ſovereign.

XVIII. This diſtinction is founded on the nature of man, and the nature and end of government. The people muſt patiently bear the ſlight injuſtices of their ſovereign, or the moderate abuſe of his power, becauſe this is no more than a juſt tribute due to humanity. 'Tis on this condition that they have inveſted him with the ſupreme authority. Kings are men as well as others, that is to ſay, liable to be miſtaken, and, in ſome inſtances, to fail in point of their duty. Of this the people cannot be ignorant, and 'tis on this footing that they have treated with their ſovereign.

XIX. If, for the ſmalleſt faults, the people had a right

right to resist their sovereign or depose him, no sovereign could retain his authority, and the society would, by this means, be continually torn to pieces; which would run directly counter both to the end and establishment of government, and of sovereignty.

XX. 'Tis therefore just, to overlook the pardonable faults of sovereigns, and to have a regard to the laborious and exalted office with which they are invested for our preservation. *Tacitus* beautifully says: "We must endure the luxury and avarice of sovereigns, as we endure the barrenness of a soil, storms, and other inconveniences of nature. There will be vices as long as there are men; but these are not continual, and are recompensed by the intermixture of better qualities *."

XXI. But if the sovereign pushes things to the last extremity, so that his tyranny becomes insupportable, and it appears evident that he has formed a design to destroy the liberty of his subjects, then they have a right to rise against him, and even to deprive him of the sovereignty.

XXII. This I prove, 1°. by the nature of tyranny, which of itself degrades the sovereign of his dignity. Sovereignty always supposes a beneficent power; we must indeed make some allowance for the

* Quomodo sterilitatem, aut nimios imbres, et cætera naturæ mala, ita luxum vel avaritiam dominantium tolerate. Vitia erunt, donec homines; sed neque hæc continua, et meliorum interventu pensantur, Hist. lib. IV. cap. 74. N. 4.

weakneſs inſeparable from humanity; but beyond that, and when the people are reduced to the laſt extremity, there is no difference between tyranny and robbery. The one gives no more right than the other, and we may always lawfully oppoſe force to violence.

XXIII. 2°. Men have eſtabliſhed civil ſociety and government for their own good, to extricate themſelves from troubles, and to deliver themſelves from the evils of a ſtate of nature. But 'tis highly evident, that if the people were obliged to ſuffer every thing from their ſovereigns, and never to reſiſt their violences, they would be reduced to a much more deplorable ſtate, than that from which they wanted to reſcue themſelves, by the eſtabliſhment of ſovereignty. It can never ſurely be preſumed, that this was the intention of men.

XXIV. 3°. Even a people, who have ſubmitted themſelves to an abſolute government, have not thereby loſt the right of aſſerting their liberty, and taking care of their preſervation, when they find themſelves reduced to extreme miſery. Abſolute ſovereignty, in itſelf, is no more than the abſolute power of doing good; now the abſolute power of procuring the good of a perſon, and the abſolute power of deſtroying him at pleaſure, have no connection with each other. Let us therefore conclude, that never any people had an intention to ſubmit themſelves to a ſovereign in ſuch a manner, as never to have it in their power to reſiſt him, not even for their own preſervation.

XXV

XXV. " Suppose, says *Grotius* *, one had asked " those who first formed the civil laws, whether " they intended to impose on all the subjects, the " fatal necessity of dying rather than taking up arms " to defend themselves against the unjust violence " of their sovereign, I know not whether they would " have answered in the affirmative. 'Tis rather " reasonable to believe that they would have declared, " that the people ought not to endure all manner of " injuries, except perhaps when matters are so si- " tuated, that resistance would infallibly produce " very great troubles in the state, or tend to the " ruin of many innocent people."

XXVI. We have already proved †, that no person can renounce his liberty to such a degree as that here mentioned. This would be selling his own life, that of his children, his religion, in a word, every advantage he enjoys, which it is not certainly in any man's power to do. This may be illustrated by the comparison of a patient and his physician.

XXVII. If therefore the subjects have always a right to resist the manifest tyranny even of an absolute prince, they must, for a stronger reason, have the same power with respect to a prince who has only a restrained and limited sovereignty, if he wants to invade the rights and properties of his people §.

* Book I. chap. 4. §. 7. N. 2.

† Part I. chap. 7. N. 22, &c.

§ *Grotius* on the Right of War and Peace, lib. I. cap. 4. § 8

XXVIII. We muſt indeed patiently ſuffer the caprice and auſterity of our maſters, as well as the bad humour of our fathers and mothers; but, as *Seneca* ſays, "Tho' a perſon ought to obey a father in all "things, yet he is not obliged to obey him when "his commands are of ſuch a nature, that he ceaſes "thereby to be a father."

XXIX. But it is here to be obſerved, that when we ſay the people have a right to reſiſt a tyrant, or even to depoſe him, we ought not, by the word people, to underſtand the vile populace or dregs of a country, nor the cabal of a ſmall number of ſeditious perſons, but the greateſt and moſt judicious part of the ſubjects of all orders in the kingdom. The tyranny, as we have alſo obſerved, muſt be notorious and accompanied with the higheſt evidence.

XXX. We may likewiſe affirm, that, ſtrictly ſpeaking, the ſubjects are not obliged to wait till the prince has entirely finiſhed the chains which he is preparing for them, and till he has put it out of their power to reſiſt him. 'Tis high time to think of their preſervation, and to take proper meaſures againſt their ſovereign, when they find that all his actions manifeſtly tend to oppreſs them, and that he is marching boldly on to the ruin of the ſtate.

XXXI. Theſe are truths of the laſt importance. 'Tis highly proper they ſhould be known, not only for the ſafety and happineſs of nations, but alſo for the advantage of good and wiſe kings.

XXXII. They, who are well acquainted with the frailty of human nature, are always diffident of themſelves; and wiſhing only to diſcharge their duty, they are contented to have bounds ſet to their authority, and by that means to be hindered from doing what they ought not to do. Taught by reaſon and experience, that the people love peace and good government, they will never be afraid of a general inſurrection, ſo long as they take care to govern with moderation, and hinder their officers from committing injuſtice.

XXXIII. However the abettors of deſpotic power and paſſive obedience, ſtart ſeveral difficulties on this ſubject.

Firſt Objection. A revolt againſt the ſupreme power includes a contradiction; for if this power is ſupreme, there is none ſuperior to it. By whom then ſhall it be judged? If the ſovereignty always inheres in the people, they have not transferred their right; and if they have transferred it, they are no longer maſters of it.

Anſwer. This difficulty ſuppoſes the point in queſtion, namely, that the people have diveſted themſelves ſo far of their liberty, that they have given full power to the ſovereign to treat them as he pleaſes, without having in any caſe reſerved to themſelves the power of reſiſting him. This is what no people ever did, nor ever could do. There is therefore no contradiction here. A power given for a certain end, is limited by that very end. The ſupreme power acknowledges none above itſelf, ſo long as the ſovereign has not forfeited his dignity. But if he he has degenerated into a tyrant, he can no longer claim a right which he has loſt by his own fault.

XXXIV. *Second Objection.* But who ſhall judge, whether the prince performs his duty, or whether he governs tyrannically? Can the people be judge in their own cauſe?

Anſwer. It certainly belongs to thoſe who have given any perſon a power, which he had not of himſelf, to judge whether he uſes it agreeably to the end for which it was given him.

XXXV. *Third Objection.* We cannot, without imprudence, grant this right of judging to the people. Political affairs are not adapted to the capacity of the vulgar, but are ſometimes of ſo delicate a nature, that even perſons of the beſt ſenſe cannot form a right judgment of them.

Anſwer. In dubious caſes, the preſumption ought always to be in favour of the ſovereign, and obedience is the duty of ſubjects. They ought even to bear a moderate abuſe of ſovereignty. But in caſes of a manifeſt and open tyranny, every one is in a condition to judge whether he is exceſſively injured or not.

XXXVI. *Fourth Objection.* But is it not expoſing the ſtate to perpetual revolutions, to anarchy, and to certain ruin, to make the ſupreme authority depend on the opinion of the people, and to grant them the liberty of riſing on ſome occaſions againſt their ſovereign.

Anſwer. This objection would be of ſome force, if we pretended that the people had a right to riſe againſt their ſovereign, or to change the form of government, thro' levity or caprice, or even for a moderate abuſe of ſovereignty. But no inconveniency will enſue, while the people only uſe this right with all the precautions, and in the circumſtances which we have ſuppoſed. Beſides, experience teaches us that it is very difficult to prevail on a people to change a government to which they have been accuſtomed. People are apt to overlook not only ſlight, but even very great faults in thoſe who govern them.

XXXVII. Our hypotheſis does not tend more than any other, to excite diſturbances in a ſtate; for a people, ill treated by a tyrannic government, will rebel as frequently as thoſe who live under eſtabliſhed laws, which they will not ſuffer to be violated. Let the abettors of deſpotic power cry up their prince as much as they pleaſe, let them ſay the moſt magnificent things of his ſacred perſon, yet the people, reduced to the laſt miſery, will trample theſe ſpecious reaſons under foot, as ſoon as they can do it with any appearance of ſucceſs.

XXXVIII. In fine, tho' the people might abuſe the liberty which we grant them, yet leſs inconveniency would ariſe from this, than from allowing all to the ſovereign, ſo as to let a whole nation periſh, rather than grant it the power of checking the iniquity of its governors.

CHAP. VIII.

Of the duty of sovereigns.

I. THERE is a sort of commerce, or reciprocal return of the duties of the subjects to the sovereign, and of his to them. After therefore having treated of the former, it remains that we take a view of the latter.

II. From what we have hitherto explained of the nature of sovereignty, of its end, extent and boundaries, the duty of sovereigns may easily be gathered. But as this is an affair of the last importance, 'tis necessary to say something more particular on it, and to collect the principal heads of it as it were into one view.

III. The higher a sovereign is raised above the level of other men, the more important are his duties: if he can do a great deal of good, he can also do a great deal of mischief. 'Tis on the good or evil conduct of princes that the happiness or misery of a whole nation or people depends. How happy is the situation, which, on all instances, furnishes occasions of doing good to so many thousands! But at the same time, how dangerous is the post which exposes every moment to the injuring of millions! Besides, the good which princes do, sometimes extends to the most remote ages; as the evils they commit are multiplied from generation to generation to latest posterity. This sufficiently discovers the importance of their duties.

VI. In order to have a proper knowledge of the duty of ſovereigns, we need only attentively conſider the nature and end of civil ſocieties, and the exerciſe of the different parts of ſovereignty.

V. 1°. The firſt general duty of princes, and which is before all things neceſſary, is carefully to inform themſelves of every thing that falls under the complete diſcharge of their truſt: for a perſon cannot well acquit himſelf in that which he has not firſt rightly learnt.

VI. It is a great miſtake to imagine that the knowledge of government is an eaſy affair; on the contrary, nothing is more difficult if princes would diſcharge their duty. Whatever talents or genius they may have received from nature, this is an employment that requires the whole man. The general rules of governing well are few in number; but the difficulty is to make a juſt application of them to times and circumſtances; and this demands the greateſt efforts of diligence and human prudence.

VII. 2°. When a prince is once convinced of the obligation he is under to inform himſelf exactly of all that is neceſſary for the diſcharge of his truſt, and of the difficulty of getting this information, he will begin with removing all obſtacles which might oppoſe it. And firſt 'tis abſolutely neceſſary, that princes ſhould retrench their pleaſures and uſeleſs diverſions, ſo far as theſe may be an obſtacle to the knowledge and practice of their duty. Then they ought to endeavour to have wiſe, prudent and experienced persons about them; and, on the contrary, to remove flatterers, buffoons, and others, whose whole merit consists in things that are frivolous and absolutely unworthy of the attention of a sovereign. Princes ought not to choose for favourites those who are most proper to divert them, but those who are most capable of governing the state.

VIII. Above all things, they cannot guard too much against flattery. No human condition has so great an occasion for true and faithful advice as that of kings. And yet princes, spoiled by flattery, take every thing, that is free and ingenuous, to be harsh and austere. They are become so delicate, that every thing, which is not flattery, offends them: But nothing ought they to be so greatly afraid of as this very flattery, since there are no miseries into which they may not be hurried by its poisonous insinuations. On the contrary, the prince is happy when but only one man is born in his reign, who is so generous as to speak the truth freely to him; such a man is the treasure of the state. Wise rulers, who have their true interests at heart, ought continually to imagine that flatterers only regard themselves and not their master; whereas a sincere counsellor, as it were, forgets himself, and thinks only on the advantage of his prince.

IX. 3°. Princes ought to use all possible application to understand the constitution of the state, and the natural temper of their subjects. They ought not in this respect to be contented with a general and superficial knowledge. They should enter into particulars,

ticulars, and carefully examine what the conſtitution of the ſtate is, what its eſtabliſhment and power, whether it is old or new, ſucceſſive or elective, acquired by legal methods or by arms, what its extent is, what its forces are, who are its allies, and what conveniences it is provided with. For according to all theſe circumſtances the ſcepter muſt be ſwayed, and the reins of government drawn in or ſlackened.

X. 4°. After this ſovereigns ought to endeavour to excel in ſuch virtues as are moſt neceſſary to ſupport the weight of ſo important a charge, and to regulate their outward behaviour in a manner worthy of their rank and dignity.

XI. We have already ſhewn that virtue in general conſiſts in that ſtrength of mind, which enables us not only to conſult right reaſon on all occaſions, but alſo to follow her counſels with eaſe, and effectually reſiſt every thing which may incline us to the contrary. This ſingle idea of virtue is ſufficient to ſhew how neceſſary it is to all men. But among all men, none have more duties to fulfil, none are more expoſed to great temptations, than ſovereigns; and none of courſe have a greater neceſſity for the aſſiſtance of virtue. Beſides, virtue in princes has this advantage, that it is the ſureſt means of rendering their ſubjects good and virtuous. For this purpoſe they need only ſhew themſelves ſuch. The example of the prince has more force than the law. It is, as it were, a living law, which has more credit and authority than precept. But to come to particulars.

XII.

XII. The virtues moſt neceſſary to ſovereigns are, 1°. *Piety*, which is certainly the foundation of all other virtues; but it muſt be a ſolid and rational piety, free from ſuperſtition and bigotry. In the high ſituation of ſovereigns, the only motive, which can moſt ſurely induce them to the diſcharge of their duty, is the fear of God. Without that, they will ſoon run into every vice which their paſſions dictate; and the people will become the innocent victims of their pride, ambition, avarice and cruelty. On the contrary, we may expect every thing that is good from a prince, who fears and reſpects God, as a ſupreme Being on whom he depends, and to whom he muſt one day give an account of his adminiſtration. Nothing can be ſo powerful a motive as this to engage princes to perform their duty, nothing can ſo well cure them of that dangerous miſtake, that being above other men, they may act as abſolute lords, and as if they were not to render an account of their conduct, and be judged in their turn, after having judged others.

XIII. 3°. The love of *Equity* and *Juſtice.* The chief deſign a prince was made for, is to take care that every one ſhould have his right. This ought to engage him to ſtudy not only the ſcience of thoſe great civilians who aſcend to the firſt juſtice, which regulates human ſociety, and which determines the principles of government and politics; but alſo that part of the law, which deſcends to the affairs of particular perſons. This branch is generally left for the gentlemen of the long robe, and not admitted into the education of princes, tho' they are every day to paſs

paſs judgment upon the fortunes, liberties, lives, honour and reputation of their ſubjects. Princes are continually talked to of valour and liberality; but if juſtice does not regulate theſe two qualities, they degenerate into the moſt odious vices: Without juſtice, valour does nothing but deſtroy; and liberality is only a fooliſh profuſeneſs.. Juſtice keeps all in order, and contains within bounds him who diſtributes it, as well as thoſe to whom it is diſtributed.

XIV. 3°. *Valour*. But it muſt be ſet in motion by juſtice, and conducted by prudence. A prince ſhould expoſe himſelf to the greateſt dangers as often as it is neceſſary. He diſhonours himſelf more by being afraid of danger in time of war, than by never going to war. The courage of him who commands others, ought not to be dubious; but neither ought he to expoſe himſelf to danger without neceſſity. Valour can no longer be a virtue than as it is guided by prudence, otherwiſe it is a ſtupid contempt of life, a brutal ardour. Inconſiderate valour is always inſecure. He, who is not maſter of himſelf in dangers, is rather fierce than brave; if he does not fly, he is at leaſt confounded. He loſes that preſence of mind which would be neceſſary for him to give proper orders, to take advantage of opportunities, and to rout the enemy. The true way of finding glory, is calmly to wait for the favourable occaſion. Virtue is the more revered, as ſhe ſhews herſelf plain, modeſt, and averſe to pride and oſtentation. In proportion as the neceſſity of expoſing yourſelf to danger augments, your foreſight and courage ought alſo to increaſe.

XV.

XV. 4°. Another virtue, very neceſſary in princes, is to be extremely reſerved in diſcovering their thoughts and deſigns. This virtue is evidently neceſſary to thoſe who are concerned in government: It includes a wiſe diffidence, and an innocent diſſimulation.

XVI. 5°. A prince muſt, above all things, accuſtom himſelf to moderate his deſires. For as he has the power of gratifying them, if he once gives way to them, he will run to the greateſt exceſs, and by deſtroying his ſubjects, he will at laſt deſtroy himſelf. In order to form himſelf to this moderation, nothing is more proper and uſeful than to accuſtom himſelf to patience. This is the moſt neceſſary of all virtues for thoſe who are to command. A man muſt be patient to become maſter of himſelf and others. Impatience, which ſeems to be a vigorous exertion of the ſoul, is only a weakneſs and inability of ſuffering pain. He who cannot wait and ſuffer, is like a perſon that cannot keep a ſecret. Both want reſolution to contain themſelves. The more power an impatient man has, the more fatal his impatience will be to him. He will not wait; he will give himſelf no time to judge; he forces every thing to pleaſe himſelf; he tears off the boughs, to gather the fruit before it is ripe; he breaks down the gates, rather than ſtay till they are opened to him.

XVII. 6°. *Goodneſs* and *Clemency* are alſo virtues very neceſſary to a prince: His office is to do good, and 'tis for this end the power is lodged in his hand. 'Tis alſo principally by this that he ought to diſtinguiſh himſelf.

XVIII.

XVIII. 7°. *Liberality*, well underſtood and well applied, is ſo much the more eſſential to a prince, as avarice is a diſgrace to a perſon to whom it coſts almoſt nothing to be liberal. To take it exactly, a king, as a king, has nothing properly his own; for he owes his very ſelf to others. But on the other hand, no perſon ought to be more careful in regulating the exerciſe of this noble virtue. This requires a great deal of circumſpection, and ſuppoſes, in the prince, a juſt diſcernment and a good taſte to know how to beſtow and diſpenſe favours on proper perſons. He ought, above all things, to uſe this virtue for rewarding merit and virtue.

XIX. But liberality has its bounds, even in the moſt opulent princes. The ſtate may be compared to a family. The want of foreſight, profuſion of treaſure, and the voluptuous inclination of princes, who are the maſters of it, do more miſchief than the moſt ſkilful miniſters can repair.

XX. To reimburſe his treaſures, ſquandered away without neceſſity, and often in criminal exceſſes, he muſt have recourſe to expedients which are fatal to the ſubjects and the ſtate. He loſes the hearts of the people, and cauſes murmurs and diſcontents which are always dangerous, and of which an enemy may take advantage. Theſe are inconveniencies that even common ſenſe might point out, if the ſtrong propenſity to pleaſure, and the intoxication of power, did not often extinguiſh the light of reaſon in princes. To what cruelty and injuſtice did not the fooliſh profuſions of *Nero* carry him? A prudent œconomy, on on the contrary, ſupplies the deficiencies of the revenue, maintains families and ſtates, and preſerves them in a flouriſhing condition. By œconomy princes not only have money in time of need, but they alſo poſſeſs the hearts of their ſubjects, who freely open their purſes upon any unforeſeen emergency, when they ſee that the prince has been ſparing in his expences; the contrary happens when he has ſquandered away his treaſures.

XXI. This is a general idea of the virtues moſt neceſſary to a ſovereign, beſides thoſe which are common to him with private people, and of which ſome are included even in thoſe we have been mentioning. *Cicero* follows almoſt the ſame ideas in the enumeration he makes of the royal virtues *.

XXII. 'Tis by the aſſiſtance of theſe virtues, of which we here have given an idea, that ſovereigns are enabled to apply themſelves with ſucceſs to the functions of government, and to fulfil the different duties of it. Let us ſay ſomething more particular on the actual exerciſe of theſe duties.

XXIII. There is a general rule which includes all the duties of a ſovereign, and by which he may eaſily judge how to proceed under every circumſtance. *Let the ſafety of the people be the ſupreme law.* This maxim ought to be the principle and end of all his actions. The ſovereign authority has been conferred

* Fortem, juſtum, ſeverum, gravem, magnanimum, largum, beneficum, liberalem dici, hæ ſunt regiæ laudes. Orat. pro rege Dejotaro, cap. 9.

upon him with this view; and the fulfilling of it is the foundation of his right and power. The prince is properly the ſervant of the public. He ought, as it were, to forget himſelf, in order to think only on the advantage and good of thoſe whom he governs. He ought not to look upon any thing as advantageous to himſelf, which is not ſo to the ſtate. This was the idea of the heathen philoſophers. They defined a good prince, one who endeavours to render his ſubjects happy; and a tyrant, on the contrary, one who aims only at his own private advantage.

XXIV. The very intereſt of the ſovereign demands, that he ſhould direct all his actions to the public good. By ſuch a conduct he wins the hearts of his ſubjects, and lays the foundation of ſolid happineſs and true glory.

XXV. Where the government is moſt deſpotic, there ſovereigns are leaſt powerful. They ruin every thing, and are the ſole poſſeſſors of the whole country; but then the ſtate languiſhes, becauſe it is exhauſted of men and money; and this firſt loſs is the greateſt and moſt irreparable. His ſubjects ſeem to adore him, and to tremble at his very looks: But ſee what will be the conſequence upon the leaſt revolution; then we find that this monſtrous power, puſhed to exceſs, cannot long endure, becauſe it has no reſource in the hearts of the people. On the firſt blow the idol tumbles down and is trampled under foot. The king, who, in his proſperity, found not a man who durſt tell him the truth, ſhall not find one, in his adverſity, that will vouchſafe either to excuſe

cuſe him, or defend him againſt his enemies. 'Tis therefore equally eſſential to the happineſs of the people and of ſovereigns, that the latter ſhould follow no other rule in their manner of governing, than that of the public good.

XXVI. 'Tis not difficult, from this general rule, to deduce thoſe of a more particular nature. The functions of the government relate either to the intereſts of the ſtate at home, or to its foreign concerns.

XXVII. As for the intereſts of the ſtate at home, the firſt care of the ſovereign ought to be, 1°. to form his ſubjects to good manners. For this purpoſe the duty of ſupreme rulers is, not only to preſcribe good laws, by which every one may know how he ought to behave in order to promote the public good; but eſpecially to eſtabliſh the moſt perfect manner of public inſtruction, and of the education of youth. This is the only method of making the ſubjects conform to the laws both by reaſon and cuſtom, rather than thro' fear of puniſhment.

XXVIII. The firſt care of a prince therefore ought to be to erect public ſchools for the education of children, and for forming them betimes to wiſdom and virtue. Children are the hope and ſtrength of a nation. 'Tis too late to correct them when they are ſpoiled. 'Tis infinitely better to prevent the evil, than to be obliged to puniſh it. The king, who is the father of all his people, is more particularly the father of all the youth, who are, as it were, the flower of the whole nation. And as it is in the flower,

flower, that fruits are prepared, so 'tis one of the principal duties of the sovereign to take care of the education of youth, and the instruction of his subjects, to plant the principles of virtue early in their minds, and to maintain and confirm them in that happy disposition. 'Tis not laws and ordinances, but good morals, that properly regulate the state.

Quid leges sine moribus
Vanæ proficiunt *.

Those who have had a bad education make no scruple to violate the nicest exactness of political constitutions; whereas they, who have been properly trained up, chearfully, and, as it were, spontaneously conform to all good establishments. In fine, nothing is more conducive to so good an end in states, than to inspire the people by times with the principles of the Christian religion, purged from all human invention. For this religion includes the most perfect scheme of morality, the maxims of which are extremely well adapted for promoting the happiness of society.

XXIX. 2°. The sovereign ought to establish good laws for the settling of such affairs, as the subjects have most frequently to transact with each other. These laws ought to be just, equitable, clear, without ambiguity and contradiction, useful, accommodated to the condition and the genius of the people, at least as far as the good of the state will permit, that, by their means, differences may be easily determined: But they are not to be multiplied without necessity.

* *Horat.* Lib. III. Od. 24. ℣. 35, 36.

XXX. I ſaid, that laws ought to be *accommodated to the condition and genius of the people*; and for this reaſon I have before obſerved, that the ſovereign ought to be thoroughly inſtructed in this point; otherwiſe one of theſe two inconveniences muſt neceſſarily happen, either the laws are not obſerved, and then it becomes neceſſary to puniſh an infinite number of people, without the ſtate reaping any advantage from it; or the authority of the laws is deſpiſed, and then the ſtate is on the brink of deſtruction.

XXXI. I mentioned alſo, that *laws ought not to be multiplied without neceſſity*; for this would only tend to lay ſnares for the ſubjects, and expoſe them to inevitable puniſhments, without any advantage to the ſociety. In fine, 'tis of great importance to regulate what relates to the adminiſtration and ordinary forms of juſtice, ſo that every ſubject may have it in his power to recover his right, without loſing much time, or being at a great expence.

XXXII. 3°. It would be of no uſe to make good laws, if people were ſuffered to violate them with impunity. Sovereigns ought therefore to ſee them properly executed, and to puniſh the delinquents without exception of perſons, according to the quality and degree of the offence. It is even ſometimes proper to puniſh ſeverely at firſt. There are circumſtances in which it is clemency to make ſuch early examples, as may ſtop the courſe of iniquity. But what is chiefly neceſſary, and what juſtice and the public good abſolutely require, is, that the ſeverity of the laws be exerciſed not only upon the ſubjects of moderate fortune and condition, but alſo upon the wealthy and powerful. It would be unjuſt that reputation, nobility, and riches, ſhould authorize any one to inſult thoſe who are deſtitute of theſe advantages. The populace are often reduced by oppreſſion to deſpair, and at laſt riſe up with a fury which throws the ſtate into convulſions.

XXXIII. 4°. Since men firſt incorporated themſelves in civil ſocieties to ſcreen themſelves from the injuries and malice of others, and to procure all the ſweets and pleaſures which can render life commodious and happy; the ſovereign is obliged to hinder the ſubjects from wronging each other, to maintain order and peace in the community by a ſtrict execution of the laws, to the end that his ſubjects may obtain the advantages which men can reaſonably propoſe to themſelves by joining in ſociety. When the ſubjects are not kept within rule, their perpetual living together, and the communication they have with each other, eaſily furniſh them with opportunities of injuring each other. But nothing is more contrary to the nature and end of civil government, than to permit ſubjects to do themſelves juſtice, and, by their own private force, to revenge the injuries they think they have ſuffered. We ſhall here add a beautiful paſſage from Mr. *De La Bruiere* upon this ſubject *. " What would it avail me or any of my " fellow-ſubjects, that my ſovereign was ſucceſsful " and crowned with glory, that my country was " powerful and the terror of neighbouring nations,

* Characters and Manners of the preſent Age, chap. 10, of the Sovereign.

 " if

" if I was forced to lead a melancholy and miser- " able life under the burthen of oppreſſion and indi- " gence? If, while I was ſecured from the incurſi- " ons of a foreign enemy, I found myſelf expoſed " at home to the ſword of an aſſaſſin, and was " leſs in danger of being robbed or maſſacred in " the darkeſt nights and in a thick foreſt, than " in the public ſtreets? If ſafety, cleanlineſs, and " good order, had not rendered living in towns " ſo pleaſant, and had not only furniſhed them with " the neceſſaries, but moreover with all the ſweets " and conveniences of life? If, being weak and " defenceleſs, I were encroached upon in the coun- " try, by every neighbouring great man? If ſo " good a proviſion had not been made to protect " me againſt his injuſtice? If I had not at hand ſo " many, and ſuch excellent maſters, to educate my " children in thoſe arts and ſciences which will one " day make their fortune? If the conveniency of " commerce had not made good ſubſtantial ſtuffs " for my clothing, and wholeſome food for my " nouriſhment, both plentiful and cheap? If, to " conclude, the care of my ſovereign had not given " me reaſon to be as well contented with my fortune, " as his princely virtues muſt needs make him with " his."

XXXIV. 5°. Since a prince can neither ſee nor do every thing himſelf, he muſt have the aſſiſtance of miniſters: But theſe, as they derive their whole authority from their maſter, all the good or the evil they do is finally imputed to him. 'Tis therefore the duty of ſovereigns to chooſe perſons of integrity and ability for the employments

employments with which they entrust them. They ought often to examine their conduct, and to punish or recompense them, according as they deserve. In fine, they ought never to refuse to lend a patient ear to the humble remonstrances and complaints of their subjects, when they are oppressed and trampled on by ministers and subordinate magistrates.

XXXV. 6°. With regard to subsidies and taxes, since the subjects are not obliged to pay them, but as they are necessary to defray the expences of the state, in war or peace; the sovereign ought to exact no more than the public necessities, or the signal advantage of the state shall require. He ought also to see that the subjects be incommoded as little as possible by the taxes laid upon them. There should be a just proportion in the tax of every individual, and there must be no exception or immunity which may turn to the disadvantage of others. The money collected ought to be laid out on the occasions of the state, and not wasted in luxury, debauchery, foolish largesses, or vain magnificence. Lastly, the expences ought to be proportioned to the revenues.

XXXVI. 7°. 'Tis the duty of a sovereign to draw no farther supplies from his subjects than he really stands in need of: The wealth of the subjects forms the strength of the state, and the advantage of families and individuals. A prince therefore ought to neglect nothing that can contribute to the preservation and increase of the riches of his people. For this purpose he ought to see that they draw all the profit they can from their lands and waters, and keep themſelves always employed in ſome induſtrious exerciſe or other. He ought to further and promote the mechanic arts, and give all poſſible encouragement to commerce. 'Tis likewiſe his duty to bring his ſubjects to a frugal method of living by good ſumptuary laws, which may forbid ſuperfluous expences, and eſpecially thoſe by which the wealth of the natives is tranſlated to foreigners.

XXXVII. 8°. Laſtly, 'tis equally the intereſt and duty of a ſupreme governour, to guard againſt factions and cabals, from whence ſeditions and civil wars eaſily ariſe. But above all, he ought to take care that none of his ſubjects place a greater dependence, under any pretext, even that of religion, on any other power, either within or without the realm, than on his lawful ſovereign. This in general is the law of the public good in regard to the domeſtic intereſts, or internal tranquillity of the ſtate.

XXXVIII. As to foreign concerns, the principal duties of the king are,

1°. To live in peace with his neighbours as much as he poſſibly can.

2°. Dexterouſly to manage the alliances and treaties he makes with other powers.

3°. To adhere faithfully to the treaties he has made.

4°. Not to ſuffer the courage of his ſubjects to be enervated, but on the contrary to maintain and augment it by a good diſcipline.

5°. In due and ſeaſonable time to make the preparations neceſſary to put himſelf in a poſture of defence.

6.

6°. Not to undertake any unjuſt or raſh war.

7°. Laſtly, even in times of peace to be very attentive to the deſigns and motions of his neighbours.

XXXIX. We ſhall ſay no more of the duties of ſovereigns. 'Tis ſufficient at preſent to have pointed out the general principles, and collected the principal heads: what we have to ſay hereafter concerning the diffrent parts of ſovereignty, will give the reader a more diſtinct idea of the particular duties attending it.

The End of the Second Part.

THE

PRINCIPLES

OF

POLITIC LAW.

PART III.

A more particular examination of the essential parts of sovereignty, or of the different rights of the sovereign, with respect to the internal administration of the state, such as the legislative power, the supreme power in matters of religion, the right of inflicting punishments, and that which the sovereign has over the Bona Reipublicæ, *or the goods contained in the common wealth.*

CHAP. I.

Of the legislative power, and the civil laws which arise from it.

I. WE have hitherto explained what relates to the nature of civil society in general, of government, and of sovereignty, which is the soul of it. Nothing remains to compleat the plan we laid down, but more

more particularly to examine the different parts of sovereignty, as well those which directly regard the internal administration of the state, as those which relate to its interests abroad, or to its concerns with foreign powers, which will afford us an opportunity of explaining the principal questions relating to these subjects; and to this purpose we design this and the subsequent part.

II. Among the essential parts of sovereignty we have given the first rank to the *legislative power*, that is to say, the power which the sovereign has of giving laws to his subjects, and of directing their actions, or of prescribing the manner in which they ought to regulate their conduct; and it is from this power that the civil laws are derived. As this right of the sovereign is, as it were, the essence of sovereignty, order requires that we should begin with the explication of whatever relates to it.

III. We shall not here repeat what we have elsewhere said of the nature of laws in general: But, supposing the principles we have established on that head, we shall only examine the nature and extent of the legislative power in society, and that of the civil laws and decrees of the sovereign which are from thence derived.

IV. *Civil Laws* then are all those, which the sovereign imposes on his subjects. The assemblage or body of these laws is what we call the *Civil Law*. In fine, civil jurisprudence is that ability, by which the civil laws are not only established, but are explained

plained in caſe of any obſcurity, and are properly applied to the actions of men.

V. The eſtabliſhment of civil ſociety ought to be fixed and perpetual, ſo as to make a ſure and undoubted proviſion for the happineſs and tranquillity of man. For this purpoſe it was neceſſary to eſtabliſh a conſtant order, and this could only be done by fixed and determinate laws.

VI. We have already obſerved that it was neceſſary to take proper meaſures to render the laws of nature as effectual as they ought to be, in order to promote the happineſs of man; and this is done by means of the civil laws.

For, 1°. They ſerve to make the laws of nature better known.

2°. They give them a new degree of force, and render the obſervance of them more ſecure, by means of their ſanction, and of the puniſhments which the ſovereign inflicts on thoſe who deſpiſe and violate them.

3°. There are ſeveral things which the law of nature preſcribes only in a general and indeterminate manner; ſo that the time, the manner, and the application to perſons are left to the prudence and diſcretion of every individual. It was however neceſſary for the order and tranquillity of the ſtate, that all this matter ſhould be regulated; which is done by the civil laws.

4°. They alſo ſerve to explain any obſcurity that may ariſe in the maxims of the law of nature.

5°. They modify, in various ways, the uſe of thoſe rights which every man naturally poſſeſſes. 6°.

6°. Laſtly, they determine the forms that are to be obſerved, and the precautions which ought to be taken, to render the different engagements that men enter into with each other effectual and inviolable; and they aſcertain the manner in which a man is to proſecute his rights in the civil court.

VII. In order therefore to form a juſt idea of the civil laws, we muſt ſay, that as civil ſociety is no other than natural ſociety itſelf, modified by the eſtabliſhment of a ſovereign whoſe buſineſs it is to maintain peace and order; in like manner the civil laws are thoſe of nature, perfected and modified in a manner ſuitable to the ſtate and advantages of ſociety.

VIII. As this is the caſe, we may very properly diſtinguiſh two ſorts of civil laws. Some are ſuch with reſpect to their authority only, and others with regard to their original. To the firſt claſs, we refer all the natural laws which ſerve as rules in civil courts, and which are alſo confirmed by a new ſanction of the ſovereign. Such are all theſe laws which determine the crimes that are to be puniſhed by the civil juſtice; and what are the obligations upon which an action may commence in the civil court, *&c.*

As for the civil laws, ſo called, becauſe of their original, theſe are arbitrary decrees, which, for their foundation, have only the will of the ſovereign, and ſuppoſe certain human eſtabliſhments; or which regulate things relating to the particular advantage of the ſtate, tho' indifferent in themſelves and undetermined by the law of nature. Such are the laws which preſcribe the neceſſary forms in contracts and teſ-

taments,

taments, the manner of proceeding in courts of justice *&c.* But it must be observed that all these regulations ought to tend to the good of the state as well as of individuals, so that they are properly appendages to the law of nature.

IX. 'Tis of great importance carefully to distinguish in the civil laws, what is natural and necessary in them, from what is only arbitrary. Those laws of nature, the observance of which is essentially conducive to the peace and tranquillity of mankind, ought certainly to have the force of a law in all states; neither is it in the power of the prince to abrogate them. As for the others, which do not so essentially interest the happiness of society, 'tis not always expedient to give them the force of a law, because the controversies about the violation of them would often be very perplexed and intricate, and would likewise lay a foundation for an infinite number of litigious suits. Besides, it was proper to give the good and virtuous an opportunity of distinguishing themselves by the practice of those duties, the violation of which incurs no human penalties.

X. What we have said of the nature of civil laws sufficiently shews, that tho' the legislative is a *supreme*, yet it is not an *abitrary*, power; but on the contrary it is limited in several respects.

1°. And as the sovereign holds the legislative power originally of the will of each member of the society, 'tis evident that no man can confer on another a right which he has not himself; and that consequently the legislative power cannot be extended

beyond

beyond this limit. The ſovereign therefore can neither command nor forbid any other actions than ſuch as are either voluntary or poſſible.

2°. Beſides, the natural laws diſpoſe of human actions antecedently to the civil laws, and men cannot recede from the authority of the former. Therefore theſe primitive laws limit the power of the ſovereign, and he can determine nothing ſo as to bind the ſubject contrary to what they either expreſly command or forbid.

XI. But we muſt be careful not to confound two things entirely diſtinct, I mean the *State of Nature* and the *Laws of Nature*. The primitive and natural ſtate of man may admit of different changes and various modifications, which are left to the diſpoſal of man, and have nothing contrary to his obligations and his duties. In this reſpect, the civil laws may produce ſome changes in the natural ſtate, and conſequently make ſome regulations unknown to the law of nature, without containing any thing contrary to that law, which ſuppoſes the ſtate of liberty in all its extent, but nevertheleſs permits men to limit and reſtrain that ſtate, in the manner which appears moſt to their advantage.

XII. We are however far from being of the opinion of thoſe writers *, who pretend that 'tis impoſſible the civil laws ſhould be repugnant to that of nature, *becauſe*, ſay they, *there is nothing either juſt or unjuſt antecedently to the eſtabliſhment of thoſe laws.* What we have juſt now advanced, and the principles

* *Hobbes.*

we

we have established in the whole course of this work; sufficiently evince the absurdity of this opinion.

XIII. 'Tis as ridiculous to assert, that before the establishment of civil laws and society, there was no rule of justice to which mankind were subject, as to pretend that truth and rectitude depend on the will of men, and not on the nature of things. It would have even been impossible for men to found societies of any durability, if, antecedently to these societies, there had been neither justice nor injustice; and if they had not, on the contrary, been persuaded that it was just to keep their word, and unjust to break it.

XIV. Such in general is the extent of the legislative power, and the nature of the civil laws, by which that power exerts itself. Hence it follows, that the whole force of civil laws consists in two things, namely, in their *Justice* and in their *Authority*.

XV. The authority of the laws consists in the force given them by the person, who, being invested with the legislative power, has a right to enact these laws; and in the Divine Will which commands us to obey him. As for the justice of civil laws, it depends on their relation to the good order of society, of which they are the rules, and on their agreement with the particular advantage of establishing them, according as times and places require.

XVI. And since the sovereignty, or right of commanding,

manding, is naturally founded on a *beneficent Power*, it neceſſarily follows that the *Authority* and *Juſtice* of laws are two characteriſtics eſſential to their nature, in default of which they can produce no true obligation. The power of the ſovereign conſtitutes the authority of his laws, and his beneficence permits him to make none but ſuch as are conformable to equity.

XVII. However certain and inconteſtable theſe general principles are, yet we ought to take care not to abuſe them in the application. 'Tis certainly eſſential to every law that it ſhould be equitable and juſt; but we muſt not from thence conclude, that private ſubjects have a right to refuſe obedience to the commands of the ſovereign, under a pretence that they do not think them altogether juſt. For beſides that ſome allowance is to be made for human infirmity, the oppoſing the legiſlative power which conſtitutes the whole ſafety of the public, muſt evidently tend to the ſubverſion of ſociety; and ſubjects are obliged to ſuffer the inconveniences which may ariſe from ſome unjuſt laws, rather than expoſe the ſtate to ruin by their diſobedience.

XVIII. But if the abuſe of the legiſlative power proceeds to exceſs, and to the ſubverſion of the fundamental principles of the laws of nature, and of the duties which it enjoins, 'tis certain that in theſe circumſtances, the ſubjects are, by the laws of God, not only authorized, but even obliged to refuſe obedience to all laws of this kind.

XIX. But this is not ſufficient. That the laws may be able to impoſe a real obligation, and be reckoned juſt and equitable, 'tis neceſſary the ſubjects ſhould have a perfect knowledge of them: now they cannot of themſelves know the civil laws, at leaſt thoſe of an arbitrary nature; theſe are, in ſome meaſure, facts of which the people may be ignorant. The ſovereign ought therefore to declare his will, and to adminiſter laws and juſtice, not by arbitrary and haſty decrees, but by mature regulations, duly made known to the public.

XX. Theſe principles furniſh us with a reflection of great importance to ſovereigns. Since the firſt quality of laws is, that they be known, ſovereigns ought to publiſh them in the cleareſt manner. In particular, 'tis abſolutely neceſſary that the laws be written in the language of the country; it would be even proper that public profeſſors ſhould not uſe a foreign language in their lectures on juriſprudence. For what can be more repugnant to the principle which directs, that the laws ſhould be perfectly known, than to uſe foreign laws, written in a dead language, which the generality of the people do not underſtand, and to render the knowledge of thoſe laws attainable only in that language. I cannot help ſaying, that this is a remains of barbarouſneſs equally contrary to the glory of ſovereigns, and the advantage of ſubjects.

XXI. If we therefore ſuppoſe the civil laws, accompanied with the conditions here mentioned, they have certainly the force of obliging the ſubjects to obſerve

observe them. Every individual is bound to submit to their regulations, so long as they include nothing contrary to the divine laws, whether natural or revealed; and this not only from a dread of the punishments annexed to the violation of them, but also from a principle of conscience, and in consequence of a maxim of natural law, which commands us to obey our lawful sovereigns in every thing we can do without committing a crime.

XXII. In order rightly to comprehend this effect of the civil laws, 'tis to be observed, that the obligation, which they impose, extends not only to external actions, but also to the inward sentiments of the mind. The sovereign, by prescribing laws to his subjects, proposes to render them truly wise and virtuous. If he commands a good action, he wants it to be done from principle; and when he forbids a crime, he not only forbids the external action, but also forbids the harbouring the thought, or forming the design of it.

XXIII. In fact, man being naturally an intelligent and free agent, he is induced to action only in consequence of his judgment, by a determination of his will, and by an internal principle. As this is the case, the most effectual means, which the sovereign can employ to procure the public happiness and tranquillity, is to work upon the mind, and on the principle of human actions, by disposing the hearts of his subjects to wisdom and virtue.

XXIV. 'Tis alſo for this end that public eſtabliſhments are formed for the education of youth. All public ſchools and profeſſors are appointed for this purpoſe. The end of all theſe inſtitutions is to inform and inſtruct mankind, and to make them early acquainted with the rules of a happy and virtuous life. Thus the ſovereign, by means of inſtruction, has an effectual method of inſtilling juſt ideas and notions into the minds of his ſubjects, and by this means his authority has a very great influence upon the internal actions, the thoughts, and inclinations of thoſe, who are ſubjected to the direction of his laws, as far at leaſt as the nature of the thing will permit.

XXV. We ſhall cloſe this chapter with the diſcuſſion of a queſtion, which naturally preſents itſelf in this place.

Some aſk, whether a ſubject can innocently execute the unjuſt commands of a ſovereign, or if he ought not rather to refuſe abſolutely to obey him, even at the hazard of his life? *Puffendorff* ſeems to anſwer this queſtion with a kind of heſitation, but at length he declares for the opinion of *Hobbes* in the following manner. " We muſt diſtinguiſh, he ſays, " whether the ſovereign commands us in our own " name to do an unjuſt action, which may be ac- " counted our own; or, whether he orders us to " perform it in his name, as inſtruments in the " execution of it, and as an action which he ac- " counts his own. In the laſt caſe, he pretends " that we may without ſcruple execute the action " ordered by the ſovereign, who is then to be con- " ſidered

" sidered as the only author of it, and to whom " the guilt ought to be solely imputed. Thus, for " example, soldiers ought always to execute the or- " ders of their prince, because they do not act in " their own name, but as instruments and in the " name of their master. But on the contrary, 'tis " never lawful to do in our own name, an action " that our conscience tells us is unjust or criminal. " Thus for example, a judge, whatever orders he " may have from the prince, ought never to con- " demn an innocent person, nor a witness depose " against the truth."

XXVI. But, in my opinion, this distinction does not remove the difficulty; for in whatever manner we pretend that a subject acts in these cases, whether in his own name, or in that of his prince, his will always concurs in some manner or other to the unjust and criminal action which he executes by order of the sovereign. We must therefore impute either both actions partly to him, or else never any of them at all.

XXVII. The surest way then, is to distinguish here between a case where the prince commands a thing evidently unjust, and that where the conscience is doubtful. As for the first, we must generally, and without any restriction, maintain, that the greatest menaces ought never to induce us, even by the order and in the name of the sovereign, to do a thing which appears to us evidently unjust and criminal; and tho' we may be very excusable before the human tribunal for having been conquered by

 such

ſuch a ſevere trial, yet we ſhall not be ſo before the tribunal of God.

XXVIII. Thus a parliament, for inſtance, commanded by the prince to regiſter an edict, which is manifeſtly unjuſt, ought certainly to refuſe to do it. The ſame I ſay of a miniſter of ſtate, whom a prince would oblige to diſpatch or put in execution ſome order full of iniquity or tyranny; of an ambaſſador whoſe maſter gives him inſtructions, attended with a manifeſt injuſtice; or of an officer, whom the king ſhould command to kill a man whoſe innocence is as clear as the day. In theſe caſes we muſt ſhew a noble courage, and with all our might reſiſt injuſtice, even at the peril of every thing that can happen to us. *'Tis better to obey God than men.* For in promiſing a faithful obedience to the ſovereign we could never do it but on condition, that he ſhould not order any thing that was manifeſtly contrary to the laws of God, whether natural or revealed. To this purpoſe there is a beautiful paſſage in a tragedy wrote by *Sophocles*. " I did not believe " (ſays *Antigone* to *Creon* king of *Thebes*) that the " edicts of a mortal man, as you are, could be of " ſuch force, as to ſuperſede the laws of the gods " themſelves, laws not written indeed, but certain " and immutable; for they are not of yeſterday or " to-day, but eſtabliſhed perpetually and for ever, " and no one knows when they began. I ought " not therefore, for fear of any man, to expoſe " myſelf, by violating them, to the puniſhment of " the gods *.

* *Sophocl.* Antigon. ỳ. 463, *&c.*

XXIX.

XXIX. But in cafes where the confcience is doubtful, the beft refolution a man can come to, is certainly to obey. The duty of obedience being of a clear and evident obligation, ought to fuperfede all doubt. Otherwife, if the obligation of the fubjects, to comply with the commands of their fovereign, permitted them to refufe obedience till they were convinced of the juftice of thefe commands; this would manifeftly reduce the authority of the prince to nothing, and fubvert all order and government. It would be neceffary that foldiers, executioners, and other inferior officers of court, fhould underftand politics and the civil law, otherwife they might excufe themfelves from their duty of obedience, under a pretence that they are not fufficiently convinced of the juftice of the orders given them; which would evidently render the prince incapable of exercifing the functions of government. 'Tis therefore the duty of the fubjects to obey in thefe circumftances; and if the action is unjuft in itfelf, it cannot be imputed to them, but the whole blame falls on the fovereign.

XXX. Let us here collect, in a few words, the principal views which the fovereign ought to have in the enacting of laws.

1°. He fhould pay a perfect regard to thefe primitive rules of juftice which God himfelf has eftablifhed, and take care that his laws be perfectly conformable to them.

2°. The laws muft be of fuch a nature that they may be eafily followed and obferved. Laws, too difficult to be put in execution, are only apt to ſhake the authority of the magiſtrates, or to lay a foundation for inſurrections capable of ſubverting the ſtate.

3°. No laws ought to be made relating to uſeleſs or unneceſſary things.

4°. The laws ought to be ſuch that the ſubjects may be inclined to obſerve them rather of their own accord than from neceſſity. For this reaſon, the ſovereign ſhould only make ſuch laws as are evidently uſeful, or at leaſt he ſhould explain and make known to the ſubjects, the reaſons and motives that have induced him to enact them.

5°. He ought not to be eaſily induced to change the eſtabliſhed laws without a great neceſſity. Frequent changes in the laws certainly leſſens their authority and that of the ſovereign.

6°. The ſovereign ought not to grant diſpenſations lightly and without good reaſons; otherwiſe he weakens the laws, and lays a foundation for jealouſies, which are always prejudicial to the ſtate and to individuals.

7°. Laws ſhould be ſo contrived as to be mutually aſſiſting to each other, that is to ſay, ſome ſhould prepare for the obſervance of others, and render the execution of them more eaſy. Thus, for example, the wiſe ſumptuary laws, which fix bounds to the expences of the ſubject, contribute greatly to the execution of thoſe laws, which order taxes and public contributions.

8°. A prince, who wants to make new laws, ought to be particularly attentive to times and circumſtances. On this principally depends the ſucceſs of a new law, and the manner in which it is received.

9°.

9°. In fine, the most effectual step a prince can take to enforce his laws, is to conform to them himself, and to shew the first example, as we have before observed.

CHAP. II.

Of the right of judging of the doctrines taught in the state: Of the care which the sovereign ought to take to form the manners of his subjects.

I. IN the enumeration before made of the essential parts of sovereignty, we have comprehended the right of judging of the doctrines taught in the state, and particularly of every thing relating to religion. This is one of the most considerable rights belonging to the sovereign, which it is of great importance to preserve and use according to the rules of justice and prudence. Let us endeavour to shew the necessity of it, to establish the foundations of it, and to point out its extent and boundaries.

II. The first duty of the sovereign ought to be to take all possible pains to form the hearts and minds of his people. In vain would it be for him to establish the best laws, and to prescribe rules of conduct in every thing that any way relates to the good of society, if he did not moreover take proper measures to convince his people of the justice and necessity of these rules, and of the advantages which naturally arise from the strict observance of them.

III. And indeed, ſince the principle of all human actions is the will, and the acts of the will depend on the ideas we form of good and evil, as well as of the rewards and puniſhments which muſt follow the commiſſion of a thing, ſo that every one is determined by his own judgment of the matter: 'tis evident that the ſovereign ought principally to take care that his ſubjects be properly inſtructed from their infancy, in all thoſe principles which can form them to an honeſt and ſober life, and in ſuch doctrines as are agreeable to the end and advantage of ſociety. This is the moſt effectual means of inducing men to a ready and ſure obedience, and of forming their manners inſenſibly. Without this the laws would not have a ſufficient force to reſtrain the ſubjects within the bounds of their duty. As long as men do not obey the laws from principle, their obedience is precarious, and uncertain; and they will always be ready to withdraw from their duty, when they think they can do it with impunity.

IV. If therefore people's manner of thinking, or the ideas and opinions commonly received, and to which they are accuſtomed, have ſo much influence on their conduct, and ſo ſtrongly contribute either to the good or evil of the ſtate; and if it is the duty of the ſovereign to attend to this article, and to beſtow all his care upon it; he ought to neglect nothing that can contribute to the education of youth, the advancement of the ſciences, and the progreſs of truth. If this be the caſe, we muſt needs grant him a right of judging of the doctrines publicly taught, and of proſcribing all thoſe which of themſelves may be oppoſite to the public good and tranquillity.

V. It belongs therefore to the ſovereign alone to eſtabliſh academies and public ſchools of all kinds, and to authorize the reſpective profeſſors. 'Tis his buſineſs to take care that nothing be taught in them, under any pretext, contrary to the fundamental maxims of natural law, to the principles of religion or good politics, in a word, nothing capable of producing impreſſions prejudicial to the happineſs of the ſtate.

VI. But ſovereigns ought to be particularly delicate as to the manner of uſing this right, and not to puſh it beyond its true bounds, but to uſe it only according to the rules of juſtice and prudence, otherwiſe great abuſes may ariſe from hence; either becauſe a thing is prepoſterouſly conſidered as detrimental to the ſtate, which, in the main, no way prejudices, but rather may be advantageous to ſociety; or becauſe, under this pretext, princes, whether of themſelves, or at the inſtigation of wicked perſons, erect inquiſitions with reſpect to the moſt indifferent and innocent, nay even the trueſt opinions, eſpecially in matters of religion.

VII. Supreme rulers cannot therefore be too much on their guard, againſt ſuffering themſelves to be impoſed on by wicked and envious men, who, under a pretext of public good and tranquillity, ſeek only their own private intereſts, and who uſe their utmoſt efforts to render certain opinions ſuſpected, only with a view to ruin honeſter men than themſelves.

VIII,

VIII. The advancement of the ſciences, and tł progreſs of truth, require that a reaſonable libert ſhould be granted to all thoſe who buſy themſelves i ſuch laudable purſuits, and that we ſhould not coı demn a man as criminal, purely becauſe in certai things he has ideas different from thoſe commonly rı ceived. Beſides, a different manner of thinking on tł ſame ſubjects, and a diverſity of ideas and opinion are ſo far from obſtructing, that they rather facil tate, the progreſs of truth; provided however thı ſovereigns take proper meaſures to oblige men of le ters to keep within the bounds of moderation, an that juſt reſpect which mankind owe to one another and that for this effect they exert their authority i checking thoſe who grow too warm in their diſpute and break thro' all rules of decency, ſo as to ir jure, calumniate, and render ſuſpected every or that is not in their way of thinking. We muſt la down as an indubitable maxim, that truth is of itſe very advantageous to men and to ſociety, that n true opinion is contrary to peace, and that all thoſı which, of their nature, are contrary to peace, mu certainly be falſe; otherwiſe we muſt aſſert, thı peace and concord are repugnant to the laws (nature.

CHAI

CHAP. III.

Of the power of the sovereign in matters of religion.

I. THE power of the sovereign, in matters of religion, is of the last importance. Every one knows the disputes which have long subsisted on this topic between the empire and the priesthood, and how fatal the consequences of it have been to states. Hence 'tis equally necessary, both to sovereigns and subjects, to form just ideas on this article.

II. My opinion is, that the supreme authority, in matters of religion, ought necessarily to belong to the sovereign; and the following are my reasons for this assertion.

III. I observe, 1°. that if the interest of society requires that laws should be established in relation to human affairs, that is, to things which properly and directly interest only our temporal happiness; this same interest cannot permit, that we should altogether neglect our spiritual concerns, or those which regard religion, and leave them without any regulation. This has been acknowledged in all ages, and among all nations; and this is the origin of the *civil Law* properly so called, and of the *sacred* or *ecclesiastic Law*. All civilized nations have established these two sorts of law.

IV. But if matters of religion have, in several respects, need of human regulation, the right of finally determining them can belong only to the sovereign.

First

First Proof. This is incontestably proved by the very nature of sovereignty, which is no more than the right of determining finally in society, and which consequently suffers nothing, not only above it, but even that is not subject to it, and embraces, in the extent of its jurisdiction, every thing that can interest the happiness of the state both *sacred* and *profane.*

V. The nature of sovereignty cannot permit any thing, that is susceptible of human direction, to be withdrawn from its authority; for what is withdrawn from the authority of the sovereign, must either be left independent, or subjected to the authority of some other person different from the sovereign himself.

VI. Were no rule established in matters of religion, this would be throwing them into a confusion and disorder, quite opposite to the good of the society, incompatible with the nature of religion, and directly contrary to the views of the Deity, who is the author of it. But if we submit these matters to some authority independent of that of the sovereign, we fall into a new inconveniency, since, by this means, we establish in the same society two sovereign powers independent of each other, which is not only incompatible with the nature of sovereignty, but a contradiction in itself.

VII. In fact, if there were, several sovereigns in the same society, they might also give contrary orders. But who does not perceive that opposite orders, with respect to the same affair, are manifestly repugnant

repugnant to the nature of things, that they cannot have their effect, nor produce a real obligation. How would it be poſſible, for inſtance, that a man, who receives different orders at the ſame time from two ſuperiors, as to repair to the camp, and to go to church, ſhould be obliged to obey both? If it be ſaid that he is not obliged to obey both, there muſt therefore be ſome ſubordination of the one to the other, the inferior will yield to the ſuperior, and it will not be true that they are both ſovereign and independent. We may here very properly apply the words of *Jeſus Chriſt*. *No man can ſerve two maſters; and a kingdom divided againſt itſelf cannot ſtand.*

VIII. *Second Proof.* I draw my ſecond proof from the end of civil ſociety and of ſovereignty. The end of ſovereignty is certainly the happineſs of the people, and the preſervation of the ſtate. Now as religion may ſeveral ways either injure or benefit the ſtate, it follows, that the ſovereign has a right over religion, at leaſt as far as it can depend on human direction. He, who has a right to the *end*, has, undoubtedly, a right alſo to the *means* which lead to it.

IX. Now that religion may ſeveral ways injure or benefit the ſtate, we have already proved in the firſt volume of this work.

1°. All men have conſtantly acknowledged, that the Deity makes his favours to a ſtate depend principally on the care which the ſovereign takes to induce his ſubjects to honour and ſerve him.

2°.

2°. Religion can of itſelf contribute greatly to render men more obedient to the laws, more attached to their country, and more honeſt to one another.

3°. The doctrines and ceremonies of religion have a conſiderable influence on the morals of people, and on the public happineſs. The ideas which men have imbibed of the Deity, have induced them to the moſt monſtrous forms of worſhip, and even prompted them to ſacrifice human victims. They have even, from theſe falſe ideas, drawn arguments in juſtification of vice, cruelty, and licentiouſneſs, as we may ſee by reading the antient poets. Since religion therefore has ſo much influence over the happineſs or miſery of ſociety, who can doubt but it is ſubject to the direction of the ſovereign?

X. *Third Proof.* What we have been ſaying evinces that 'tis incumbent on the ſovereign, and one of his moſt eſſential duties, to make religion, which includes the moſt valuable intereſts of mankind, the principal object of his care and application. He ought to promote the eternal, as well as the preſent and temporal happineſs of his ſubjects: This is therefore a point properly ſubject to his juriſdiction.

XI. *Fourth Proof.* In fine, we can in general acknowledge only two ſovereigns, God and the prince. The ſovereignty of God is a tranſcendent, univerſal, and abſolute ſupremacy, to which even princes themſelves are ſubject; the ſovereignty of the prince holds the ſecond rank, and is ſubordinate to that of God, but in ſuch a manner, that the prince has a right

right to regulate every thing, which interests the happiness of society, and by its nature is susceptible of human direction.

XII. After having thus established the right of the sovereign in matters of religion, let us examine into the extent and bounds of this right; whereby it will appear, that these bounds are not different from those which the sovereignty admits of in all other matters. We have already observed, that the power of the sovereign extended to every thing susceptible of human direction and command. Hence it follows, that the first boundary we ought to fix to the authority of the sovereign, but which indeed is so obvious as scarce needs mentioning, is, that he can order nothing impossible in its nature, either in religion, or any thing else; as for example, to fly into the air, to believe contradictions, *&c.*

XIII. The second boundary, but which does not more particularly interest religion than every thing else, is deduced from the laws of God: for 'tis evident that all human authority, being subordinate to that of God; whatever God has determined by some law, whether *natural* or *positive*, cannot be changed by the sovereign. This is the foundation of that maxim, *'Tis better to obey God than men.*

XIV. 'Tis in consequence of these principles, that no human authority can, for example, forbid the preaching of the gospel, or the use of the sacraments, nor eſtabliſh a new article of faith, nor introduce a new worſhip: for God having given us a rule of religion, and forbidden us to alter this rule, 'tis not in the power of any man to do it; and it would be abſurd to imagine that any man can either believe or practiſe any thing as conducive to his ſalvation, in oppoſition to that which God has declared.

XV. 'Tis alſo on the footing of the limitations we have here eſtabliſhed, that the ſovereign cannot lawfully aſſume to himſelf an empire over conſciences, as if it was in his power to impoſe the neceſſity of believing ſuch or ſuch an article in matters of religion. Nature itſelf and the divine laws are equally contrary to this pretenſion. 'Tis therefore no leſs fooliſh than impious to endeavour to conſtrain conſciences, and, as it were, to extort religion by force of arms. The natural puniſhment of thoſe who are in an error is to be taught *. As for the reſt we muſt leave the care of the ſucceſs to God.

XVI. The authority of the ſovereign, in matters of religion, cannot therefore extend beyond the bounds we have aſſigned to it; but theſe are the only bounds, neither do I imagine it poſſible to think of any others. But what is principally to be obſerved, is, that theſe bounds of the ſovereign power, in matters of religion, are, in no reſpect, different from thoſe he ought to acknowledge in every other matter; that on the contrary they are preciſely the ſame; that they agree indifferently with all the parts of the ſove-

* Errantis pœna eſt doceri.

reignty,

reignty, and that they are not leſs applicable to common things than to thoſe of religion. For example, it would be no more lawful for a father to neglect the nouriſhment and education of his children, tho' the prince ordered him to neglect it, than it would be for paſtors or Chriſtians to abandon the ſervice of God, tho' they were commanded ſo to do by ſome impious ſovereign. The reaſon of this is, becauſe the law of God equally forbids both, and the exception drawn from this law is invincible, and ſuperior to all human authority.

XVII. However, tho' the power of the ſovereign, in matters of religion, cannot change what God has determined, we may nevertheleſs ſay that theſe very things are, in ſome meaſure, ſubmitted to the authority of the ſovereign. Thus, for example, the ſovereign has certainly a right to remove the external obſtacles which may prevent the obſervance of the laws of God, and to make ſuch an obſervance eaſy. This is even one of his firſt duties. Hence alſo ariſes his right of regulating every thing relating to the functions of the clergy and the circumſtances of external worſhip, that the whole may be performed with more order, as far, at leaſt, as the law of God has left theſe things to the direction of men. In a word, 'tis certain that the ſovereign may alſo give an additional degree of force, and obligation to the divine laws by temporal rewards and puniſhments. We muſt therefore acknowledge the right of the ſovereign in regard to religion, and that this right cannot belong to any one elſe on earth.

XVIII. However, the defenders of the rights of the priesthood start many difficulties on this subject, which we must answer. If God, say they, delegates to men the authority he has over his church, it is rather to his pastors and ministers of the gospel, than to sovereigns and magistrates. The magistrate does not belong to the essence of the church. God, on the contrary, has established pastors over his church, and regulated all the functions of their ministry; and in their office they are so far from being the vicegerents of sovereigns, that they are not even obliged to obey them in all things. What is still more, they exercise their functions on the sovereign, as well as on private persons; and the whole scripture and church history attribute a right of government to them.

Answer. When they say that the magistrate does not belong to the essence of the church, they would explain themselves more properly, if they said that the church may subsist tho' there were no magistrates. This is true, but we cannot from hence conclude, that the magistrate has no authority over the church; for, by the same reasoning, we might prove that merchants, physicians, and every person else do not depend on the sovereign; because it is not essential to merchants, physicians, and men in general, to have magistrates, and they can subsist without them. However, reason and scripture subject them to the *superior powers*.

XIX. 2°. What they add is very true, that God has established pastors, and regulated their functions, and that in this quality they are not the vicegerents of human powers; but 'tis easy to convince them by examples, that, from this, they can draw no consequence to the prejudice of the sovereign authority. The function of a physician comes from God as the Author of nature; and that of a pastor comes also from the Deity as the Author of religion. This however does not hinder the physician from having a dependance on the sovereign. The same may be said of agriculture, commerce, and all the arts. Besides, the judges hold their charges and places from the sovereign, yet they do not receive all the rules they are to follow from him. 'Tis God himself who orders them to take no bribe, and to do nothing thro' hatred or favour *&c.* Nothing more is requisite to shew how unjust a consequence it is to pretend, that, because a thing is established by God, it should be, for that reason, independent of the sovereign.

XX. 3°. But, say they, pastors are not always obliged to obey the sovereign. We agree with them in this point, but we have observed that this can only take place in things directly opposite to the law of God; and we have shewn that this right appertains indifferently to every person in common affairs as well as in religion, and consequently this takes away nothing from the authority of the sovereign.

XXI. 4°. Neither can we deny that the pastoral functions are exeecised on kings, not only as members of the church, but also in particular as kings. But this proves nothing; for what function is there that does not regard the sovereign? In particular, does the physician less exercise his profession on the prince, than on other people? Does he not equally prescribe for him a regimen and the medicines necessary for health? Does not the office of a counsellor regard also the sovereign, and even in his quality of sovereign? and yet who ever thought of exempting these persons from a subjection to the supreme authority?

XXII. 5°. But lastly, say they, is it not certain, that scripture and antient history every where ascribe the government of the church to pastors? 'This is also true, but we need only examine what the nature of that government is which is proper to the ministers of religion, to be convinced that it does not at all oppose or diminish the authority of the sovereign or the preeminence of his government.

XXIII. There is a government of *simple direction*, and a government of *authority*. The first consists in giving counsel, or teaching the rules which ought to be followed. But it supposes no authority in him who governs, neither does it in any thing restrain the liberty of those who are governed, except in as much as the laws they are taught imply an obligation of themselves. Such is the government of physicians with respect to health, of lawyers with respect to civil affairs, and of counsellors of state with respect to politics. The opinions of all these persons are not obligatory in indifferent things; and in necessary things they are not obligatory of themselves, but only so far as they teach the laws established by nature, or by the sovereign, and this is the species of government which belongs to pastors.

XXIV.

XXIV. But there is alſo a government of *juriſdiction and authority*, which contains in itſelf the right of making regulations, and really obliges thoſe who are ſubjected to it. This government, which ariſes from a ſovereign authority, obliges by the eminence of the authority itſelf, which gives a right and power to compel. But 'tis to be remarked, that true authority is inſeparable from the right of conſtraining and obliging. Theſe are the natural effects of it by which alone we may know it. 'Tis this laſt ſpecies of government which we aſcribe to the ſovereign; and of which we ſay that it does not belong to paſtors *.

XXV. We therefore ſay, that the government, which belongs to paſtors, is a government of counſel, inſtruction and perſuaſion, and whoſe entire force and authority conſiſts in the word of God, which they ought to teach the people, and by no means in a perſonal authority. Their power is to declare the orders of God, and their commiſſion goes no farther.

XXVI. If at preſent we compare theſe different ſpecies of government, we ſhall eaſily perceive that they are not oppoſite to each other, even in matters of religion. The government of ſimple direction, which we give to paſtors, has nothing that can claſh with the ſovereign authority; on the contrary, it may find an advantage in its aid and aſſiſtance. Thus there is no contradiction in ſaying, that the ſo-

* See the goſpel according to St. *Luke*, chap. xii. ỳ. 14. firſt Epiſtle to the *Corinthians*; chap. x. ỳ. 4. *Epheſ.* chap. vi. ỳ. 17. *Philip.* iii. ỳ. 20.

vereign governs the paſtors, and that he is alſo governed by them, provided we attend to the different kinds of government. Theſe are the general principles of this important doctrine, and 'tis eaſy to apply them to particular caſes.

CHAP. IV.

Of the power of the ſovereign over the lives and fortunes of his ſubjects in criminal caſes.

I. THE principal end of civil government and ſociety, is to ſecure all the natural advantages of man, and eſpecially his life. However this end neceſſarily requires that the ſovereign ſhould have ſome right over the lives of his ſubjects, either in an *indirect manner*, for the defence of the ſtate, or in a *direct manner*, for the puniſhment of crimes.

II. The power of the ſovereign over the lives of the ſubjects, with reſpect to the defence of the ſtate, regards the right of war, of which we ſhall treat hereafter. We intend to ſpeak here only of the power of inflicting puniſhments.

III. The firſt queſtion which preſents itſelf, is to know what is the origin and foundation of this part of the ſovereign power; a queſtion, which cannot be anſwered without ſome difficulty. Puniſhment, 'tis ſaid, is an evil which a perſon ſuffers in a compulſive way: A man cannot puniſh himſelf; and conſequently it it ſeems that individuals could not transfer to the ſovereign a right which they had not over themſelves.

IV. Some civilians pretend, that when a ſovereign inflicts puniſhments on his ſubjects, he does it by virtue of their own conſent; becauſe, by ſubmitting to his authority, they have promiſed to acquieſce in every thing he ſhould do with reſpect to them; and in particular a ſubject, who voluntarily determines to commit a crime, conſents thereby to ſuffer the puniſhment eſtabliſhed againſt ſuch a crime, which puniſhment is perfectly known to him.

V. But it ſeems difficult to determine the right of the ſovereign on a preſumption of this nature, eſpecially with reſpect to capital puniſhments; neither is it neceſſary to have recourſe to this pretended conſent of criminals, in order to eſtabliſh the right of the ſovereign. 'Tis better to ſay that the right of the ſovereign, to puniſh malefactors, derives its origin from that which every individual originally had in the ſociety of nature, to puniſh the crimes committed againſt himſelf, or againſt the members of the ſociety, yielded and transferred to the ſovereign.

VI. In a word, the right of executing the natural laws, and of puniſhing thoſe who violate them, belongs originally to human ſociety, and to each individual with reſpect to all the reſt; otherwiſe the laws which nature and reaſon impoſe on man, would be entirely uſeleſs in a ſtate of nature, if no body had the power of putting them in execution, or of puniſhing the violation of them.

VII. Whoever violates the laws of nature, testifies thereby, that he tramples on the maxims of reason and equity, which God has prescribed for the common safety; and thus he becomes an enemy of mankind. Since therefore every man has an inconteſtable right to take care of his own preservation and that of society, he may, without doubt, inflict on such a man punishments capable of producing repentance in him, and of hindering him from committing the like faults for the future, or even of deterring others by his example. In a word, the same laws of nature which forbid vice, also give a right of pursuing the perpetrator of it, and of punishing him in a just proportion.

VIII. 'Tis true, in a state of nature, these kinds of chastisements are not inflicted by authority, and it might happen that the criminal could shelter himself from the punishments he has to dread from other men, or even repel their attacks. But the right of punishment is not for that either less real or less well founded. The difficulty of putting it in execution does not destroy it: This was one of the inconveniences of the primitive state, which men have efficaciously remedied by the establishment of sovereignty.

IX. By following these principles, it is easy to comprehend that the right of a sovereign, to punish crimes, is no other than that natural right which human society and every individual had originally to execute the law of nature, and to take care of their own safety, yielded and transferred to the sovereign, who,

who, by means of the authority with which he is invested, exercises it in a sure manner, from which it is very difficult for wicked men to screen themselves. Besides, whether we call this natural right of punishing crimes the *right of revenge*, or whether we refer it to a kind of *right of war*, is a matter of indifference, neither does it change its nature on that account.

X. These are the true foundations of the right of the sovereign with respect to punishments. This being granted, I define punishment an evil, with which the sovereign threatens those who are disposed to violate his laws, and which he actually inflicts, and in a just proportion, when they violate them, independently of the reparation of the damage, with a view to some future good, and finally for the safety and tranquillity of the society.

XI. I say, 1°. that punishment is an evil, and this evil may be of a different nature, according as it affects the life of a person, his body, his reputation, or his estate. Besides, it is indifferent whether this evil consists in some hard and toilsome labour, or in suffering something painful.

XII. I add, in the second place, that 'tis the sovereign who awards punishments; not that every punishment in general supposes sovereignty, but because we here speak of the right of punishing in civil society, and as being a branch of the sovereign power. 'Tis therefore the sovereign alone who can award punishments in civil society, and individuals

duals cannot do themſelves juſtice, without encroaching on the rights of the ſovereign.

XIII. I afterwards ſay, 3°. *with which the ſovereign threatens &c.* to denote the firſt intention of the ſovereign. He threatens firſt, and then puniſhes, if the threatning is not ſufficient to prevent the crime. Hence it alſo appears that puniſhment always ſuppoſes guilt, and conſequently we ought not to reckon among puniſhments properly ſo called, all the evils to which men are expoſed, without their having antecedently committed ſome crime.

XIV. I add, 4°. that puniſhment is inflicted *independently of the reparation of the damage,* to ſhew that theſe are two things very diſtinct, and we ought not to confound them. Every crime is accompanied with two obligations; the firſt is, to repair the injury which a man has done; and the ſecond is, to ſuffer the puniſhment; and the delinquent ought to ſatisfy both. 'Tis alſo to be obſerved on this occaſion, that the right of puniſhment in civil ſociety is transferred entirely to the magiſtrate, who may conſequently by his own authority, if he pleaſes, pardon a criminal; but this is not the caſe with reſpect to the right of requiring ſatisfaction or reparation of damages. The magiſtrate cannot acquit the offender in this point, and the injured perſon always retains his own right; ſo that he is wronged, if he is hindered from the ſatisfaction which is due to him.

XV. Laſtly, 5°. by ſaying *that puniſhment is inflicted with a view to ſome good.* By this we point out

out the end which the ſovereign ought to propoſe to himſelf in inflicting puniſhments, and this we ſhall now explain more particularly.

XVI. The ſovereign, as ſuch, has not only a right, but is alſo obliged to puniſh crimes. The uſe of puniſhments is ſo far from being contrary to equity, that it is abſolutely requiſite for the public tranquillity. The ſovereign power would be uſeleſs, if it was not inveſted with a right, and armed with a force, ſufficient to deter the wicked by the dread of ſome evil, and to make them actually ſuffer that evil, when they diſturb the ſociety by their enormities. It was even neceſſary that this power ſhould extend ſo far as to make them ſuffer the greateſt of natural evils, which is *death*; in order effectually to repreſs the moſt daring audaciouſneſs, and, as it were, to balance the different degrees of human wickedneſs by a counterpoiſe ſufficiently powerful.

XVII. Such is the right of the ſovereign. But if the ſovereign has a right to puniſh, the criminal muſt be under ſome obligation in this reſpect; for we cannot poſſibly conceive a right without ſome obligation correſponding to it. But wherein does this obligation of the criminal conſiſt? Is he obliged wantonly to betray himſelf, and voluntarily expoſe himſelf to puniſhment? I anſwer, that this is not neceſſary for the end propoſed in the eſtabliſhment of puniſhments, and we cannot reaſonably require that a man ſhould thus betray himſelf; but this does not hinder him from lying under ſome reciprocal obligation.

XVIII. 1°. 'Tis certain, that when there is a ſimple pecuniary puniſhment, to which a man is lawfully condemned, he ought to pay it without being forced by the magiſtrate; not only prudence requires it, but alſo the rules of juſtice, which demand that we ſhould repair damages, and obey lawful judges.

XIX. 2°. There is more difficulty in what relates to afflictive, and eſpecially to capital, puniſhments. The natural inſtinct which renders us fond of life, and the averſion we have to infamy, do not permit us to lay a criminal under an obligation of accuſing himſelf voluntarily, and preſenting himſelf to puniſhment; and indeed neither the public good, nor the rights of the perſon who is intruſted with the ſupreme authority, demand it.

XX. 3°. In conſequence of this ſame principle, a criminal may innocently ſeek his own ſafety in flight, and is not obliged to remain in priſon if he perceives the doors open, or if he can eaſily force them. But it is not lawful for him to procure his liberty by the commiſſion of ſome new crime, as by cutting the throats of the jailors, or by killing thoſe ſent to apprehend him.

XXI. 4°. But in fine, if we ſuppoſe that the criminal is known, that he is taken, that he cannot make his eſcape from priſon, and that, after a mature examination or trial, he is convicted of the crime, and conſequently condemned to condign puniſhment; he is in this caſe certainly obliged to undergo the puniſhment, to acknowledge the lawful-

neſs

neſs of his ſentence, that there is no injury done him, and that he cannot reaſonably complain of any one except himſelf: Much leſs can he withdraw from puniſhment by the ways of violence, and oppoſe the magiſtrate in the exerciſe of his right. In this properly conſiſts the obligation of the criminal with reſpect to puniſhment. Let us now enquire more particularly what end the ſovereign ought to propoſe to himſelf in inflicting them.

XXII. In general, 'tis certain that the ſovereign ought never to inflict puniſhments but with a view to ſome public advantage. To make a man ſuffer purely becauſe he has done a thing, and to attend only to what has paſſed, is a piece of cruelty condemned by reaſon; for after all 'tis impoſſible that the evil done ſhould be undone. In ſhort, the right of puniſhing is a part of ſovereignty: now ſovereignty is founded ultimately on a beneficent power: it follows therefore that even when the ſovereign makes uſe of his power of the ſword, he ought always to aim at ſome advantage, or ſome future good, agreeably to what is required of him by the very nature and foundation of his authority.

XXIII. The principal and laſt end of puniſhment is therefore the ſafety and tranquillity of ſociety; but as there may be different means of arriving at this end, according to different circumſtances, the ſovereign alſo, in inflicting puniſhments, propoſes different and particular views, which are always ſubordinate to the principal end we have mentioned, and are all finally reducible to it. What we have ſaid

ſaid very well agrees with the obſervation of *Grotius* *. "In puniſhments, ſays he, we muſt have the good of "the criminal in view, or the advantage of him whoſe "intereſt it was that the crime ſhould not have been "committed, or the good of all indifferently."

XXIV. Thus the ſovereign ſometimes propoſes to correct the criminal, and make him loſe the propenſity of falling into the ſame crime, in curing the evil by its contrary, and taking away the ſweets of the crime, which are allurements to it, by the bitterneſs of the puniſhment. This puniſhment, if the criminal is reformed by it, tends to the public good. But if he ſhould perſevere in his crime, the ſovereign muſt have recourſe to more violent remedies, and even to death.

XXV. Sometimes the ſovereign propoſes to deprive criminals of the means of committing freſh crimes, as for example, by taking from them the arms which they might uſe, by ſhutting them up in a priſon, by baniſhing them, or even by putting them to death. At the ſame time he takes care of the public ſafety, not only with reſpect to the criminals themſelves, but alſo with regard to thoſe inclined to commit the ſame crime, in deterring them by theſe examples. For this reaſon, nothing is more agreeable to the end of puniſhments, than to inflict them publicly, and with ſuch a ſolemnity as is moſt proper to make an impreſſion on the minds of the vulgar.

XXVI. All theſe particular ends of puniſhment

* Lib. II. cap. 20. §. 6. N. 2.

ought

ought to be conſtantly ſubordinate and referred to the principal and laſt end, which is the ſafety of the public, and the ſovereign ought to uſe them all as means of obtaining the principal end; ſo that he ſhould not have recourſe to the moſt rigorous puniſhments, till theſe of greater lenity are inſufficient to procure the public tranquillity.

XXVII. But here a queſtion ariſes, whether all actions, contrary to the laws, can be lawfully puniſhed? I anſwer, that the very end of puniſhment, and the conſtitution of human nature, evince there may be actions, in themſelves evil, which however it is to no purpoſe for human juſtice to puniſh.

XXVIII. And, 1°. acts purely internal, or ſimple thoughts which do not diſcover themſelves by any external acts prejudicial to ſociety; for example, the agreeable idea of a bad action, the deſire of committing it, the deſign of it without proceeding to the execution, *&c.* all theſe are not ſubject to the ſeverity of human puniſhment, even tho' it ſhould accidentally happen that they are afterwards diſcovered.

XXIX. On this ſubject we muſt however make the following few remarks. The firſt is, that if theſe kinds of vicious actions are not ſubject to human puniſhment, it is becauſe the weakneſs of mand oes not permit, even for the good of ſociety, that he ſhould be treated with the utmoſt rigour. We ought to have a juſt regard for humanity in things, which, tho' bad in themſelves, yet do not greatly affect the public order and tranquillity. The ſecond remark is, is, that tho' acts, purely internal, are not ſubject to civil puniſhment, we muſt not for this reaſon conclude, that theſe acts are not under the direction of the civil laws. We have before eſtabliſhed the contrary *. In a word, 'tis evident that the laws of nature expreſly condemn ſuch actions, and that they are puniſhed by God.

XXX. 2°. It would be too rigorous to puniſh every peccadillo; ſince human frailty, notwithſtanding the greateſt caution and attention to our duty, cannot avoid a multitude of ſlips and infirmities. This is a conſequence of the toleration due to humanity.

XXXI. 3°. In a word, we muſt neceſſarily leave unpuniſhed, thoſe common vices which are the conſequences of a general corruption; as for inſtance, ambition, avarice, inhumanity, ingratitude, hypocriſy, envy, pride, wrath, *&c.* for if a ſovereign wanted to puniſh theſe, and ſimilar vices, with rigour, he would be reduced to a neceſſity of reigning in a deſert. 'Tis ſufficient to puniſh theſe vices when they prompt men to enormous and open exceſſes.

XXXII. 'Tis not even always neceſſary to puniſh crimes which are in themſelves puniſhable, for there are caſes in which the ſovereign may pardon; and of this we muſt judge by the very ends of puniſhment.

* Chap. 1. §. 22, *&c.*

XXXIII. The public good is the ultimate end of all punishments. If therefore there are circumstances, in which, by pardoning, as much or more advantage is procured than in punishing, then there is no obligation to punish, and the sovereign even ought to shew clemency. Thus if the crime is concealed, or is only known to a few, it is not always necessary, nay it would sometimes be dangerous, to make it public by punishment; for many abstain from evil, rather from their ignorance of vice, than from a knowledge and love of virtue. *Cicero* observes, with regard to *Solon*'s having no law against parricide, that this silence of the legislator has been looked upon as a great mark of prudence; forasmuch as he made no prohibition of a thing of which there had been yet no example, lest by speaking of it, he should seem to give the people a notion of committing it, rather than deter them from it.

We may also consider the personal services which the criminal, or some of his family, have done to the state, and whether he can still be of great advantage to it, so that the impression made by the sight of his punishment is not likely to produce so much good as he himself is capable of doing. Thus at sea, when the pilot has committed a crime, and when there is none on board capable of navigating the ship, it would be destroying all those in the vessel to punish him. This example may also be applied to the general of an army.

In a word, the public advantage, which is the measure of punishments, sometimes requires that the sovereign should pardon because of the great number of criminals. The prudence of the government requires that the juſtice, eſtabliſhed for the preſervation of ſociety, ſhould not be exerciſed in ſuch a manner as to deſtroy the ſtate.

XXXIV. All crimes are not equal, and 'tis but juſtice that there ſhould be a due proportion between the crime and the puniſhment. We may judge of the greatneſs of a crime in general by its object, by the intention and malice of the criminal, and by the prejudice ariſing to ſociety from it; and to this laſt conſequence, the two others muſt be finally referred.

XXXV. According as the object is more or leſs noble, that is, as the perſons offended are more or leſs conſiderable, the action is alſo more or leſs criminal. In the firſt claſs, we muſt place thoſe crimes which intereſt human ſociety in general, then thoſe which diſturb the order of civil ſociety, and laſtly thoſe which relate to individuals; and theſe laſt are more or leſs atrocious, according as the good of which they deprive us is more or leſs valuable. Thus he, who kills his father, commits a more atrocious murder than if he had killed a ſtranger. He, who injures a magiſtrate, is more criminal than if he had injured his equal. A robber, who kills travellers, is more guilty than he who only ſtrips them of what they have.

XXXVI. The greater or ſmaller degree of malice, alſo contributes very much to the enormity of the crime, and is to be deduced from ſeveral circumſtances.

1°. From the motives which engage men in crimes, and which may be more or lefs eafy to refift. Thus he, who robs or murders in cold blood, is more criminal than he who yields to temptation by the violence of fome furious paffion.

2°. From the particular character of the criminal, which, befides the general reafons, ought to retain him in his duty; "The higher a man's birth is, "fays *Juvenal*, or the more exalted he is in dignity, "the more enormous is the crime he commits *. "This takes place efpecially with refpect to princes, "and fo much the more, becaufe the confequences "of their bad actions are very fatal to the ftate, "from the great number of perfons who endeavour "to imitate them." This is the judicious remark made by *Cicero* †. The fame obfervation may alfo be applied to magiftrates and clergymen.

3°. We muft alfo confider the circumftances of time and place, in which the crime has been committed, the manner of committing it, the inftruments ufed for that purpofe *&c.*

4°. Laftly, we are to confider whether the criminal has made a cuftom of committing fuch a crime, or, if he is but rarely guilty of it; whether he

* *Omne animi vitium tanto confpectius in fe*
Crimen habet, quanto major qui peccat habetur.
Juv. Sat. VIII. ℣. 140, 141.

† De Leg. lib. III. cap. 14. *Nec enim tantum mali eft peccare principes, quanquam eft magnum hoc per feipfum malum; quantum illud, quod permulti imitatores principum exiftunt: quo perniciofius de republica merentur vitiofi principes, quod non folum vitia concipiunt ipfi, fed ea infundunt in civitatem. Neque folum obfunt, quod ipfi corrumpuntur, fed etiam quod corrumpunt; plufque exemplo, quam peccato, nocent.*

has committed it of his own accord, or has been ſeduced by others *&c.*

XXXVII. We may eaſily perceive that the different concurrence of theſe circumſtances more or leſs intereſts the happineſs and tranquillity of ſociety, and conſequently either augments or diminiſhes the enormity of the crime.

XXXVIII. There are therefore crimes more or leſs great than others, and conſequently they do not all deſerve to be puniſhed with equal ſeverity; but the kind and preciſe degree of puniſhment depends on the prudence of the ſovereign. The following are the principal rules which he ought to follow.

1°. The degree of puniſhment ought always to be proportioned to the end propoſed, that is, to repreſs the inſolence and malignity of the wicked, and to procure the internal tranquillity and ſafety of the ſtate. 'Tis upon this principle that we muſt augment or diminiſh the rigour of the puniſhment. The puniſhment is too rigorous, if we can, by milder means, obtain the ends propoſed in puniſhing; and, on the contrary, it is too moderate when it has not ſharpneſs enough to produce theſe effects, and when the criminals themſelves deſpiſe it.

2°. According to this principle, every crime in particular may be puniſhed in proportion as the public good requires, without conſidering whether there is an equal or ſmaller puniſhment eſtabliſhed for another crime, which in itſelf appears leſſer or greater: thus robbery, for inſtance, is in itſelf much leſs criminal than murder; and yet robbers may, without

injuſtice,

injuſtice, be puniſhed with death in certain caſes, as well as murderers.

3°. The equality which the ſovereign ought always to obſerve in the exerciſe of juſtice, conſiſts in puniſhing thoſe alike who have treſpaſſed alike, and in not pardoning a perſon, without very good reaſons, who has committed a crime for which others have been puniſhed.

4°. It muſt be alſo obſerved, that we cannot multiply the kinds and degrees of puniſhment *in infinitum*; and as there is no greater puniſhment than death, 'tis neceſſary that certain crimes, tho' unequal in themſelves, ſhould be equally ſubject to capital puniſhments. All that can be ſaid, is, that death may be more or leſs terrible, according as we employ a mild and ſhort method, or ſlow and cruel torments, to deprive a perſon of life.

5°. We ought, as much as poſſible, to incline to the merciful ſide, when there are not ſtrong reaſons for the contrary. This is the ſecond part of clemency. The firſt conſiſts in a total exemption from puniſhment, when the good of the ſtate permits it. This is alſo one of the rules of the *Roman* law *.

6°. On the contrary, 'tis ſometimes neceſſary and convenient to heighten the puniſhment, and to ſet ſuch an example as will intimidate the wicked, when the evil can be prevented only by violent remedies †.

* In pœnalibus cauſis, benignius interpretandum eſt, lib. CV. §. 2 ff. de Reg. Jur. vid. ſup. §. 33.

† Nonnunquam evenit, ut aliquorum maleficiorum ſupplicia exacerbantur, quoties nimirum, multis perſonis graſſantibus, exemplo opus ſit, lib. XVI. §. 10. ff. de pœnis.

7°. The ſame puniſhment does not make the ſame impreſſion on all kinds of people, and conſequently has not the ſame force to deter them from vice. We ought therefore to conſider, both in the general penal ſanction and in the application of it, the perſon of the criminal, and in that, all thoſe qualities of age, ſex, ſtate, riches, ſtrength, and the like, which may either increaſe or diminiſh the ſenſe of puniſhment. A particular fine, for inſtance, will diſtreſs a poor man, while it is nothing to a rich: The ſame mark of ignominy will be very mortifying to a perſon of honour and quality, which would paſs for a trifle with a vulgar fellow. Men have more ſtrength to ſupport puniſhments than women, and full-grown people more than thoſe of tender years, *&c.* Let us alſo obſerve, that it equally belongs to the juſtice and prudence of the government, always to follow the order of judgments and of the judiciary procedure in the infliction of puniſhments. This is neceſſary, not only that we may not commit injuſtice in an affair of ſuch importance, but alſo that the ſovereign may be ſecured againſt all ſuſpicion of injuſtice and partiality. However, there are ſometimes extraordinary and preſſing circumſtances where the good of the ſtate and the public ſafety do not permit us exactly to obſerve all the formalities of the criminal procedure; and provided, in theſe circumſtances, the crime is duly proved, the ſovereign may judge ſummarily, and without delay puniſh a criminal, whoſe puniſhment cannot be deferred without imminent danger to the ſtate. Laſtly, 'tis alſo a rule of prudence, that if we cannot puniſh a criminal without expoſing the ſtate to great danger, the ſovereign

reign ought not only to grant a pardon, but alſo to do it in ſuch a manner as that it may appear rather to be the effect of *clemency* than of *neceſſity*.

XXXIX. What we have ſaid relates to puniſhments inflicted for crimes of which a perſon is the ſole and proper author. With reſpect to crimes committed by ſeveral, the following obſervations may ſerve as principles.

1°. 'Tis certain that thoſe, who are really accomplices of the crime of any perſon, ought to be puniſhed in proportion to the ſhare they have in it, and according as they ought to be conſidered as principal cauſes, or ſubordinate and collateral inſtruments. In theſe caſes, ſuch perſons ſuffer rather for their own crime than for that of another.

2°. As for crimes committed by a body or community, thoſe only are really criminal who have given their actual conſent to them; but they, who have been of a contrary opinion, are abſolutely innocent. Thus *Alexander*, having given orders to ſell all the *Thebans* after the taking of their city, excepted thoſe, who, in the public deliberations, had oppoſed the breaking of the alliance with the *Macedonians*.

3°. Hence it is, that, with reſpect to crimes committed by a multitude, reaſons of ſtate and humanity direct, that we ſhould principally puniſh thoſe who are the ring-leaders, and pardon the reſt. The ſeverity of the ſovereign to ſome will repreſs the audaciouſneſs of the moſt reſolute; and his clemency to others will gain him the heart of the multitude *.

* *Quintil.* Declam. cap. VII. p. m. 237.

4°. If the ring-leaders have ſheltered themſelves by flight, or otherwiſe, or if they have all an equal ſhare in the crime, we muſt have recourſe to a decimation, or ſome other means to puniſh ſome of them. By this means the terror reaches all, while but few fall under the puniſhment.

XL. Beſides, 'tis a certain and inviolable rule, that no perſon can be lawfully puniſhed for the crime of another, in which he has had no ſhare. All merit and demerit is intirely perſonal and incommunicable; and we have no right to puniſh any but thoſe who deſerve it.

XLI. It ſometimes happens, however, that innocent perſons ſuffer on account of the crimes of others; but we muſt make two remarks on this ſubject.

1°. Not every thing that occaſions uneaſineſs, pain, or loſs to a perſon, is properly a puniſhment; for example, when ſubjects ſuffer ſome grievances from the miſcarriages and crimes of their prince, it is not in reſpect to them a puniſhment, but a misfortune.

The ſecond remark is, that theſe kinds of evils, or indirect puniſhments, if we may call them ſo, are inſeparable from the conſtitution of human affairs, and the neceſſary conſequences of it.

XLII. Thus if we confiſcate the effects of a man, his children ſuffer indeed for it; but it is not properly a puniſhment to them, ſince theſe effects ought to belong to them only on ſuppoſition their father had kept them till his death. In a word, we muſt either almoſt entirely aboliſh the uſe of puniſhments, or at leaſt acknowledge, that theſe inconveniencies, inſeparable from the conſtitution of human affairs, and from the particular relations which men have to each other, have nothing in themſelves unjuſt.

XLIII. Laſtly, 'tis to be obſerved, that there are crimes ſo enormous, and which ſo eſſentially affect ſociety, that the public good authoriſes the ſovereign to take the ſtrongeſt precautions againſt them, and even if it is neceſſary, to make a part of the puniſhment fall on the perſons who are moſt dear to the criminal. Thus the children of traitors or ſtate criminals, may be excluded from poſts and honours. The father is certainly puniſhed by this means, ſince he ſees he is the cauſe why the perſons who are deareſt to him, are reduced to live in obſcurity. But this is not properly a puniſhment in regard to the children; for the ſovereign having a right to give public employments to whom he pleaſes, he may, when the public good requires it, exclude even perſons who have done nothing to render themſelves unworthy of theſe employments. I confeſs that this is indeed a hardſhip, but neceſſity authoriſes it, to the end that the tenderneſs of a father for his children may make him more careful to undertake nothing againſt the ſtate. But equity ought always to direct theſe judgments, and to mitigate them according to circumſtances.

XLIV. I am not of opinion that we can juſtly puſh things beyond theſe bounds, neither does the public good require it. 'Tis therefore a real piece of injuſtice, which is eſtabliſhed with ſeveral nations,

nations, namely, to banish or kill the children of a tyrant or traitor, and sometimes all his relations, tho' they had no share in his crimes. What has been said is sufficient to shew us what we ought to think of the famous law of *Arcadius* * the Christian emperor.

* Cod. ad L. Jul. Maj. lib. IX. tit. 8. leg. 5.

CHAP. V.

Of the power of sovereigns over the Bona Reipublicæ; *or the goods contained in the commonwealth.*

I. THE right of the sovereign over the goods contained in the commonwealth, relates either to the goods of the subject, or to the public goods which belong to the commonwealth itself as such.

II. The right of the sovereign over the goods of the subject may be established two different ways; for this right may either be founded on the very nature of the sovereignty, or on the particular manner in which it was acquired.

III. If we suppose, that a sovereign primitively possesses, with a full right of property, all the goods contained in the commonwealth, and that he has collected, as it were, his own subjects, who originally hold their estates of him, then 'tis certain that the sovereign has as absolute a power over these estates, as every master of a family has over his own patrimony; and that the subjects cannot enjoy or dispose of these goods or eſtates, except in as far as the ſovereign permits. In theſe circumſtances, as long as the ſovereign has remitted nothing of his right by irrevocable grants, his ſubjects poſſeſs their eſtates in a *precarious* manner, revocable at pleaſure, whenever the prince thinks fit; they can only ſupply themſelves with ſuſtenance and other neceſſaries from them: In this caſe the ſovereignty is accompanied with a right of abſolute property.

IV. But, 1°. this manner of eſtabliſhing the power of the ſovereign over the goods of the ſubjects cannot be of great uſe; and if it has ſometimes taken place, it has only been among the oriental nations, who eaſily ſubmit to deſpotic government.

2°. Experience teaches us, that this abſolute dominion of the ſovereign over the goods of the ſubjects does not tend to the advantage of ſtates. A modern traveller obſerves, that the countries, where this propriety of the prince prevails, however beautiful and fertile of themſelves, become daily more deſolate, poor, and barbarous; or that at leaſt they are not ſo flouriſhing as moſt of the kingdoms of *Europe*, where the ſubjects poſſeſs their eſtates as their own property excluſive of the prince.

3°. Sovereignty does not of itſelf require, that the prince ſhould have this abſolute dominion over the eſtates of the ſubjects. The property of individuals is prior to the formation of ſtates, and there is no reaſon which can induce us to ſuppoſe that theſe individuals have entirely transferred to the ſovereign the right they had over their own eſtates; on on the contrary, it is to ſecure a quiet and eaſy poſſeſſion of their properties, that they have eſtabliſhed government and ſovereignty among them.

4°. Beſides, if we ſhould ſuppoſe an abſolute ſovereignty acquired by arms, yet this does not of itſelf give an abſolute dominion over the properties of the ſubjects. The ſame is true even of a patrimonial ſovereignty, which gives a right of alienating the crown; for this right of the ſovereign does not hinder the ſubjects from enjoying their ſeveral properties.

V. Let us therefore conclude, that, in general, the right of the prince over the goods of the ſubjects is not an abſolute dominion over their properties, but a right founded on the nature and end of ſovereignty, which gives him the power of diſpoſing of thoſe eſtates in different manners, for the benefit of individuals as well as of the ſtate, without depriving the ſubjects of the right they have to their properties, except in caſes where it is abſolutely neceſſary for the public good.

VI. This being premiſed, the prince, as ſovereign, has a right over the eſtates of his ſubjects principally in three different manners.

The firſt conſiſts in regulating, by wiſe laws, the uſe which every one ought to make of his goods and eſtate, for the advantage of the ſtate and that of individuals.

The ſecond, in raiſing ſubſidies and taxes.

The

The third, in using the rights of ſovereign or *tranſcendental* propriety *.

VII. To the firſt head we muſt reduce all *ſumptuary laws*, by which bounds are ſet to unneceſſary expences, which ruin families, and conſequently impoveriſh the ſtate. Nothing is more conducive to the happineſs of a nation, or more worthy of the care of the ſovereign, than to oblige the ſubjects to œconomy, frugality, and labour.

When luxury has once prevailed in a nation, the evil becomes almoſt incurable. As too great authority ſpoils kings, ſo luxury poiſons a whole people. The moſt ſuperfluous things are looked upon as neceſſary, and new neceſſities are daily invented. Thus families are ruined, and individuals diſabled from contributing to the expences neceſſary for the public good. An individual, for inſtance, who ſpends only three fifths of his income, and pays one fifth for the public ſervice, will not hurt himſelf, ſince he lays up a fifth to increaſe his ſtock. But if he ſpends all his income, he either cannot pay the taxes, or he muſt break in upon his capital.

Another inconveniency is, that not only the eſtates of individuals are ſquandered away by luxury, but what is ſtill worſe, they are generally carried abroad into foreign countries, in purſuit of thoſe things which flatter luxury and vanity.

The impoveriſhing of individuals produces alſo another evil for the ſtate, by hindering marriages. On the contrary, people are more inclined to marri-

* Dominium eminens.

age,

age, when a moderate expence is ſufficient for the ſupport of a family.

This the emperor *Auguſtus* was very ſenſible of; for when he wanted to reform the manners of the *Romans*, among the various laws which he either made or renewed, he re-eſtabliſhed both the ſumptuary law, and that which obliged people to marry.

When luxury is once introduced, it ſoon becomes a general evil, and the contagion inſenſibly ſpreads from the firſt men of the ſtate to the very dregs of the people. The king's relations want to imitate his magnificence; the nobility that of his relations; the gentry, or middle ſort of people, want to equal the nobility; and the poor would fain paſs for gentry: Thus every one living beyond what he has, the people are ruined, and all orders and diſtinctions confounded.

Hiſtory informs us, that, in all ages, luxury has been one of the cauſes which has more or leſs contributed to the ruin and decay even of the moſt powerful ſtates, becauſe it ſenſibly enervates courage, and deſtroys virtue. *Suetonius* obſerves, that *Julius Cæſar* invaded the liberties of his country only becauſe he knew not how to pay his debts contracted by his exceſſive prodigality, nor how to ſupport his expenſive way of living. Many ſided with him becauſe they had not wherewith to ſupply that luxury to which they had been accuſtomed, and they were in hopes of getting by the civil wars enough to maintain their former pride *.

We muſt obſerve, in fine, that to render the ſumptuary laws more effectual, princes and magi-

* See Sall. ad Cæſar. de Repub. ordinand.

ſtrates

ſtrates ought, by the example of their own moderation, to put thoſe out of countenance who love extravagance, and to encourage the prudent, who would eaſily ſubmit to follow the pattern of a good œconomy and honeſt frugality.

VIII. To this right of the ſovereign of directing the ſubjects in the uſe of their eſtates and goods, we muſt alſo reduce the laws againſt gaming and prodigality, thoſe which ſet bounds to grants, legacies, and teſtaments; and, in fine, thoſe againſt idle and lazy people, and againſt perſons that ſuffer their eſtates to run to ruin, purely by careleſſneſs and neglect.

IX. Above all, it is of great importance to uſe every endeavour to baniſh idleneſs, that fruitful ſource of a thouſand diſorders. The want of a uſeful and honeſt occupation is the foundation of an infinite number of miſchiefs. The human mind being of ſo active a nature as it is, cannot remain in a ſtate of inaction, and if it is not employed on ſomething good, it will inevitably apply itſelf to ſomething bad, as is certain from the experience of all ages. It were therefore to be wiſhed, that there were laws againſt idleneſs, to prevent its pernicious effects, and that no perſon was permitted to live without ſome honeſt occupation either of the mind or body. Eſpecially young people, who aſpire after political, eccleſiaſtical, or military employments, ought not to be permitted to paſs in ſhameful idleneſs, the time of their life moſt proper for the ſtudy of morality, politics, and religion. 'Tis eaſy to perceive that a wiſe prince may,

may, from these reflexions, draw very important instructions for government.

X. The second manner, in which the prince can dispose of the goods or estates of his subjects, is, by demanding taxes or subsidies of them. That the sovereign has this right, will evidently appear, if we consider that taxes are no more than a contribution which individuals pay to the state for the preservation and defence of their lives and properties, a contribution absolutely necessary both for the ordinary and extraordinary expences which the care of the government requires, and which the sovereign neither can nor ought to furnish out of his own fund: He must therefore have a right to take away part of the goods of the subject by way of tax for that end and purpose.

XI. *Tacitus* relates a memorable story on this subject. " *Nero*, he says, once thought to abolish all " taxes, and to make this magnificent grant to the " *Roman* people; but the senate moderated his ar- " dour; and, after having commended the emperor " for his generous design, they told him that the " empire would inevitably fall, if its foundations " were sapped; that most of the taxes had been " established by the consuls and tribunes during the " very height of the liberty of the republic, and that " they were the only means of supplying the im- " mense expences necessary for the support of so " great an empire."

XII. Nothing is then generally more unjust and unreason-

unreaſonable than the complaints of the populace, who frequently aſcribe their miſery to taxes, without reflecting that theſe are, on the contrary, the foundation of the tranquillity and ſafety of the ſtate, and that they cannot refuſe to pay them without prejudicing their own intereſts.

XIII. However, the end and prudence of civil government require not only that the people ſhould not be over-charged in this reſpect, but alſo that the taxes ſhould be raiſed in as gentle and imperceptible a manner as poſſible.

XIV. And, 1°. the ſubjects muſt be equally charged, that they may have no juſt reaſon of complaint. A burthen equally ſupported by all, is lighter to every individual; but if a conſiderable number releaſe or excuſe themſelves, it becomes much more heavy and inſupportable to the reſt. As every ſubject equally enjoys the protection of the government, and the ſafety which it procures; ſo 'tis juſt that they ſhould all contribute to its ſupport in a proper equality.

XV. 2°. But 'tis to be obſerved, that this equality does not conſiſt in paying equal ſums of money, but in equally bearing the burthen impoſed for the good of the ſtate; that is, there muſt be a juſt proportion between the burthen of the tax and the benefit of peace; for tho' all equally enjoy peace, yet the advantages, which all reap from it, are not equal.

XVI. 3°. Every man ought therefore to be taxed in proportion to his income, both in ordinary and extraordinary exigencies.

XVII. 4°. Experience ſhews, that the beſt method of raiſing taxes is to lay them on things which are daily conſumed in life.

XVIII. 5°. As for merchandizes imported, 'tis to be obſerved, that if they are not neceſſary, but only ſubſervient to luxury, very great duties may juſtly be laid on them.

XIX. 6°. When foreign merchandizes conſiſt of ſuch things as may grow, or be manufactured at home, by the induſtry and application of our own people, the impoſts ought to be raiſed higher upon them.

XX. 7°. As to the exportation of commodities of our own growth, if it be the intereſt of the ſtate, that they ſhould not go out of the country, it may be right to raiſe the cuſtoms upon them; but on the contrary, if it is for the public advantage that they ſhould be ſent to foreign markets, then the duty of exportation ought to be diminiſhed, or abſolutely taken away. In ſome countries, by a wiſe piece of policy, rewards are given to the ſubjects, who export ſuch commodities as are in too great plenty, and more than the wants of the inhabitants require.

XXI. 8°. In a word, in the application of all theſe maxims, the ſovereign muſt always attend to the good of trade, and take all proper meaſures to favour it and make it flouriſh.

XXII. 'Tis not neceſſary to obſerve, that the right of the ſovereign, with reſpect to taxes, being founded on the wants of the ſtate, he ought never to raiſe them but in proportion to theſe wants, and that he ought never to employ them but with theſe views, and not to apply them to his own private uſes.

XXIII. He ought alſo to attend to the conduct of the officers who collect them, to hinder their importunity and impertinence. Thus *Tacitus* commends a very wiſe edict of the emperor *Nero*'s, "who ordered "that the magiſtrates of *Rome* and of the provinces "ſhould receive complaints againſt the publicans at "all times, and regulate them upon the ſpot."

XXIV. The *ſovereign* or *tranſcendental* property *, which, as we have ſaid, conſtitutes the third part of the ſovereign's power over the eſtates of his ſubjects, conſiſts in the right he has of making uſe of every thing the ſubject poſſeſſes, to anſwer the neceſſities of the ſtate.

XXV. Thus, for example, if a town is to be fortified, he may take the gardens, lands, or houſes of private ſubjects, which are ſituated in the place where the ramparts or ditches are to be made. In ſieges, he may beat down houſes and trees belonging to private perſons, that the enemy may not be ſheltered by them, or the beſieged incommoded.

* Dominium eminens.

XXVI. There are great disputes, among politicians, concerning this *transcendental property*. Some absolutely condemn it and will not admit of it; but the dispute turns more upon the word than the thing. It is certain that the very nature of sovereignty authorises a prince, in case of necessity, to make use of the goods and fortunes of his subjects; since, in conferring the sovereign authority upon him, they have at the same time given him the power of doing and exacting every thing that is necessary for the preservation and advantage of the state. Whether this is called *transcendental property*, or by some other name, is altogether indifferent, provided we are agreed about the right itself.

XXVII. To say something more particular concerning this *transcendental property* of the sovereign, we must observe, that it is really a maxim of natural equity, that when contributions are to be made for the necessities of the state, and for the preservation of some particular thing, by persons that enjoy it in common, every man ought to pay his quota, and should not be forced to bear more of the burthen than another.

XXVIII. But since it may happen that the pressing wants of the state, and particular circumstances, will not permit this rule to be literally followed, there is a necessity that the sovereign may deviate from it, and have a right to seize on something in the possession of some private subject, the use of which, in the present circumstances, is become necessary to the public. Hence this right takes place only in a necessity of state, which ought not to have too great an extent, but should be tempered as much as possible with the rules of equity.

XXIX. 'Tis therefore just in these cases, that the proprietors should be indemnified, either by their fellow-subjects, or by the Exchequer, for what exceeds their proper share, at least as near as possible. But if the subjects have voluntarily exposed themselves to suffer this loss by building houses in a place where they are to be pulled down in time of war, then the state is not in rigour obliged to indemnify them, and they may be reasonably thought to have consented to this loss. This is sufficient for what relates to the right of the sovereign over the estates of the subjects.

XXX. But besides these rights of the sovereign, of which we have been speaking, he has also originally a power of disposing of certain places which are called *public goods*, because they belong to the state as such: but as all these public goods are not of the same kind, the right of the sovereign in this respect also varies.

XXXI. There are goods intended for the support of the king and the royal family, and others to defray the public expences for the preservation of the government. The first are called the crown lands or the patrimony of the prince, and the other the public treasure or the revenue of the state.

XXXII. As to the first, the sovereign has the full and entire profits, and may dispose of the revenues

 arising

arising from them as he absolutely pleases. So that what he lays up out of his income makes an accession to his own private patrimony, unless the laws of the kingdom have determined otherwise. With regard to the other public goods, he has only the simple administration of them, in which he ought to propose only the advantage of the state, and to express as much care and fidelity as a guardian with respect to the estate of his pupil.

XXXIII. By this distinction, and these princi- ciples, we may judge to whom the acquisitions belong, which a prince has made during his reign; for if these acquisitions arise from the goods intended to defray the public expences, they ought certainly to accrue to the public, and not to his own private patrimony. But if a king has undertaken and supported a war at his own expence, and without engaging or charging the state in the least, he may lawfully appropriate the acquisitions he has made in such an expedition.

XXXIV. From the principles we have here established, it follows also that the king cannot, without the consent of the people or their representatives, alienate the least part either of the public patrimony, or of the crown lands, of which he has only the use. But we must distinguish between the goods themselves and the profits or produce of them. The king may dispose of the revenues or profits as he thinks proper, tho' he cannot alienate the principal.

XXXV. A prince indeed, who has a right of lay-

ing

ing taxes when he thinks proper for good reaſons, may, when the neceſſities of the commonwealth require it, mortgage a part of the public patrimony: for it is the ſame thing to the people, whether they give money to hinder the mortgage, or it be levied upon them afterwards to redeem it.

XXXVI. Beſides, all that has been ſaid is to be underſtood upon ſuppoſition, that things are not otherways regulated by the fundamental laws of the ſtate.

XXXVII. As for the alienation of the kingdom, or ſome part of it; by the principles hitherto eſtabliſhed, we may eaſily learn what to think of it.

And, 1°. if there can be any ſuch thing as a patrimonial kingdom, 'tis evident that the ſovereign may alienate ſuch a kingdom, and, by a ſtronger reaſon, ſome part of it *.

XXXVIII. 2°. Except in this caſe, and if the kingdom is not poſſeſſed as a patrimony, the king cannot, by his own authority, transfer or alienate any part of it; for this purpoſe the conſent of the people is neceſſary. Sovereignty cannot of itſelf imply the right of alienation, and as the people cannot take the crown from the prince againſt his will, ſo neither has the king a power of ſubſtituting another ſovereign in his place without their conſent.

XXXIX. 3°. But if only a part of the kingdom is to be alienated, beſides the approbation of the

* See *Grotius*, lib. II. cap. 6.

king and that of the people, 'tis neceſſary that the part, which is to be alienated, ſhould alſo conſent; and this laſt conſent even ſeems to be the moſt neceſſary. 'Tis to no purpoſe that the other provinces of the kingdom conſent to the alienation of this, if its inhabitants themſelves oppoſe it. The right of the plurality of ſuffrages does not extend ſo far as to cut off from the body of the ſtate thoſe who have not violated their engagements, and the laws of ſociety.

XL. In fact, 'tis evident, that thoſe who firſt erected the commonwealth, and thoſe who voluntarily came into it afterwards, bound themſelves, by mutual compact, to form a permanent body or ſociety, under one and the ſame government, ſo long at leaſt as they incline to remain in the territories of the ſame ſtate; and it is with a view to the advantages which accrued to them in common from this reciprocal union, that they firſt erected the ſtate. This is the foundation of their compacts in this reſpect. Hence, by virtue of ſuch a compact, they cannot, againſt their wills, be deprived of the right they have acquired of being a part of a certain body politic, except by way of puniſhment. Beſides, in this caſe, the *obligation* correſponds to the *right*. The ſtate, by virtue of the ſame compact, has acquired a right over each of its members, by which no ſubject can put himſelf under a foreign government, nor diſclaim the authority of his natural ſovereign.

XLI. 4°. 'Tis however to be obſerved, that there are two general exceptions to the principles we have here

here eſtabliſhed, and which are both founded on the right and privileges ariſing from neceſſity. The firſt is, that tho' the body of the ſtate has not the right of alienating any of its parts, ſo as to oblige that part, againſt its will, to ſubmit to a new maſter, this does not hinder the ſtate from a power of lawfully abandoning one of its parts, when there is an evident danger of periſhing if they continue united.

XLII. 'Tis true that even in theſe circumſtances, the ſovereign cannot directly force one of his towns or provinces to ſubmit to another government. He can only withdraw his forces, or abandon the inhabitants; but they retain the right of defending themſelves if they can: ſo that if they perceive themſelves ſtrong enough to reſiſt the enemy, there is no reaſon why they ſhould not; and if they ſucceed, they may erect themſelves into a diſtinct commonwealth. Hence the conqueror becomes the lawful ſovereign of this country only by the conſent of the inhabitants, or by their ſwearing allegiance to him.

XLIII. It may be ſaid, that, properly ſpeaking, the ſtate or the ſovereign do not alienate, in this caſe, ſuch a part, but only renounce a ſociety whoſe engagements are at an end by virtue of a tacit exception ariſing from neceſſity. After all, 'twould be in vain for the body to perſiſt in defending ſuch a part, ſince we ſuppoſe it unable to preſerve or defend itſelf. 'Tis therefore a pure misfortune which muſt be ſuffered by the abandoned part.

XLIV.

XLIV. 5°. But if this be the right of the body with respect to the part, the part has also, in like circumstances, the same right with respect to the body. Thus we cannot condemn a town, which, after having made the best resistance it could, chooses rather to surrender to the enemy, than be pillaged and exposed to fire and sword.

XLV. In a word, every one has a natural primitive right to take care of his own preservation by all possible means; and 'tis principally for the better attainment of this end, that men have entered into civil societies. If therefore the state can no longer defend and protect the subjects, they are disengaged from the ties they were under before, and they resume their primitive right of taking care of themselves independently of the state, in the manner they think most proper. Thus things are equal on both sides, and the sentiment of *Grotius*, who wants to establish the contrary, and refuses the body of the state, with respect to the part, the same right which he grants the part with respect to the body, cannot be maintained.

XLVI. We shall end this chapter with two remarks. The first is, that the maxim which some politicians inculcate so strongly, namely, that the goods appropriated to the crown are absolutely unalienable, is not true, except on the terms, and agreeably to the principles we have here established. What the same politicians add, that an alienation, succeeded by a peaceable possession for the longest course of years, does not hinder a future right to what belonged to the

the crown, and the resumption of it by main force, on the first occasion, is altogether unreasonable.

The second observation is, that since it is not lawful for a king, independently of the will of the people or of their representatives, to alienate the whole or any part of his kingdom, it is not lawful for him to render it feudatory to some other prince; for this is evidently a kind of alienation.

The End of the Third Part.

THE

THE

PRINCIPLES

OF

POLITIC LAW.

PART IV.

In which are conſidered the different rights of ſovereignty with reſpect to foreign ſtates; the right of war, and every thing relating to it; public treaties, and the right of ambaſſadors.

CHAP. I.

Of war in general, and firſt of the right of the ſovereign, in this reſpect, over his ſubjects.

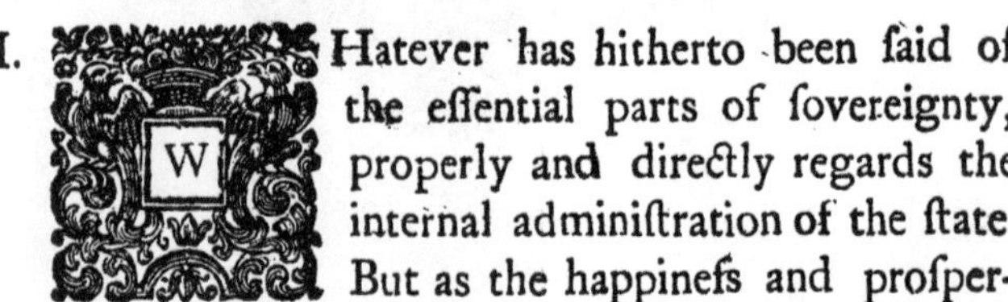

I. WHatever has hitherto been ſaid of the eſſential parts of ſovereignty, properly and directly regards the internal adminiſtration of the ſtate. But as the happineſs and proſperity of a nation demands not only that order and peace ſhould be maintained at home, but alſo that the ſtate ſhould be ſheltered from the inſults of enemies abroad, and ſhould obtain all the advantages it can

can from other nations; we ſhall now proceed to examine theſe parts of ſovereignty which directly regard the ſafety and external advantages of the ſtate, and treat of the moſt eſſential queſtions which relate to this ſubject.

II. To trace things from their original, we muſt firſt obſerve, that mankind being divided into ſeveral particular ſocieties called *ſtates* or *nations*, and theſe different political bodies forming a kind of ſociety among themſelves, they are alſo ſubjected to thoſe primitive and general laws, which God has given to all mankind, and that they are conſequently obliged to practiſe certain duties towards each other.

III. 'Tis the ſyſtem or aſſemblage of theſe laws that is properly called the law of *nations*: and theſe are no more than the laws of nature, which men, conſidered as members of human ſociety, in general, ought to practiſe towards each other; or, in other words, the law of nations is no more than the general law of *ſociability*, applied not to the individuals who compoſe the ſociety, but to men, conſidered as forming different bodies called *ſtates* or *nations*.

IV. The natural ſtate of nations, with reſpect to each other, is certainly that of ſociety and peace. Such is the natural and primitive ſtate of one man with reſpect to every other man; and whatever particular alteration mankind may have made in regard to their primitive ſtate, they cannot, without violating their duties, break in upon that ſtate of peace and ſociety, in which nature has placed them, and which, by by her *laws*, ſhe has ſo ſtrongly recommended to them.

V. Hence proceed ſeveral maxims of the law of nations; for example, that all nations ought to look upon themſelves as naturally equal and independent of each other, and to treat one another as ſuch on all occaſions. That they ought to do no harm to each other, but, on the contrary, repair that which they may have done. Hence alſo ariſes their right of endeavouring to provide for their ſafety and happineſs, and of employing force and arms againſt thoſe who declare themſelves their enemies. Fidelity in treaties and alliances, and the reſpect due to ambaſſadors, alſo ariſe from the ſame principle. This is the idea we ought to form of the law of nations in general.

VI. We do not here propoſe to enter minutely into all the political queſtions which may occur concerning the law of nations; we ſhall only examine theſe three articles, which, being the moſt conſiderable, include almoſt all the reſt, I mean the *right of war*, that of *treaties and alliances*, and that of *ambaſſadors*.

VII. The ſubject of the right of war being equally important and extenſive, conſequently merits to be treated with great exactneſs. We have already obſerved, that it is a fundamental maxim of the law of nature and nations, that individuals and ſtates ought to live in a ſtate of union and ſociety, that they ought not to hurt each other, nor occaſion any mutual

tual damage; on the contrary, that they ought to exercise the duties of humanity to one another.

VIII. When men practise these duties, they are said to be in a state of peace. This state is certainly the most agreeable to human nature, the most capable of promoting its happiness, and indeed that which the law of nature was given to men principally to establish and preserve.

IX. The opposite state to this of union and peace, is what we call *war*, which, in the most general sense, is no more than the state of those who try to determine their differences by the ways of force, considered as such. I say, this is the most general sense, for, in a more limited signification, common use has restrained the word *war* to that carried on between sovereign powers *.

X. Tho' a state of peace and mutual benevolence is certainly most natural to man, and most agreeable to the laws which he ought to follow, war is nevertheless permitted in certain circumstances, and is sometimes necessary both for individuals and nations. This we have sufficiently shewn in the second part of this work, by establishing the rights which nature gives to men for their own preservation, and the means which they may lawfully employ for that purpose. All the principles of this kind, which we have established with respect to particulars, equally, and even for stronger reasons, are applicable to nations.

* See afterwards, chap. 3.

XI. The law of God no leſs enjoins a whole nation to take care of their preſervation, than it does private men. It is therefore juſt that they ſhould employ force againſt thoſe, who, declaring themſelves their enemies, violate the law of ſociability towards them, refuſe them their due, ſeek to deprive them of their advantages, and even to deſtroy them. It is therefore for the good of ſociety, that people ſhould be able effectually to repreſs the malice and efforts of thoſe who ſubvert the foundations of it; otherwiſe the human ſpecies would become the victims of robbery and licentiouſneſs: for the right of making war is, properly ſpeaking, the moſt powerful means of maintaining peace.

XII. Hence it is certain that the ſovereign, in whoſe hands the intereſt of the whole ſociety is lodged, has a right to make war: but if it is ſo, we muſt of courſe give him a right of employing all the means neceſſary for that purpoſe. In a word, we muſt give him the power of levying troops, enliſting ſoldiers, and obliging them to perform the moſt dangerous duties even at the peril of their lives. And this is one branch of the right of life and death which manifeſtly belongs to the ſovereign.

XIII. But as the ſtrength and valour of troops depend, in a great meaſure, on their being accuſtomed to military exerciſes, the ſovereign ought, even in times of peace, to train the ſubjects up to theſe exerciſes, that they may, when occaſion calls, be more able to ſuſtain the fatigues of war, and perform the different duties of it.

XIV. The obligation, under which ſubjects are in this reſpect, is ſo rigorous and ſtrong, that, ſtrictly ſpeaking, no man can be exempted from taking up arms when occaſion requires; and the refuſal of it would be a juſt reaſon not to tolerate ſuch perſons any longer in the ſociety. If in moſt governments there are ſome ſubjects exempted from military litary exerciſes, this immunity is not a privilege that belongs to them by right; it is only a toleration which has no force, but when there are troops enough beſides for the defence of the commonwealth, and the perſons to whom it is granted follow ſome other uſeful and neceſſary employment. Excepting this caſe, in time of need all the members of a ſtate ought to take the field, and none can be lawfully exempted.

XV. In conſequence of theſe principles, military diſcipline ſhould be very rigorous; the ſmalleſt neglect, or the leaſt fault is often of the laſt importance, and for that reaſon may be ſeverely puniſhed. Other judges make ſome allowance for the weakneſs of human nature, or the violence of paſſions; but in a council of war, there is not ſo much indulgence; death is often inflicted on a ſoldier, whom the dread of that very evil has induced to quit his poſt.

XVI. 'Tis therefore the duty of thoſe who are once enliſted, to maintain the poſt where the general has placed them, and to fight bravely, even tho' they run a riſque of loſing their lives. To conquer or die, is the law of ſuch engagements; and 'tis certainly much better to loſe one's life glorioully, by endeavouring to deſtroy that of the enemy, than to die in a cowardly manner. Hence ſome judgment may be formed of what we ought to think of thoſe captains of ſhips, who, by the orders of their ſuperior, blow themſelves up into the air, rather than fall into the hands of the enemy. Suppoſe the number of ſhips equal on both ſides, if one of our ſhips is taken, the enemy will have two more than we; whereas if one of ours is ſunk they will have but one more; and if the veſſel, which wants to take ours, ſinks with it, which often happens, the forces will remain equal.

XVII. As for the queſtion, whether ſubjects are obliged to take up arms, and ſerve in an unjuſt war, we muſt judge of it by the principles we have already eſtabliſhed at the end of the firſt chapter of the third part, which treats of *the legiſlative power*.

XVIII. Theſe are the obligations of ſubjects with reſpect to war and to the defence of the government; but this part of the ſovereignty being of great importance, it requires the utmoſt precaution in the ſovereign to exerciſe it in ſuch a manner as may prove advantageous to the ſtate. We ſhall here point out the principal maxims of politics in this reſpect.

XIX. Firſt then it is evident, that the force of a ſtate, with reſpect to war, conſiſts chiefly in the number of its inhabitants; ſovereigns therefore ought to neglect nothing that can either ſupport or augment the number of them.

XX. Among the other means, which may be uſed

ufed for this purpofe, there are three of great efficacy. The firft is, eafily to receive all ftrangers of a good character, who want to fettle among us; to let them tafte all the fweets of government; and to make them fhare the advantages of civil liberty. Thus the ftate is filled with fubjects, who bring with them the arts, commerce, and riches; and among whom we may, in time of need, find a confiderable number of good foldiers.

XXI. Another thing, conducive to the fame end, is to favour and encourage marriages, which are the pledges of the ftate; and to make good laws for this purpofe. The mildnefs of the government may, among other things, greatly contribute to incline the fubjects to marry. People loaded with taxes, who can hardly, by their labour, find wherewithal to fupply the wants of life and the public charges, are not inclined to marry, left their children fhould ftarve for hunger.

XXII. Laftly, another means, very proper for maintaining and augmenting the number of inhabitants, is liberty of confcience. Religion is one of the greateft advantages of mankind, and all men view it in that light. Every thing which tends to deprive them of this liberty, appears infupportable. They cannot eafily accuftom themfelves to a government which tyrannizes over them in this article. *France*, *Spain*, and *Holland* prefent us with fenfible proofs of the truth of thefe obfervations. Perfecutions have deprived the firft of a great part of her inhabitants; by which means fhe has been confiderably weakened. The ſecond is almoſt unpeopled; and this depopulation is occaſioned by the barbarous and tyrannical eſtabliſhment called the *Inquiſition*, an eſtabliſhment equally affrontive to God and pernicious to human ſociety, and which has made a kind of deſert of one of the fineſt countries in *Europe*. The third, in conſequence of an entire liberty of conſcience, which ſhe offers to all the world, is conſiderably improved even amidſt wars and diſaſters. She has raiſed herſelf, as it were, on the ruins of other nations, and enjoys a credit and proſperity for which ſhe is indebted to the number of her inhabitants, who have brought power, commerce and riches into her boſom.

XXIII. The great number of the inhabitants of a country is therefore its principal ſtrength. But, for this purpoſe the inhabitants muſt alſo be formed betimes to labour and virtue. Luxury, effeminacy, and pleaſures, impair the body and enervate the mind. A prince therefore, who wants good troops, and deſires to put the military ſtate on a good footing, muſt take great care of the education of youth, eſtabliſh a good diſcipline, procure his ſubjects the means of forming themſelves to bodily exerciſes, and prevent luxury and pleaſures from rendering their manners effeminate, or weakening their courage.

XXIV. Laſtly, one of the moſt efficacious means of having good troops, is to make them obſerve the military order and diſcipline with all poſſible care and exactneſs; to take particular care that the ſoldiers be punctually paid; to ſee that the ſick be properly looked after, and to furniſh them with the aſſiſtances they

they ſtand in need of; laſtly, to preſerve among them a knowledge of religion and of the duties it preſcribes, by procuring them the means of inſtruction. Theſe are the principal maxims which good policy ſuggeſts to ſovereigns, and by means of which they may reaſonably hope always to find good troops among their ſubjects, troops diſpoſed to fight bravely in defence of their country.

CHAP. II.

Of the cauſes of war.

I. IF war is ſometimes lawful, and even neceſſary, as we have already ſhewn; this is to be underſtood when it is undertaken only for juſt reaſons, and on condition that he, who undertakes it, propoſes, by that means, to obtain a ſolid and laſting peace. A war may therefore be either juſt or unjuſt, according to the cauſe which has produced it.

II. A war is juſt if it is undertaken for juſt reaſons; and unjuſt if it is entered into without a cauſe, or at leaſt without a juſt and ſufficient cauſe.

III. To render the thing more plain, we may, with *Grotius*, diſtinguiſh between the juſtifying reaſons, and the motives of the war. The firſt are thoſe which render, or ſeem to render, the war juſt with reſpect to the enemy, ſo that in taking up arms againſt him we do not think we do him injuſtice. The motives are the views of intereſt which determine us to declare war. Thus in the war of *Alexander* againſt *Darius*, the juſtifying reaſon of the former was, to revenge the injuries which the *Greeks* had received from the *Perſians*. The motives were, the ambition, vanity, and avarice of that conquerour, who took up arms the more chearfully, as the expeditions of *Xenophon* and *Ageſilaus* made him conceive great hopes of an eaſy ſucceſs. The juſtifying reaſon of the ſecond *Punic* war was, a diſpute about the city of *Saguntum*. The motive was, an old grudge entertained by the *Carthaginians* againſt the *Romans* for the hard terms they were obliged to ſubmit to when reduced to a low condition, and the encouragement given them by the good ſucceſs of their arms in *Spain*.

IV. In a war, in every reſpect innocent and perfectly juſt, the juſtifying reaſons muſt not only be lawful, but alſo be blended with the motive; that is to ſay, we muſt never undertake a war but thro' the neceſſity we are reduced to of defending ourſelves againſt another's inſults, of recovering what is our undoubted right, or of obtaining ſatisfaction for a manifeſt injury.

V. Thus a war may be vicious or unjuſt, with reſpect to the cauſes, four different ways.

1°. When we undertake it without any juſtifying reaſon, or ſo much as an apparent motive of advantage, but only from a fierce and brutal fury, which delights in blood and ſlaughter. But it may be juſtly doubted, whether we can find an example of ſo barbarous a war.

VI.

VI. 2°. When we attack others only for our own intereſt, without their having done us any injury; that is, when we have no juſtifying cauſes: and theſe wars are, with reſpect to the aggreſſor, downright robberies.

VII. 3°. When we have ſome motives founded on juſtifying cauſes, but which have ſtill only an apparent equity, and when well examined, are found at the bottom to be unlawful.

VIII. 4°. Laſtly, we may ſay that a war is alſo unjuſt, when tho' we have good juſtifying reaſons, yet we undertake it from other motives, which have no relation to the wrong received; as for inſtance, thro' vain glory, or the deſire of extending our dominions, &c.

IX. Of theſe four ſorts of war, the undertaking of which includes ſome injuſtice, the third and laſt are very common, for there are few nations ſo barbarous as to take up arms without alledging ſome ſort of juſtifying reaſons. It is not difficult to diſcover the injuſtice of the third; as for the fourth, tho' perhaps very common, it is not ſo much unjuſt in itſelf, as with reſpect to the views and diſpoſition of him who undertakes it. But it is very difficult to convince him of it, the motives being generally impenetrable, or at leaſt moſt princes taking great care to conceal them *.

* See the explication of theſe principles in *Budeus*'s Juriſprud. hiſt. ſpecim. §. 28, &c.

X. From the principles here eſtabliſhed we may conclude, that every juſt war muſt be made, either to defend ourſelves and properties againſt thoſe who endeavour to injure us by aſſaulting our perſons, and by taking away or ruining our eſtates; or to conſtrain others to yield up to us what they ought to do, when we have a perfect right to require it of them; or laſtly, to obtain ſatisfaction for the damages we have injuriouſly ſuſtained, and to force thoſe who did the injury to give ſecurity for their future good behaviour.

XI. From hence we eaſily conceive what the cauſes of war may be. But to illuſtrate the ſubject more, we ſhall give ſome examples of the principal unjuſt cauſes of war.

1°. Thus for example, to have a juſt reaſon for war, it is not ſufficient that we are afraid of the growing power of a neighbour. All we can do, in theſe circumſtances, is innocently to try to obtain *real caution*, that he will attempt nothing againſt us; and to put ourſelves in a poſture of defence. But acts of hoſtility are not permitted except when they are neceſſary, and they are never neceſſary ſo long as we are not morally certain that the neighbour we dread has not only the power, but alſo the inclination to attack us. We cannot, for inſtance, juſtly declare war againſt a neighbour purely becauſe he orders citadels or fortifications to be built, which he may ſome time or other employ againſt us.

XII. 2°. Neither does utility alone give the ſame right as neceſſity, nor is it ſufficient to render

a war

a war lawful. Thus, for example, we cannot lawfully take up arms to make ourſelves maſters of a place which lies conveniently for us, and is proper to cover our frontiers.

XIII. 3°. We muſt ſay the ſame of the deſire of changing our former ſettlements, and of removing from marſhes and deſerts to a more fertile ſoil.

4°. Nor is it leſs unjuſt to invade the rights and liberty of a people under a pretext of their not being ſo poliſhed in their manners, or of ſuch quick underſtanding as ourſelves. It was therefore unjuſt in the *Greeks* to treat the *Barbarians* as people who were naturally their enemies, on account of the diverſity of their manners, and perhaps becauſe they did not appear to have ſo much ſenſe as themſelves.

XIV. 5°. It would alſo be an unjuſt war to take up arms againſt a nation in order to bring them under ſubjection, upon pretence of its being their intereſt to be governed by us. Though a thing may be advantageous to a perſon, yet this does not give us a right to compel him to ſubmit to it. Whoever has the uſe of reaſon ought to have the liberty of chooſing what he thinks advantageous to himſelf.

XV. We muſt alſo obſerve, that the duties which nations ought to practiſe towards each other, are not all equally obligatory, and that their deficiency in this reſpect does not always lay a foundation for a juſt war. Among nations as well as individuals, there are duties attended with a rigorous and perfect obligation, the violation of which implies *an*

in-

injury properly ſo called; and duties of an imperfect obligation, which give to another only an imperfect and leſs rigorous right. And as we cannot, in a diſpute between individuals, have recourſe to judges, to recover what in this ſecond manner is our due; ſo neither can we, in conteſts between different powers, conſtrain them by force of arms.

XVI. We muſt however except from this rule, the caſes of neceſſity in which the *imperfect* is *changed* into the *perfect right*; ſo that, in theſe caſes, the refuſal of him, who will not give us our due, furniſhes us with a juſt reaſon for a war. But every war, undertaken on account of the refuſal of what a man is not obliged by the laws of humanity to grant, is unjuſt.

XVII. To apply theſe principles we ſhall give ſome examples. The right of paſſing over the lands of another is really founded on humanity, when we deſign to uſe that permiſſion only on a lawful account; as when people, expelled their own country, want to ſettle elſewhere; or when, in the proſecution of a juſt war, it is neceſſary to paſs thro' the territories of a neutral people, *&c.* But this is only an office of humanity which is not due to another in virtue of a perfect and rigorous right, and the refuſal of which does not authoriſe a nation to challenge it in a forcible manner.

XVIII. *Grotius* however, examining this queſtion, pretends, " that we are not only obliged to grant a " paſſage over our lands to a ſmall number of men

" unarmed, and from whom we have consequently " nothing to fear; but moreover that we cannot re- " fuse it to a large army, notwithstanding the just " apprehension we may have that this passage will " do us a considerable injury, which is likely to arise " either from that army itself, or from those against " whom it marches: provided, continues he, 1°. that " this passage is asked on a just account. 2°. That " it is asked before an attempt is made to pass by " force."

XIX. This author then pretends, that, in these circumstances, the refusal authorises us to have recourse to arms, and that we may lawfully procure by force, what we could not obtain by favour, even tho' the passage may be had elsewhere by taking a larger circuit. He adds, " That the suspicion of " danger from the passing of a great number of " armed men, is not a sufficient reason to refuse it, " because good precautions may be taken against it. " Nor is a fear of provoking that prince, against " whom the other marches his army, a sufficient " reason for refusing him passage, if the latter has a " just reason for undertaking the war."

XX. *Grotius* founds his opinion on this reason, that the establishment of property was originally made with the tacit reservation of the right of using the property of another in time of need, as far as it can be done without injuring the owner.

XXI. But I cannot embrace the opinion of this celebrated writer, for, 1°. whatever may be said, it is is certain that the right of paſſing thro' the territories of another is not a perfect right, the execution of which can be rigorouſly demanded. If a private perſon is not obliged to ſuffer another to paſs thro' his ground, much leſs is a nation obliged to grant a paſſage to a foreign army, without any compact or conceſſion intervening.

XXII. 2°. The great inconveniences which may follow ſuch a permiſſion, authoriſe this refuſal. By granting ſuch a paſſage we run a riſque of making our own country the ſeat of war. Beſides, if they, to whom we grant the paſſage, are repulſed and vanquiſhed, let the reaſons they had for making war be ever ſo juſt, yet will not the enemy revenge himſelf upon us who did not hinder thoſe troops from invading him? But farther, ſuppoſe that we live in friendſhip with both the princes who are at war, we cannot favour one to the prejudice of the other, without giving this other a ſufficient reaſon to look upon us as enemies, and as defective in that part of our duty which we owe to our neighbours. It would be in vain, on this occaſion, to diſtinguiſh between a juſt and an unjuſt war, pretending that the latter gives a right of refuſing the paſſage, but that the former obliges us to grant it. This diſtinction does not remove the difficulty; for beſides that it is not always eaſy to decide whether a war is juſt or unjuſt, it is a piece of raſhneſs to thruſt in our arbitration between two armed parties, and to intermeddle with their differences.

XXIII. 3°. But is there nothing to fear from the

troops to whom the paſſage is granted? The abettors of the contrary opinion agree there is, for which reaſon they allow that many precautions ought to be obſerved. But whatever precautions we may take, none of them can ſecure us againſt all events; and ſome evils and loſſes are irreparable. Men that are always in arms are eaſily tempted to abuſe them, and to commit outrages, eſpecially if they are numerous, and find an opportunity of making a conſiderable booty. How often have we ſeen foreign armies ravage and appropriate to themſelves the eſtates of a people who have called them to their aſſiſtance? Nor have the moſt ſolemn treaties and oaths been able to deter them from this black perfidiouſneſs *? What then may we expect from thoſe who are under no ſuch ſtrict engagements?

XXIV. 4°. Another obſervation we may make, which is of great uſe in politics, that almoſt all ſtates have this in common, that the further men advance into the heart of a country, they find it more weak and unarmed. The *Carthaginians*, otherwiſe invincible, were vanquiſhed near *Carthage* by *Agathocles* and *Scipio*. *Hannibal* ſaid the *Romans* could not be conquered except in *Italy*. 'Tis therefore dangerous to lay open theſe ſecrets to a multitude of ſtrangers, who, having arms at hand, may take advantage of our weakneſs, and make us repent our imprudence.

XXV. 5°. To this we muſt add, that in every ſtate there are almoſt always mutinous and turbulent ſpirits, who are ready to ſtir up ſtrangers either againſt their

* See Juſt. lib. IV. cap 4 & 8. and Liv. lib. VII. cap. 38.

fel-

fellow-citizens, their ſovereign, or their neighbours. Theſe reaſons ſufficiently prove, that all the precautions which can be taken cannot ſecure us from danger.

6°. Laſtly, we may add the example of a great many nations, who have been very ill requited for letting foreign troops paſs thro' their country.

XXVI. We ſhall finiſh the examination of this queſtion by making two remarks. The firſt is, that 'tis evident from the whole of what has been ſaid, that this is a matter of prudence; and that tho' we are not obliged to grant a paſſage to foreign troops, and the ſafeſt way is to refuſe it, yet when we are not ſtrong enough to reſiſt the violence of thoſe who want to paſs at any rate, and by reſiſting we muſt involve ourſelves in a troubleſome war, we ought certainly to grant a paſſage; and the neceſſity to which we are reduced, is a ſufficient juſtification to the prince whoſe territories thoſe troops are going to invade.

XXVII. My ſecond remark is, that if we ſuppoſe on the one hand, that the war which the prince, who demands a paſſage thro' our country, makes, is juſt and neceſſary, and on the other, that we have nothing to fear either from him that is to paſs, or him againſt whom he marches; we are then indiſpenſibly obliged to grant a paſſage. For if the law of nature obliges every one to aſſiſt thoſe whom he ſees manifeſtly oppreſſed, when he can do it without danger and with hopes of ſucceſs, much leſs ought he to be a hindrance to ſuch as undertake their own defence.

XXVIII.

XXVIII. By following the principles here eftablifhed, we may judge of the right of tranfporting merchandizes thro' the territories of another. This is alfo only an imperfect right, and a duty of humanity, which obliges us to grant it to others; the obligation is not rigorous, and the refufal cannot be a juft reafon for war.

XXIX. Truly fpeaking, the laws of humanity indifpenfibly oblige us to grant a paffage to fuch foreign commodities as are abfolutely neceffary for life, which our neighbours cannot procure by themfelves, and with which we cannot furnifh them. But, except in this cafe, we may have good reafons for hindering foreign commodities from paffing thro' our country to be carried farther. Too great a refort of ftrangers is fometimes dangerous to a ftate; and befides, why fhould not a fovereign procure to his own fubjects that profit, which would otherwife be made by foreigners, by means of the paffage granted them?

XXX. It is not however contrary to humanity to require toll or cuftom for foreign commodities to which a paffage is granted. This is a juft reimburfement for the expences the fovereign is obliged to be at in repairing the high roads, bridges, harbours, *&c.*

XXXI. We muft reafon in the fame manner in regard to commerce in general between different ftates. I fay the fame of the right of being fupplied with wives by our neighbours; a refufal on their fide, tho' there be great plenty of women among them, authorize us to declare war.

XXXII.

XXXII. We ſhall here ſubjoin ſomething concerning wars undertaken on account of religion. The law of nature, which permits a man to defend his life, his ſubſtance, and all the other advantages which he enjoys, againſt the attacks of an unjuſt aggreſſor, certainly grants him the liberty alſo of defending himſelf againſt thoſe who would, as it were, by force, deprive him of his religion, by hindering him to profeſs that which he thinks the beſt, or by conſtraining him to embrace that which he thinks to be falſe.

XXXIII. In a word, religion is one of the greateſt bleſſings man can enjoy, and includes his moſt eſſential intereſts. Whoever oppoſes him in this reſpect, declares himſelf his enemy; and conſequently he may juſtly uſe forcible methods to repel the injury, and to ſecure himſelf againſt the evil intended him. It is therefore lawful, and even juſt, to take up arms, when we are attacked for the cauſe of religion.

XXXIV. But tho' we are allowed to defend ourſelves in the cauſe of religion, yet we are not permitted to make war in order to propagate that which we profeſs, and to conſtrain thoſe who have ſome principle or practice different from ours. The one is a neceſſary conſequence of the other. It is not lawful to attack him who has a right to defend himſelf. If the defenſive war is juſt, the offenſive muſt needs be criminal. The very nature of religion does not permit that violent means ſhould be uſed for its propagation; it conſiſts in the internal ſentiments of the mind. The right of mankind, in regard to the propagation of religion, is to inform and inſtruct thoſe who

who are in an error, and to use the soft and gentle methods of persuasion. Men must be persuaded, and not compelled. To act otherwise, is to commit a robbery on them; a robbery so much the more criminal, as those who commit it endeavour to authorise it by the most sacred pretext. There is therefore no less folly, than impiety, in such a conduct.

XXXV. In particular, nothing is more contrary to the spirit of Christianity, than to employ the force of arms for its propagation. Jesus Christ, our divine master, taught men, but used no violence against them. The apostles followed his example; and the enumerations which St. Paul makes of the arms which he employed for the conversion of mankind, is a beautiful lesson to Christians *.

XXXVI. So far is a simple difference of opinion, in matters of religiom, from being a just reason for pursuing, by force of arms, or disturbing in the least, those whom we think in an error; that, on the contrary, such as act in this manner, furnish others with a just reason of making war against them, and of defending those whom they unjustly oppress. Upon which occasion the following question occurs: *Whether protestant princes may not, with a good conscience, enter into a confederacy to destroy the Inquisition, and oblige the powers, who suffer it in their dominions, to disarm that cabal, under which Christianity has so long groaned, and which, under a false pretence to zeal and piety, exercises a tyranny most horrible in itself, and most contrary to human nature?*

* 2 Corinth. chap. vi. ver. 4, &c. and chap. x. ver. 4.

nature? Be that as it may, it is at leaſt certain, that never would any hero have ſubdued monſters more furious and deſtructive to mankind, than he who could accompliſh the deſign of purging the earth of theſe wicked men, who ſo impudently and cruelly abuſe the ſpecious ſhew of religion, only to procure wherewith to live in luxury and idleneſs, and to make both princes and ſubjects dependent on them.

XXXVII. Theſe are the principal remarks which occur on the cauſes of war. To which let us here add, that as we ought not to make war, which of itſelf is a very great evil, but to obtain a ſolid peace, it is abſolutely neceſſary to conſult the rules of prudence before we undertake it, however juſt it may otherwiſe appear. We muſt, above all things, exactly weigh the good or evil, which we may bring upon ourſelves by it: For if in making war, there is reaſon to fear that we ſhall draw greater evils on ourſelves, or thoſe that belong to us, than the good we can propoſe from it; it is better to put up with the injury, than to expoſe ourſelves to more conſiderable evils, than that for which we ſeek redreſs by arms.

XXXVIII. In the circumſtances here mentioned we may lawfully make war, not only upon our account, but alſo for others; provided that he, in whoſe favour we engage, has juſt reaſon to take up arms, and that we are likewiſe under ſome particular tie or obligation to him, which authoriſes us to treat as enemies thoſe who have done us no injury.

XXXIX.

XXXIX. Now among those, whom we may and ought to defend, we must give the first place to such as depend on the defender, that is, to the subjects of the state; for 'tis principally with this view of protection that men, before independent, incorporated themselves into civil society. Thus the *Gibeonites* having submitted themselves to the government of the *Israelites*; the latter took up arms on their account, under the command of *Joshua*. The Romans also proceeded in the same manner. But sovereigns in these cases ought to observe the maxim we have established in sect. 37. They ought to beware in taking up arms for some of their subjects, not to bring a greater inconveniency on the body of the state. The duty of the sovereign regards first and principally the interest of the whole, rather than that of a part; and the greater the part is, the nearer it approaches to the whole.

XL. 2°. Next to subjects come our allies, whom we are expresly engaged by treaty to assist in time of need; and this, whether they have put themselves entirely under our protection, and so depend upon it; or whether assistance be agreed upon for mutual help and security.

XLI. But the war must be justly undertaken by our ally; for we cannot innocently engage to help any one in a war, which is manifestly unjust. Let us add here, that we may, even without prejudice to the treaty, defend our own subjects preferably to our allies, when there is no possibility of assisting

 them

them both at the ſame time; for the engagements of a government to its ſubjects always ſuperſede thoſe into which it enters with ſtrangers.

XLII. As for what *Grotius* ſays, that we are not obliged to aſſiſt an ally, when there is no hope of ſucceſs; it is to be underſtood in this manner. If we evidently ſee that our united forces are not ſufficient to oppoſe the enemy, and that our ally, tho' able to treat with him on tolerable terms, is yet obſtinately bent to expoſe himſelf to certain ruin; we are not obliged, by the treaty of alliance, to join with him in ſo extravagant and deſperate an attempt. But then it is alſo to be conſidered, that alliances would become uſeleſs, if, in virtue of this union, we were not obliged to expoſe ourſelves to ſome danger, or to ſuſtain ſome loſs in the defence of an ally.

XLIII. Here it may be enquired; when ſeveral of our allies want aſſiſtance, which ought to be helped firſt, and preferably to the reſt? *Grotius* anſwers, that when two allies unjuſtly make war upon each other, we ought to help neither of them; but if the cauſe of one ally is juſt, we muſt not only aſſiſt him againſt ſtrangers, but alſo againſt another of our allies, unleſs there is ſome particular article in a treaty, which does not permit us to defend the former againſt the latter, even tho' the latter has committed the injury. And, in fine, that if ſeveral of our allies enter into a league againſt a common foe, or make war ſeparately againſt particular enemies, we muſt aſſiſt them all equally, and

and according to treaties; but when there is no poſſibility of aſſiſting them all at once, we muſt give the preference to the oldeſt ally.

XLIV. 3°. Friends, or thoſe with whom we are united by particular ties of kindneſs and affection, hold the third rank. For tho' we have not promiſed them a certain aſſiſtance, determined by a formal treaty; yet the nature of friendſhip itſelf lays a mutual engagement on friends to help each other, as far as the ſtricter obligations they are under will permit; and the concern for each other's ſafety ought to be much ſtronger, than that which is demanded by the ſimple connection of humanity.

XLV. I ſay that we may take up arms for our friends, who are engaged in a juſt war; for we are not under a ſtrict obligation to aſſiſt them: and this condition ought to be underſtood, if we can do it eaſily, and without any great inconveniency to ourſelves.

XLVI. 4°. In fine, we may affirm that the ſingle relation, in which all mankind ſtand to each other, in conſequence of their common nature and ſociety, and which forms the moſt extenſive connection, is ſufficient to authoriſe us in aſſiſting thoſe who are unjuſtly oppreſſed; at leaſt if the injuſtice is conſiderable, and manifeſt, and the party injured calls us to his aſſiſtance; ſo that we act rather in his name, than in our own. But even here we muſt make this remark, which is, that we have a right to ſuccour the diſtreſſed purely from humanity, but that we are not under a ſtrict obligation of doing it. 'Tis a duty of an imperfect obligation, and which binds us only ſo far as we can practiſe it, without bringing a conſiderable inconveniency upon ourſelves; for all circumſtances being equal, we may, and even ought to prefer our own preſervation to that of another.

XLVII. It is another queſtion, whether we can undertake a war in defence of the ſubjects of a foreign prince, againſt his invaſions and oppreſſions, merely from the principle of humanity? I anſwer, that this is permitted only in caſes where the tyranny is riſen to ſuch a height, that the ſubjects themſelves may lawfully take up arms, to ſhake off the yoke of the tyrant, according to the principles already laid down.

XLVIII. 'Tis true, that ſince the eſtabliſhment of civil ſocieties, the ſovereign has acquired a peculiar right over his ſubjects; in virtue of which he can puniſh them, without any other power having any buſineſs to interfere. But 'tis no leſs certain, that this right has its bounds, and that it cannot be lawfully exerciſed, except when the ſubjects are really culpable, or at leaſt when their innocence is dubious. Then the preſumption ought to be in favour of the ſovereign, and a foreign power has no right to intermeddle with what paſſes in another ſtate.

XLIX. But if the tyranny is arrived at its greateſt height, if the oppreſſion is manifeſt, as when a

Buſiris,

Busiris, or *Phalaris* oppress their subjects in so cruel a manner, as must be condemned by every reasonable man living; we cannot refuse the subjects, thus oppressed, the protection of the laws of human society. Every man, as such, has a right to claim the assistance of other men when he is really in necessity; and every one is obliged to give it him, when he can, by the laws of humanity. Now 'tis certain, that we neither do, nor can renounce these laws, by entering into society, which could never have been established to the prejudice of the laws of humanity: tho' we may be justly supposed to have engaged, not to implore a foreign aid for slight injuries, or even for great ones, which affect only a few persons.

But when all the subjects, or a considerable part of them, groan under the oppression of a tyrant, the subjects, on the one hand, re-enter into all the rights of natural liberty, which authorises them to seek assistance wherever they can find it; and, on the other hand, those who are in a condition of giving it them, without any considerable damage to themselves, not only may, but ought to do all they can to deliver the oppressed; for this single reason, that they are men, and members of human society, of which civil societies are parts.

L. It appears indeed, from antient and modern history, that the desire of invading the states of others is often covered by similar pretexts; but the bad use which men make of a thing, does not always hinder it from being just in itself. Pirates sail on the seas, and robbers wear swords, as well as others.

CHAP. III.

Of the different kinds of war:

I. BESIDES the diſtinction abovementioned of war into juſt and unjuſt, there are ſeveral others, which it is proper to conſider here. And firſt, war is diſtinguiſhed into *offenſive* and *defenſive*.

II. Defenſive wars are thoſe undertaken for the defence of our perſons, or the preſervation of our properties. Offenſive wars are thoſe which are made to conſtrain others to give us our due, in virtue of a perfect right we have to exact it of them; or to obtain ſatisfaction for damage unjuſtly done us, and to force them to give caution for the future.

III. 1°. We muſt therefore take care not to confound this with the former diſtinction; as if every defenſive war was juſt, and, on the contrary, every offenſive war unjuſt. 'Tis now-a-days the cuſtom to excuſe the moſt unjuſt wars, by ſaying they are purely defenſive. Some people think that all unjuſt wars ought to be called offenſive, which is not true; for if there are offenſive wars which are juſt, as there is no doubt of it, there are alſo defenſive wars which are unjuſt; as when we defend ourſelves againſt a prince who has reaſon to attack us.

IV. 2°. Neither are we to believe, that he who firſt injures another, begins by that an offenſive war, and that the other, who demands ſatisfaction for the in-

injury received, is always upon the defenſive. There are a great many unjuſt acts which may kindle a war, and which however are not the war; as the ill treatment of a prince's ambaſſadour, the plundering of his ſubjects, &c. If therefore we take up arms to revenge ſuch an unjuſt act, we commence an offenſive, but a juſt war; and the prince who has done the injury, and will not give ſatisfaction, makes a defenſive, but an unjuſt war. An offenſive war is therefore unjuſt only, when it is undertaken without a lawful cauſe; and then the defenſive war, which on other occaſions might be unjuſt, becomes juſt.

V. We muſt therefore affirm, in general, that the firſt who takes up arms, whether juſtly or unjuſtly, commences an offenſive war; and he who oppoſes him, whether with or without a reaſon, begins a defenſive war. Thoſe who look upon the word *offenſive war* to be an odious term, as always implying ſomething unjuſt; and who, on the contrary, conſider a defenſive war as inſeparable from equity, confound ideas, and perplex a thing, which of itſelf ſeems to be ſufficiently clear. It is with princes as with private perſons. The plaintiff who commences a ſuit at law, is ſometimes in the wrong, and ſometimes in the right. 'Tis the ſame with the defendant. It is wrong to refuſe to pay a ſum which is juſtly due; and it is right to forbear paying what we do not owe.

VI. In the third place, *Grotius* diſtinguiſhes war into *private*, *public*, and *mix'd*. *Public war* he calls that which is made on both ſides by the authority of the civil power : *Private war*, that which is made between private perſons, without any public authority : and, laſtly, *mix'd war*, that which, on one ſide, is carried on by public authority, and, on the other, by mere private perſons.

VII. We may obſerve concerning this diviſion, that if we take the word *war* in the moſt general and extenſive ſenſe, and underſtand by it *all taking up arms with a view to decide a quarrel*, in contradiſtinction to the way of deciding a difference by recourſe to a common judge, then this diſtinction may be admitted ; but cuſtom ſeems to explode it, and has reſtrained the ſignification of the word *war* to that carried on between ſovereign powers. In a civil ſociety, private perſons have not a right to make war ; and as for the ſtate of nature, we have already treated of the right which men have in that ſtate to defend and preſerve their perſons and properties ; ſo that as we are here treating only of the right of ſovereigns, with regard to each other, 'tis properly public, and not private war, that falls under our preſent enquiry.

VIII. 4°. War is alſo diſtinguiſhed into *ſolemn according to the laws of nations*, and *not ſolemn*. To render a war ſolemn, two things are requiſite ; the firſt, that it be made by the authority of the ſovereign ; the ſecond, that it be accompanied with certain formalities, as a formal declaration, *&c.* but of this we ſhall treat more fully in its proper place. War not ſolemn, is that which is made either without a formal declaration, or againſt mere private perſons. We ſhall here only hint at this diviſion, referring a more particular examination of it, and an enquiry into its effects, till we come to treat of the formalities which uſually precede war.

IX. But a queſtion is moved, relating to this ſubject, which is, whether a magiſtrate, properly ſo called, and as ſuch, has a power of making war of his own accord? *Grotius* anſwers, that judging independently of the civil laws, every magiſtrate ſeems to have as much right, in caſe of reſiſtance, to take up arms in order to exerciſe his juriſdiction, and to ſee his commands executed, as to defend the people intruſted to his care. *Puffendorf*, on the contrary, takes the negative, and criticiſes on the opinion of *Grotius*.

X. But 'tis eaſy to reconcile theſe two authors, the diſpute between them being merely about words. *Grotius* fixes a more vague and general idea to the term *war* *: according to him, therefore, when a ſubordinate magiſtrate takes up arms to maintain his authority, and to reduce thoſe to reaſon who refuſe to ſubmit to him, he is ſuppoſed to act with the approbation of the ſovereign; who, by entruſting him with a ſhare in the government of the ſtate, has at the ſame time inveſted him with the power neceſſary to exerciſe it. And thus the queſtion is only, whether every magiſtrate, as ſuch, has need on this occaſion of an expreſs order from the ſovereign; ſo that the conſtitution of civil ſocieties in general re-

* See above, Sect. VII.

quire

quire it, independently of the civil laws of each particular ſtate.

XI. Now I aſk, if a magiſtrate can have recourſe to arms for the reduction of one perſon, of two, ten, or twenty, who either refuſe to obey him, or attempt to hinder the exerciſe of his juriſdiction, why may he not uſe the ſame means againſt fifty, a hundred, a thouſand? *&c.* The greater the number is, the more he will have occaſion for force to overcome their reſiſtance. Now this is what *Grotius* includes under the term *war*.

XII. *Puffendorf* agrees to all this in the main; but he pretends that this coercive power, which belongs to a magiſtrate over diſobedient ſubjects, is not a right of war; war ſeeming to be intirely between equals, or at leaſt ſuch as pretend to be ſo. The idea of *Puffendorf*'s is certainly more regular, and agreeable to cuſtom; but 'tis evident, that the difference between him and *Grotius* conſiſts only in the greater or ſmaller extent which each of them gives to the word *war*.

XIII. If it be objected, that it is dangerous to leave ſo much power to a ſubordinate magiſtrate; this may be true: but then it proves only that legiſlators act wiſely, in ſetting bounds to the power of the magiſtrate, in order to reſtrain that, which otherwiſe might be a neceſſary conſequence of the very deſign for which the magiſtrate is eſtabliſhed.

XIV.

XIV. But to judge of the power of the magiſtrates, or of generals and leaders, in reſpect to war, properly ſo called, and which is carried on againſt a foreign enemy, we need only to attend to the extent of their commiſſions; for it is evident that they cannot lawfully undertake any act of hoſtility of their own head, and without a formal order of the ſovereign, at leaſt reaſonably preſumed, in conſequence of the circumſtances which they are under.

XV. Thus, for example, a general ſent upon an expedition with an unlimited authority, may act againſt the enemy offenſively, as well as defenſively, and in ſuch a manner as he ſhall judge moſt advantageous; but he can neither levy any new war, nor make peace of his own head. But if his power is limited, he ought never to paſs the bounds preſcribed to him, unleſs he is unavoidably reduced to it by the neceſſity of ſelf-defence; for whatever he does in that caſe, is ſuppoſed to be with the conſent and approbation of the ſovereign. Thus, if an admiral has orders to be upon the defenſive, he may, notwithſtanding ſuch a confinement, break in upon the enemy's fleet, and ſink and burn as many of their ſhips as he can, if they come to attack him: all that he is forbidden, is to challenge the enemy firſt.

XVI. In general, the governors of provinces and cities, if they have troops under their command, may by their own authority defend themſelves againſt an enemy who attacks them; but they ought not to carry the war into a foreign country, without an expreſs order from their ſovereign.

XVII.

XVII. 'Twas in virtue of this privilege, arifing from neceffity, that *Lucius Pinarius* *, governour of *Enna* in *Sicily* for the *Romans*, upon certain information that the inhabitants defigned to revolt to the *Carthaginians*, put them all to the fword, and thus preferved the place. But, except in fuch a cafe of neceffity, the inhabitants of a town have no right to take up arms, to obtain fatisfaction for thofe injuries which the prince neglects to revenge.

XVIII. A mere prefumption of the will of the fovereign, would not even be fufficient to excufe a governour, or any other officer, who fhould undertake a war, except in a cafe of neceffity, without either a general or particular order. For 'tis not fufficient to know what part the fovereign would probably act, if he were confulted, in fuch a particular pofture of affairs; but it fhould rather be confidered in general, what it is probable a prince would defire fhould be done without confulting him, when the matter will allow time, and when the affair is dubious. Now certainly fovereigns will never confent that their minifters fhould, whenever they think proper, undertake, without their orders, a thing of fuch importance as an offenfive war, which is the proper fubject of the prefent inquiry.

XIX. In thefe circumftances, whatever part the fovereign would have thought proper to act, if he had been confulted; and whatever fuccefs the war, undertaken without his orders, may have had; it is left to the fovereign whether he will ratify, or con-

* Livy, lib. XXI. cap. 18.

demn

demn the aƈtion of his miniſter. If he ratifies it, this approbation renders the war ſolemn, by reflecting back, as it were, an authority upon it, ſo that it obliges the whole commonwealth. But if the ſovereign condemn the aƈtion of the governour, the hoſtilities committed by the latter ought to paſs for a ſort of robbery, the fault of which by no means affects the ſtate, provided the governour is delivered up, or puniſhed according to the laws of the country, and proper ſatisfaction be made for the damages ſuſtained.

XX. We may here further obſerve, that in civil ſocieties, when a particular member has done an injury to a ſtranger, the governour of the commonwealth is ſometimes reſponſible for it, ſo that war may be declared againſt him on that account. But to ground this kind of imputation, we muſt neceſſarily ſuppoſe one of theſe two things, ſufferance, or reception, *viz.* either that the ſovereign has ſuffered this harm to be done to the ſtranger, or that he afforded a retreat to the criminal.

XXI. In the firſt caſe it muſt be laid down as a maxim, that a ſovereign, who knowing the crimes of his ſubjects, as for example, that they practiſe piracy on ſtrangers; and being alſo able and obliged to hinder it, does not hinder it, renders himſelf criminal, becauſe he has conſented to the bad action, the commiſſion of which he has permitted, and conſequently furniſhed a juſt reaſon of war.

XXII. The two conditions abovementioned, I mean

mean the knowledge and sufferance of the sovereign, are absolutely necessary, the one not being sufficient without the other, to communicate any share in the guilt. Now 'tis presumed, that a sovereign knows what his subjects openly and frequently commit; and as to his power of hindering the evil, this likewise is always presumed, unless the want of it be clearly proved.

XXIII. The other way, in which a sovereign renders himself guilty of the crime of another, is by allowing a retreat and admittance to the criminal, and screening him from punishment. *Puffendorf* pretends, that if we are obliged to deliver up a criminal who takes shelter among us, it is rather in virtue of some treaty on this head, than in consequence of a common and indispensable obligation.

XXIV. But *Puffendorf*, I think, has, without sufficient reasons, abandoned the opinion of *Grotius*, which seems to be better founded. The principles of the latter, in regard to the present question, may be reduced to these following.

1°. Since the establishment of civil societies, the right of punishing offences against human society, which every particular person, if not chargeable himself with any such crime, had in the state of nature, has been transferred to the respective sovereigns, so that they alone have the privilege of punishing, as they think proper, those faults of their subjects, which properly interest the commonwealth.

XXV. But this right of punishing offences against human

human ſociety, is not ſo excluſively theirs, but that either public bodies, or their governours, have a right to procure the puniſhment of them in the ſame manner, as the laws of a particular ſtate allow every one an action for a certain crime.

XXVI. 3°. And much more have they this right, with reſpect to crimes, by which they are directly offended, and with regard to which they have a perfect right of puniſhing, for the ſupport of their honour and ſafety. In theſe circumſtances, therefore, the ſtate, or the governour of the ſtate, where the criminal retires, ought not to obſtruct the right which belongs to the other power.

XXVII. 4°. Now as one prince does not generally permit another to ſend armed men into his territories, upon the ſcore of exacting puniſhment, (for this would indeed be accompanied with terrible inconveniences) 'tis reaſonable the ſovereign, in whoſe dominions the convicted offender lives, or has taken ſhelter, ſhould either puniſh the criminal according to his demerits, or elſe deliver him up, to be puniſhed at the diſcretion of the injured ſovereign. This is that delivering up, of which we have ſo many examples in hiſtory.

XXVIII. 5°. The principles here laid down, concerning the obligation of puniſhing or delivering up, regard not only the criminals who have always been ſubjects of the government they now live under, but alſo thoſe who, after the commiſſion of ſome crime, have taken ſhelter in the country.

XXIX. 6°. In fine, we muſt obſerve that the right of demanding fugitive delinquents to puniſhment, has not for ſome ages laſt paſt been inſiſted upon by ſovereigns, in moſt parts of *Europe*, except in crimes againſt the ſtate, or thoſe of a very heinous nature. As for leſſer faults, they are connived at on both ſides, unleſs 'tis otherwiſe agreed on by ſome particular treaty.

XXX. Beſides all theſe kinds of war, hitherto mentioned, we may alſo diſtinguiſh them into *perfect* and *imperfect* wars. A perfect war, is that which entirely, and in all reſpects, breaks the peace and tranquillity of the ſtate, and lays a foundation for all poſſible acts of hoſtility. An imperfect war, on the contrary, is that which does not break the peace in all reſpects, but only in certain particulars, the tranquillity of the ſtate ſubſiſting in other affairs uninterrupted.

XXXI. This laſt ſpecies of war is generally called repriſals, of the nature of which we ſhall give here ſome account. By repriſals then we mean *that imperfect kind of war, or thoſe acts of hoſtility which ſovereigns exerciſe againſt each other, or, with their conſent, their ſubjects, by ſeizing the perſons or effects of the ſubjects of a foreign commonwealth, that refuſeth to do us juſtice; with a view to obtain ſecurity, and to recover our right, and in caſe of refuſal, to do juſtice to ourſelves, without any other interruption of the public tranquillity.*

XXXII. *Grotius* pretends, that repriſals are not founded

founded on the law of nature and neceſſity, but only on a kind of arbitrary law of nations, by which moſt of them have agreed, that the goods belonging to the ſubjects of a foreign ſtate ſhould be a pledge or ſecurity, as it were, for what that ſtate, or the governour of it, might owe us, either directly, and in their own names, or by rendering themſelves reſponſible for the actions of others, by refuſing to adminiſter juſtice.

XXXIII. But this is far from being an arbitrary right, founded upon any pretended law of nations, whoſe exiſtence we cannot prove, and where all is reduced to a cuſtom, more or leſs extended, but which, in itſelf, has never the force of a law. The right we here ſpeak of, is a conſequence of the conſtitution of civil ſocieties, and an application of the maxims of the law of nature to that conſtitution.

XXXIV. In the independence of the ſtate of nature, and before there was any civil government, if a perſon had been injured, he could come upon thoſe only who had done the wrong, or upon their accomplices; becauſe there was then no tie between men, in virtue of which a perſon might be deemed to have conſented, in ſome manner, to what others did even without his participation.

XXXV. But ſince civil ſocieties have been formed, that is to ſay, communities, whoſe members are all united together, for their common defence, there has neceſſarily ariſen from thence a conjunction of intereſts and wills; which is the reaſon, that as the ſociety, or the powers which govern it, engage to defend each other againſt the inſults of every other, whether citizen or foreigner; ſo every individual may be alſo deemed to have engaged to anſwer for what the ſociety, of which he is a member, or the powers which govern it, do or owe.

XXXVI. No human eſtabliſhment, no connection into which mankind enter, can ſuperſede the obligation of that general and inviolable law of nature, *that the damage we have done to another ſhould be repaired*; except thoſe, who are thereby expoſed to ſuffer, have manifeſtly renounced their right of demanding reparation. And when ſuch eſtabliſhments hinder, in certain reſpects, thoſe who are injured, from obtaining ſatisfaction ſo eaſily as they might without them, this difficulty muſt be made up, by furniſhing the perſons intereſted with all the other poſſible methods of doing themſelves juſtice.

XXXVII. Now 'tis certain that ſocieties, or the powers which govern them, by being armed with the force of the whole body, are ſometimes encouraged to laugh at ſtrangers with impunity, who come to demand ſomething which is their due; and that every ſubject contributes, one way or other, to enable them to act in this manner; ſo that he may be ſuppoſed to conſent to it in ſome meaſure. But if he does not in reality conſent, there is, after all, no other manner of facilitating, to injured ſtrangers, the proſecution of their rights, which is become difficult by the united force of the whole body, than to authoriſe them to come upon all thoſe who are members of it.

XXXVIII.

XXXVIII. Let us therefore conclude, that in consequence of the constitution of civil societies, every subject, so long as he continues such, is responsible to strangers for what the society, or he who governs it, do or owe: with this clause, however, that he may demand indemnification, when there is any fault or injustice on the part of his superiors. But if it should be any man's misfortune to be disappointed of this indemnification, he must look upon it as one of those inconveniences which, in a civil state, the constitution of human affairs renders almost inevitable. If to all these we add the reasons alledged by *Grotius*, we shall plainly see, that there is no necessity for supposing here a tacit consent of the people to found the right of reprisals.

XXXIX. As reprisals are an act of hostility, and often the prelude or forerunner of a compleat and perfect war, 'tis plain that none but the sovereign can lawfully use this right, and that the subjects can make no reprisals but by his order and authority.

XL. Besides, 'tis proper that the wrong or injustice done us, and which occasions the reprisals, should be clear and evident, and that the thing in dispute be of great consequence. For if the wrong is dubious, or of no importance, it would be equally unjust and dangerous to proceed to this extremity, and to expose ourselves to all the calamities of an open war. Neither ought we to come to reprisals, before we have tried, by the ordinary means, to obtain justice for the injury committed. For this purpose we must apply to the prince, whose subject has done us the injustice; and if the prince takes no notice, or refuses satisfaction, we may then make reprisals, in order to obtain it.

XLI. In a word, we must not have recourse to reprisals, except when all the ordinary means of obtaining our due have failed; so that, for instance, if a subordinate magistrate has refused us the justice we ask, we are not permitted to use reprisals before we apply to the sovereign himself, who will perhaps do us justice. In these circumstances, we may therefore either detain the subjects of a foreign state, if they detain ours; or we may seize their goods and effects. But whatever just reason we may have to make reprisals, we can never directly, and for that reason alone, put those to death whom we have seized upon, but only secure them, and not use them ill, till we have obtained satisfaction; so that, during all that time, they are to be considered as hostages.

XLII. As for the goods seized by right of reprisals, we must take care of them till the time, in which satisfaction ought to be made, is expired; after which we may adjudge them to the creditor, or sell them for the payment of the debt; returning to him, from whom they were taken, the overplus, when all charges are deducted.

XLIII. We must also observe, that it is not permitted to use reprisals, except with regard to subjects, properly so called, and their effects; for as to strangers,

ſtrangers, who do but paſs through a country, or only come to make a ſhort ſtay in it, they have not a ſufficient connection with the ſtate, of which they are only members but for a time, and in an imperfect manner; ſo that we cannot indemnify ourſelves by them, for the loſs we have ſuſtained by any original and perpetual ſubject, and by the refuſal of the ſovereign to render us juſtice. We muſt farther except ambaſſadors, who are ſacred perſons, even in the height of war. But as for women, clergymen, men of letters, *&c.* the law of nature grants them no privilege in this caſe, if they have not otherwiſe acquired it by virtue of ſome treaty.

XLIV. Laſtly, ſome political writers diſtinguiſh thoſe wars which are carried on between two or more ſovereigns, from thoſe of the ſubjects againſt their governours. But 'tis plain, that when ſubjects take up arms againſt their ſovereign, they either do it for juſt reaſons, and according to the principles eſtabliſhed in this work; or without any juſt and lawful cauſe. In this laſt caſe, it is rather a revolt or inſurrection, than a war, properly ſo called. But if the ſubjects have juſt reaſon to reſiſt their ſovereign, 'tis ſtrictly a war; ſince, in this caſe, there are neither ſovereign nor ſubjects, all dependance and obligation having ceaſed. The two oppoſite parties are then in a ſtate of nature and equality, trying to obtain juſtice by their own proper ſtrength, which conſtitutes what we underſtand properly by the term *war*.

CHAP. IV.

Of those things which ought to precede war.

I. HOwever juſt reaſon we may have to make war, yet as it inevitably brings along with it an incredible number of calamities, and often injuſtices, 'tis certain that we ought not to proceed too eaſily to a dangerous extremity, which may perhaps prove fatal to the conqueror himſelf.

II. The following are the meaſures which prudence directs ſovereigns to obſerve in theſe circumſtances.

1°. Suppoſing the reaſon of the war is juſt in itſelf, yet the diſpute ought to be about ſomething of great conſequence to us; ſince 'tis better even to relinquiſh part of our right, when the thing is not conſiderable, than to have recourſe to arms to defend it.

2°. We ought to have, at leaſt, ſome probable appearance of ſucceſs; for it would be a criminal temerity, and a real folly, wantonly to expoſe ourſelves to certain deſtruction, and to run into a greater, in order to avoid a leſſer evil.

3°. Laſtly, there ſhould be a real neceſſity for taking up arms; that is, we ought not to have recourſe to force, but when we can employ no milder method of recovering our right, or of defending ourſelves from the evils with which we are menaced.

III. Theſe meaſures are agreeable not only to the prin-

principles of prudence, but alſo to the fundamental maxims of ſociability, and the love of peace; maxims of no leſs force, with reſpect to nations, than individuals. By theſe a ſovereign muſt therefore be neceſſarily directed; even the juſtice of the government obliges him to it, in conſequence of the very nature and end of authority. For as he ought always to take particular care of the ſtate, and of his ſubjects, conſequently he ſhould not expoſe them to all the evils with which war is attended, except in the laſt extremity, and when there is no other expedient left but that of arms.

IV. 'Tis not therefore ſufficient that the war is juſt in itſelf, with reſpect to the enemy; it muſt alſo be ſo with reſpect to ourſelves, and our ſubjects. *Plutarch* informs us, "that among the ancient *Ro*-" *mans*, when the *Feciales* had determined that a " war might be juſtly undertaken, the ſenate after-" wards examined whether it would be advantage-" ous to engage in it."

V. Now among the methods of deciding differences between nations without a war, there are three moſt conſiderable. The firſt is an amicable conference between the contending parties; with reſpect to which *Cicero* judiciouſly obſerves, "that this " method of terminating a difference by a diſcuſſion " of reaſons on both ſides, is peculiarly agreeable " to the nature of man; that force belongs to " brutes, and that we never ought to have recourſe " to it, but when we cannot redreſs our grievances " by any other method."

VI.

VI. The ſecond way of terminating a difference between thoſe who have not a common judge, is to put the matter to arbitration. The more potent indeed often neglect this method, but it ought certainly to be followed by thoſe who have any regard to juſtice and peace; and it is a way that has been taken by great princes and people.

VII. The third method, in fine, which may be ſometimes uſed with ſucceſs, is that of caſting lots. I ſay, we may ſometimes uſe this way; for it is not always lawful to refer the iſſue of a difference, or of a war, to the deciſion of lots. This method cannot be taken juſt as we think proper, except when the diſpute is about a thing, in which we have a full propriety, and which we may renounce whenever we pleaſe. But in general, the obligation of the ſovereign to defend the lives, the honour, the religion, and ſuch like of the ſubjects, as alſo his obligation to maintain the honour of the ſtate, are of too ſtrong a nature to ſuffer him to renounce the moſt natural and probable means of his own, and others ſecurity, and to refer immediately his caſe to chance, which in its nature is entirely uncertain.

VIII. But this excepted, if upon due examination he, who has been unjuſtly attacked, finds himſelf ſo weak, that he has no probability of making any conſiderable reſiſtance, he may reaſonably decide the difference by the way of lot, in order to avoid a certain, by expoſing himſelf to an uncertain danger; which, in this caſe, it is the leaſt of two inevitable evils.

IX. There is alſo another method, which has ſome relation to lots. This conſiſts in ſingle combats, which have often been uſed to terminate ſuch differences as were likely to cauſe a war between two nations. And indeed, to prevent a war, and its concomitant evils, I ſee no reaſon that can hinder us from referring matters to a combat between a certain number of men agreed upon by both parties. Hiſtory furniſhes us with ſeveral examples of this kind, as that of *Turnus* and *Eneas*, *Menelaus* and *Paris*, the *Horatii* and the *Curiatii*.

X. 'Tis a queſtion of ſome importance, to know whether it is lawful thus to expoſe the intereſt of a whole ſtate to the fate of theſe combats. It appears on the one hand, that by that means we ſpare the effuſion of human blood, and ſhorten the calamities of war; and, on the other hand, it promiſeth fairer, and looks like a better venture, to ſtand the ſhock even of a bloody war, than by one blow to riſque the liberty and ſafety of the ſtate by a deciſive combat; ſince, after the loſs of one or two battles, the war may be ſet on foot again, and a third perhaps may prove ſucceſsful.

XI. However, it may be ſaid, that if otherwiſe there is no proſpect of making a good end of a war, and if the liberty and ſafety of the ſtate are at ſtake, there ſeems to be no reaſon againſt taking this ſtep, as the leaſt of two evils.

XII. *Grotius*, in examining this queſtion, pretends that theſe combats are not reconcileable to internal

ternal juſtice, though they are approved by the external right of nations; and that private perſons cannot innocently expoſe their lives, of their own accord, to the hazard of a ſingle combat, though ſuch a combat may be innocently permitted by the ſtate or ſovereign, to prevent greater miſchiefs. But it has been juſtly obſerved, that the arguments uſed by this great man, to ſupport his opinion, either prove nothing at all, or prove, at the ſame time, that it is never lawful to venture one's life in any combat whatever.

XIII. We may even affirm, that *Grotius* is not very conſiſtent with himſelf, ſince he permits this kind of combats, when otherwiſe there is the greateſt probability that he who proſecutes an unjuſt cauſe will be victorious, and thereby deſtroy a great number of innocent perſons: For this exception evinces that the thing is not bad in itſelf, and that all the harm, which can be in this caſe, conſiſts in expoſing our own, or the life of others, without neceſſity, to the hazard of a ſingle combat. The deſire of terminating, or preventing a war, which has always terrible conſequences, even to the victorious, is ſo commendable, that it may excuſe, if not intirely juſtify thoſe, who engage either themſelves or others even imprudently in a combat of this kind. Be this as it may, it is certain that in ſuch a caſe, thoſe who combat by the order of the ſtate, are entirely innocent; for they are no more obliged to examine whether the ſtate acts prudently or not, than when they are ſent upon an aſſault, or to fight a pitched battle.

XIV.

XIV. We muſt however obſerve, that it was a fooliſh ſuperſtition in thoſe people who looked upon a ſet combat as a lawful method of determining all differences, even between individuals, from a perſuaſion that the deity gave always the victory to the good cauſe; for which reaſon they called this kind of combats *the judgments of God.*

XV. But if, after having uſed all our endeavours to terminate differences in an amicable manner, there remains no further hope, and we are abſolutely conſtrained to undertake a war, we ought firſt to declare it in form to the enemy.

XVI. This declaration of war conſidered in itſelf, and independently of the particular formalities of each people, does not ſimply belong to the law of nations, taking this word in the ſenſe of *Grotius*, but to the law of nature itſelf. Indeed prudence, and natural equity, equally require, that before we take up arms againſt any ſtate, we ſhould try all amicable methods, to avoid coming to ſuch an extremity. We ought then to ſummon him, who has injured us, to make a ſpeedy ſatisfaction, that we may ſee whether he will not have regard to himſelf, and not put us to the hard neceſſity of purſuing our right by the force of arms.

XVII. From what has been ſaid it follows, that this declaration takes place only in *offenſive wars*; for when we are actually attacked, that alone gives us reaſon to believe that the enemy is reſolved not to liſten to an accommodation.

XVIII.

XVIII. From thence it alſo follows, that we ought not to commit acts of hoſtility immediately upon declaring war, but we ſhould wait, ſo long at leaſt as we can without doing ourſelves a prejudice, 'till he who has done us the injury plainly refuſes to give us ſatisfaction, and has put himſelf in condition to receive us with bravery and reſolution; otherwiſe the declaration of war would be only a vain ceremony. For we ought to neglect no means to convince all the world, and even the enemy himſelf, that it is only abſolute neceſſity that obliges us to take up arms, for the recovery or defence of our juſt rights; after having try'd every other method, and given the enemy full time to conſider.

XIX. Declarations of war are diſtinguiſhed into *conditional* and *abſolute*. The *conditional* is that which is joined with a ſolemn demand of reſtitution, and with this condition, that if the injury is not repaired, we ſhall do ourſelves juſtice by arms. The *abſolute* is that which includes no condition, and by which we abſolutely renounce the friendſhip and ſociety of him againſt whom we declare war. But every declaration of war, in whatever manner it be made, is of its own nature conditional *; for we ought always to be diſpoſed to accept of a reaſonable ſatisfaction, as ſoon as the enemy offers it; and on this account ſome writers reject this diſtinction of the declaration of war into conditional and abſolute. But it may nevertheleſs be maintained, by ſuppoſing that he, againſt whom war is declared purely and ſimply, has already ſhewn, that he had no deſign

* See above, Numb. XVIII.

to

to ſpare us the neceſſity of taking up arms againſt him. So far therefore the declaration may, at leaſt as to the form of it, be pure and ſimple, without any prejudice to the diſpoſition in which we ought always to be, if the enemy will hearken to reaſon: but this relates to the concluſion, rather than the commencement of war; to the latter of which the diſtinction of conditional and abſolute declarations properly belongs.

XX. As ſoon as war has been declared againſt a ſovereign, it is preſumed to be declared at the ſame time not only againſt all his ſubjects, who, in conjunction with him, form one moral perſon; but alſo againſt all thoſe who ſhall afterwards join him, and who are, with reſpect to the principal enemy, to be looked upon only as acceſſories, or adherents.

XXI. As to the formalities obſerved by different nations in declaring war, they are all arbitrary in themſelves. 'Tis therefore a matter of indifference, whether the declaration is made by envoys, heralds, or letters; whether to the ſovereign in perſon, or to his ſubjects, provided the ſovereign cannot plead ignorance of it.

XXII. With reſpect to the reaſons why a ſolemn denunciation was required unto ſuch a war, as by the law of nations is called juſt; *Grotius* pretends it was, that the people might be aſſured that the war was not undertaken by a private authority, but by the conſent of one or other of the nations, or of their ſovereigns.

XXIII.

XXIII. But this reaſon of *Grotius*'s ſeems to be inſufficient; for are we more aſſured that the war is made by a public authority, when a herald, for inſtance, comes to declare it with certain ceremonies, than we ſhould be, when we ſee an army upon our frontiets, commanded by ſome principal perſon of the ſtate, and ready to enter the country? Might it not, on the contrary, more eaſily happen that a perſon, or ſome few perſons, ſhould aſſume the character of heralds, than that a ſingle man ſhould, by his own authority, raiſe an army, and march at the head of it to the frontiers, without the ſovereign's knowledge?

XXIV. The truth is, the principal end of declarations of war, or at leaſt what has occaſioned them to be eſtabliſhed, is to let all the world know that there was juſt reaſon to take up arms, and to ſignify to the enemy himſelf, that it had been, and ſtill was, in his power to avoid it. The declarations of war, and the manifeſtos publiſhed by princes, are marks of the due reſpect they have for each other, and for the ſociety in general, to which by this means they give, in ſome meaſure, an account of their conduct, in order to obtain their approbation. This appears particularly by the manner in which the *Romans* made theſe denunciations. The perſon ſent for this purpoſe took the gods to witneſs, that the nation, againſt whom they had declared war, had acted unjuſtly, by refuſing to comply with what law and juſtice required.

XXV. Laſtly, it is here to be obſerved, that we ought

ought not to confound the *declaration* with the *publication* of war. This last is made in favour of the subjects of the prince who declares the war, and to inform them that they are henceforth to look upon such or such a nation as their enemies, and to take their measures accordingly.

CHAP. V.

General rules to know what is allowable in war.

I. IT is not enough that a war be undertaken with justice, or for a lawful reason, and that we observe the other conditions hitherto mentioned; but we ought also, in the prosecution of it, to be directed by the principles of justice and humanity, and not to carry the liberties of hostility beyond these bounds.

II. *Grotius*, in treating this subject, establishes three general rules, as so many principles, which serve to explain the extent of the rights of war.

III. The *first* is, that every thing which has a connection morally necessary with the end of the war, is permitted, and no more. For it would be to no purpose to have a right to do a thing, if we could not make use of the necessary means to bri g it about. But, at the same time, it would not be just, that, under a pretence of defending our right, we should think every thing lawful, and should proceed, without any manner of neceſſity, to the laſt extremity.

IV. *The ſecond rule.* The right we have againſt an enemy, and which we purſue by arms, ought not to be conſidered only with reſpect to the cauſe which gave riſe to the war; but alſo with reſpect to the freſh cauſes which happen afterwards, during the courſe of the war: Juſt as at law, one of the parties often acquires ſome new right before the ending of the ſuit. This is the foundation of the right we have to act againſt thoſe who join our enemies, during the courſe of the war, whether they are his dependents or not.

V. The *third rule*, in fine, is, that there are a great many things, which, tho' otherwiſe unlawful, are yet permitted in war, becauſe they are inevitable conſequences of it, and happen contrary to our intention, and without any formal deſign. Otherwiſe there would never be any way of making war without injuſtice; and the moſt innocent actions would be looked upon as unjuſt; ſince there are but few, from which ſome evil may not accidentally ariſe, contrary to the intention of the agent.

VI. Thus, for example, in recovering our own, if juſt ſo much as is preciſely our due cannot be had, we have a right to take more, but under the obligation of returning the value of the overplus. Thus we may attack a ſhip full of pirates, tho' there may be women, or children, or other innocent perſons on board, who muſt needs be expoſed to the danger of being

being involved in the ruin of thoſe whom we may juſtly deſtroy.

VII. This is the extent of the right we have againſt an enemy, in conſequence of a ſtate of war. By a ſtate of war, that of ſociety is aboliſhed; ſo that whoever declares himſelf my enemy, gives me a liberty to uſe violence againſt him *in infinitum*, or as far as I pleaſe; and that not only till I have repulſed the danger that threatened me, or till I have recovered, or forced from him, what he either unjuſtly deprived me of, or refuſed to pay me, but till I have further obliged him to give me good ſecurity for the future. It is not therefore always unjuſt to return a greater evil for a leſs.

VIII. But it is alſo to be obſerved, that tho' theſe maxims are true, according to the ſtrict right of war, yet the law of humanity fixes bounds to this right. That law directs us to conſider, not only whether ſuch or ſuch acts of hoſtility may, without injury, be committed againſt an enemy; but alſo, whether they are worthy of a humane or generous conqueror. Thus, as far as is poſſible, and our own defence and future ſecurity will permit, we muſt moderate the evils we inflict upon an enemy, by the principles of humanity.

IX. As to the manner of acting lawfully againſt an enemy, it is evident that violence and terror are the proper characteriſtics of war, and the method moſt commonly uſed. Yet it is alſo lawful to employ ſtratagem and artifice, provided it be without treachery, or breach of promiſe. Thus we may deceive an enemy by falſe news, and fictitious relations, but we ought never to violate our compacts or engagements with him, as we ſhall ſhew more particularly hereafter.

X. By this we may judge of the right of ſtratagems; neither is it to be doubted but we may innocently uſe fraud and artifice, wherever it is lawful to have recourſe to violence and force. The firſt means have even the advantage over the laſt, in this, that they are attended by fewer evils, and preſerve the lives of a great many innocent people.

XI. It is true, ſome nations have rejected the uſe of ſtratagem and deceit in war; this, however, was not becauſe they thought them unjuſt, but from a certain magnanimity, and often from a confidence in their own ſtrength. The *Romans*, 'till very near the end of the ſecond *Punic war*, thought it a point of honour to uſe no ſtratagem in war.

XII. Theſe are the principles by which we may judge to what degree the liberties of hoſtility may be carried. To which let us add, that moſt nations have fixed no bounds to the rights which the law of nature gives us to act againſt an enemy: and the truth is, it is very difficult to determine, preciſely, how far it is proper to extend acts of hoſtility even in the moſt legitimate wars, in defence of our perſons, or for the reparation of damages, or for obtaining caution for the future; eſpecially as thoſe, who engage in war, give each other, by a kind of tacit agree-

agreement, an entire liberty to moderate or augment the violence of arms, and to exercise all acts of hostility, as each shall think proper.

XIII. And here it is to be observed, that tho' generals usually punish their soldiers, who have carried acts of hostility beyond the orders prescribed; yet this is not because they suppose the enemy is injured, but because it is necessary the general's orders should be obeyed, and that military discipline should be strictly observed.

XIV. It is also, in consequence of these principles, that those who, in a just and solemn war, have pushed slaughter and plunder beyond what the law of nature permits, are not generally looked upon as murderers or robbers, nor punished as such. The custom of nations is to leave this point to the conscience of the persons engaged in war, rather than involve themselves in troublesom broils, by taking upon them to condemn either party.

XV. It may be even said, that this custom of nations is founded on the principles of the law of nature. Let us suppose, that in the independence of the state of nature, thirty heads of families, inhabitants of the same country, should have entered into a league to attack or repulse a body, composed of other heads of families: I say, that neither during that war, nor after it is finished, those of the same country, or elsewhere, who had not joined the league of either side, ought, or could punish, as murderers or robbers, any of the two parties who ſhould happen to fall into their hands.

XVI. They could not do it during the war; for that would be eſpouſing the quarrel of one of the parties; and ſince they continued neuter in the beginning, they had clearly renounced the right of interfering with what ſhould paſs in the war: much leſs could they intermeddle after the war is over; becauſe, as the war could not be ended without ſome accommodation or treaty of peace, the parties concerned were reciprocally diſcharged from all the evils they had done to each other.

XVII. The good of ſociety alſo required that we ſhould follow theſe maxims. For if thoſe, who continued neuter, had ſtill been authoriſed to take cognizance of the acts of hoſtility, exerciſed in a foreign war, and conſequently to puniſh ſuch as they believed to have committed any injuſtice, and to take up arms on that account; inſtead of one war, ſeveral might have ariſen, and proved a ſource of broils and troubles. The more wars became frequent, the more neceſſary it was, for the tranquillity of mankind, not to eſpouſe raſhly other people's quarrels. The eſtabliſhment of civil ſocieties only rendered the practice of theſe rules more neceſſary; becauſe wars then became, if not more frequent, at leaſt more extenſive, and attended with a greater number of evils.

XVIII. Laſtly it is to be obſerved, that all acts of hoſti-

hoſtility, which can be lawfully committed againſt an enemy, may be exerciſed either in his territories, or ours, in places that belong to no-body, or at ſea.

XIX. This does not hold good in a neutral country; that is to ſay, whoſe ſovereign has taken no ſhare in the war. In ſuch countries, we cannot lawfully exerciſe any acts of hoſtility, neither on the perſons of the enemy, nor on their effects; not in virtue of any right of the enemy themſelves, but through a juſt reſpect to the ſovereign, who having taken neither ſide, lays us under a neceſſity of reſpecting his juriſdiction, and of forbearing to commit any acts of violence in his territories. To this we may add, that the ſovereign, by continuing neuter, has tacitly engaged not to ſuffer either party to commit any acts of hoſtility within his dominions.

CHAP. VI.

Of the rights which war gives over the perſons of the enemy, and of their extent and bounds.

I. WE ſhall now enter into the particulars of the different rights which war gives over the enemy's perſon and goods; and to begin with the former.

1°. It is certain that we may lawfully kill an enemy; I ſay lawfully, not only according to the terms of external juſtice, which paſſes for ſuch among all

 nations,

nations, but alſo according to internal juſtice, and the laws of conſcience. Indeed the end of war neceſſarily requires that we ſhould have this power, otherwiſe it would be in vain to take up arms, and the law of nature would permit it to no purpoſe.

II. If we conſulted only the cuſtom of countries, and what *Grotius* calls the *law of nations*, this liberty of killing an enemy would extend very far; we might ſay that it had no bounds, and might even be exerciſed on innocent perſons. However, tho' it be certain that war is attended with numberleſs evils, which in themſelves are acts of injuſtice, and real cruelty, but, under particular circumſtances, ought rather to be conſidered as unavoidable misfortunes; it is nevertheleſs true, that the right which war gives over the perſon and life of an enemy has its bounds, and that there are meaſures to be obſerved, which cannot be innocently neglected.

III. In general, we ought always to be directed by the principles eſtabliſhed in the preceding chapter, in judging of the degrees to which the liberties of hoſtility may be carried. The power we have of taking away the life of an enemy, is not therefore unlimited; for if we can attain the legitimate end of war, that is, if we can defend our lives and properties, aſſert our rights, and recover ſatisfaction for damages ſuſtained, and good ſureties for the future, without taking away the life of the enemy, it is certain that juſtice and humanity directs us to forbear it, and not to ſhed human blood unneceſſarily.

IV. It is true, in the application of these rules to particular cases, it is sometimes very difficult, not to say impossible, to fix precisely their proper extent and bounds; but it is certain, at least, that we ought to come as near to them as possible, without prejudicing our real interests. Let us apply these principles to particular cases.

V. 1°. It is often disputed, whether the right of killing an enemy regards only those who are actually in arms; or whether it extends indifferently to all those in the enemy's country, subjects or foreigners? My answer is, that with respect to those who are subjects, the point is incontestable. These are the principal enemies, and we may exercise all acts of hostility against them, by virtue of the state of war.

VI. As to strangers, those who settle in the enemy's country after a war is begun, of which they had previous notice, may justly be looked upon as enemies, and treated as such. But in regard to such as went thither before the war, justice and humanity require that we should give them a reasonable time to retire; and if they neglect that opportunity, they are accounted enemies.

VII. 2°. As to old men, women and children, it is certain that the right of war does not, of itself, require that we should push hostilities so far as to kill them; it is therefore a barbarous cruelty to do so. I say, that the end of war does not require this of itself; but if women, for instance, exercise acts

acts of hostility; if, forgetting the weakness of their sex, they usurp the offices of men, and take up arms against us, then we are certainly excused in availing ourselves of the rights of war against them. It may also be said, that when the heat of action hurries the soldiers, as it were, in spite of themselves, and against the orders of their superiors, to commit these acts of inhumanity; as for example, at the siege of a town, which, by an obstinate resistance, has irritated the troops; we ought to look upon these evils rather as misfortunes, and as the unavoidable consequences of war, than as crimes that deserve to be punished.

VIII. 3°. We must reason almost in the same manner, with respect to prisoners of war. We cannot, generally speaking, put them to death, without being guilty of cruelty. I say generally speaking; for there may be cases of necessity so pressing, that the care of our own preservation obliges us to proceed to extremities, which in any other circumstances than these would be absolutely criminal.

IX. In general, even the laws of war require that we should abstain from slaughter as much as possible, and that we should not shed human blood without necessity. We ought not, therefore, directly and deliberately to kill prisoners of war, nor those who ask quarter, or surrender themselves, much less old men, women and children; and in general, all those whose age and profession render them unfit to carry arms, and who have no other share in the war, than their being in the country, or party of the enemy.

enemy. We may alſo eaſily conceive, that the rights of war do not extend ſo far, as to authoriſe the outrages committed upon the honour and chaſtity of women; for this contributes nothing either to our defence or ſafety, or to the ſupport of our rights, but only ſerves to ſatisfy the brutality of the ſoldiers *.

X. Again a queſtion is here moved, whether in caſes, where it is lawful to kill the enemy, we may not, for that purpoſe, uſe all kinds of means indifferently? I anſwer, that to conſider the thing in itſelf, and in an abſtract manner, it is no matter which way we kill an enemy, whether by open force, or by fraud and ſtratagem, by the ſword, or by poiſon.

XI. It is however certain that, according to the ideas and cuſtoms of civilized nations, it is looked upon as a criminal cowardice, not only to cauſe any poiſonous draught to be given to the enemy, but alſo to poiſon wells, fountains, ſprings, rivers, arrows, darts, bullets, or other weapons uſed againſt him. Now it is ſufficient, that this cuſtom of looking on the uſe of poiſon as criminal, is received among the nations at variance with us, to ſuppoſe we comply with it, when, in the beginning of the war, we do not declare that we are at liberty to act otherwiſe, and leave it to our enemy's option to do the ſame.

XII. We may ſo much the more ſuppoſe this

* Grotius, lib. III. cap. iv. ſect. 19.

tacit

tacit agreement, as humanity, and the intereſt of both parties equally require it; eſpecially ſince wars are become ſo frequent, and are often undertaken on ſo ſlight occaſions; and ſince the human mind, ingenious in inventing the means to hurt, has ſo greatly multiplied thoſe which are authoriſed by cuſtom, and looked upon as honeſt. Beſides, it is beyond all doubt, that when we can obtain the ſame end by milder and more humane meaſures, which preſerve the lives of many, and particularly of thoſe in whoſe preſervation human ſociety is intereſted, humanity directs that we ſhould take this courſe.

XIII. Theſe are therefore juſt precautions, which men ought to follow for their own advantage. It is for the common benefit of mankind, that dangers ſhould not be augmented without end. In particular, the ſociety is intereſted in the preſervation of the lives of kings, generals of armies, and other perſons of the firſt rank, on whoſe ſafety that of ſocieties generally depends. For if the lives of theſe perſons are in greater ſafety than thoſe of others, when attacked only by arms; they are, on the other hand, more in danger of poiſon, *&c.* and they would be every day expoſed to periſh in this manner, if they were not protected by a regard to ſome ſort of law, or eſtabliſhed cuſtom.

XIV. Let us add, in fine, that all nations that ever pretended to juſtice and generoſity, have always followed theſe maxims; and the *Roman* Conſuls, in a letter they wrote to *Pyrrhus*, informing him that one of his people had offered to poiſon him,

him, ſaid, that it was the intereſt of all nations not to ſet ſuch examples.

XV. It is likewiſe diſputed whether we may lawfully ſend a perſon to aſſaſſinate an enemy? I anſwer, 1°. that he who for this purpoſe employs only ſome of his own people, may do it juſtly. When it is lawful to kill an enemy, it is no matter whether thoſe employed are many or few in number. Six hundred *Lacedæmonians*, with *Leonidas*, entered the enemy's camp, and went directly to the *Perſian* king (*Xerxes*'s) pavilion; now a ſmaller number might certainly have done the ſame. The famous attempt of *Mucius Scevola* is commended by all antiquity; and *Porſenna* himſelf, whoſe life was aimed at, acknowledged this to be an act of great valour.

XVI. But it is not ſo eaſy to determine whether we may for this purpoſe employ aſſaſſins, who by undertaking this taſk muſt be guilty of falſehood and treaſon; ſuch as ſubjects with regard to their ſovereign, and ſoldiers to their general. In this reſpect there are, in my opinion, two points to be diſtinguiſhed. Firſt, whether we do any wrong even to the enemy himſelf, againſt whom we employ traitors; and ſecondly, whether ſuppoſing we do him no wrong, we commit nevertheleſs a bad action.

XVII. 3°. As for the firſt queſtion, to conſider the thing in itſelf, and according to the rigorous law of war, it ſeems, that admitting the war to be juſt, no wrong is done to the enemy, whether we take advantage

vantage of the opportunity of a traitor who freely offers himſelf, or whether we ſeek for it, and bring it about ourſelves.

XVIII. The ſtate of war, into which the enemy has put himſelf, and which it was in his own power to prevent, permits of itſelf every method that can be uſed againſt him; ſo that he has no reaſon to complain whatever we do. Beſides, we are no more obliged, ſtrictly ſpeaking, to reſpect the right he has over his ſubjects, and the fidelity they owe him as ſuch, than their lives and fortunes, of which we may certainly deprive them by the right of war.

XIX. 4°. And yet I believe that this is not ſufficient to render an aſſaſſination, in theſe circumſtances, entirely innocent. A ſovereign, who has the leaſt tenderneſs of conſcience, and is convinced of the juſtice of his cauſe, will not endeavour to find out perfidious methods to ſubdue his enemy, nor be ſo ready to embrace thoſe which may preſent themſelves to him. The juſt confidence he has in the protection of heaven, the horror he conceives at the traitor's perfidy, the dread of becoming his accomplice, and of ſetting an example, which may fall again on himſelf and others, will make him deſpiſe and reject all the advantage he might propoſe to himſelf from ſuch a means.

XX. 5°. Let us alſo add, that ſuch a means cannot always be looked upon as entirely innocent, even with reſpect to the perſon who employs it. The ſtate of hoſtility, which ſuperſedes the intercourſe of good offices, and authorises to hurt, does not therefore dissolve all ties of humanity, nor remove our obligation to avoid, as much as possible, the giving room for some bad action of the enemy, or his people; especially those, who of themselves have had no part in the occasion of the war. Now every traitor certainly commits an action equally shameful and criminal.

XXI. 6°. We must therefore conclude with *Grotius*, that we can never in conscience seduce, or sollicit the subjects of an enemy to commit treason, because that is positively and directly inducing them to commit an abominable crime, which otherwise would, in all probability, have been very remote from their thoughts.

XXII. 7°. It is quite another thing, when we only take advantage of the occasion and the dispositions we find in a person, who has had no need to be sollicited to commit treason. Here, I think, the infamy of the perfidy does not fall on him who finds it intirely formed in the heart of the traitor; especially if we consider, that in these cases between enemies, the thing, with respect to which we take advantage of the bad disposition of another, is of such a nature, that we may innocently and lawfully do it ourselves.

XXIII. 8°. Be that as it may, for the reasons above alledged, we ought not to take advantage of a treason which offered itself, except in an extraordinary case, and from a kind of necessity. And tho' the

the custom of several nations has nothing obligatory in itself, yet as the people, with whom we are at variance, look upon the very acceptance of these offers of a certain kind of perfidy to be unlawful, as that of assassinating one's prince or general, we are reasonably supposed to comply with it by a tacit consent.

XXIV. 9°. Let us observe, however, that the law of nations makes some difference between a fair and legitimate enemy, and rebels, pirates, or highwaymen. The most religious princes make no difficulty to propose even rewards to those who will betray such persons; and the public odium of all, which men of this stamp lie under, is the cause that no body thinks the measure hard, or blames the conduct of the prince in using every method to destroy them.

XXV. Lastly, it is permitted to kill an enemy wherever we find him, except in a neutral country; for violent means are not suffered in a civilised society, where we ought to implore the assistance of the magistrate. In the time of the second *Punic war* *, seven *Carthaginian* galleys rode in a harbour belonging to *Syphax*, who was then in peace both with the *Romans* and *Carthaginians*, and *Scipio* came that way with two galleys only. The *Carthaginians* immediately prepared to attack the *Roman* galleys, which they might easily have taken before they had entered the port, but being forced by a strong wind into the harbour, before the *Carthaginians* had time to weigh

* Livy, lib. XXVIII. cap. xvii. numb. 12, & seq.

anchor,

anchor, they durſt not attack them, becauſe it was in a neutral prince's haven.

XXVI. Here it may be proper to ſay ſomething concerning priſoners of war. In former times, it was a cuſtom almoſt univerſally eſtabliſhed, that thoſe who were made priſoners in a juſt and ſolemn war, whether they had ſurrendered themſelves, or been taken by main force, became ſlaves, the moment they were conducted into ſome place dependent on the conqueror. And this right was exerciſed on all perſons whatſoever taken, even on thoſe who happened unfortunately to be in the enemy's country, at the time the war ſuddenly broke out.

XXVII. Further, not only the priſoners themſelves, but their poſterity for ever, were reduced to the ſame condition; that is to ſay, thoſe born of a woman after ſhe had been made a ſlave.

XXVIII. The effects of ſuch a ſlavery had no bounds; every thing was permitted to a maſter with reſpect to his ſlave, he had the power of life and death over him, and all that the ſlave poſſeſſed, or could afterwards acquire, belonged of right to the maſter.

XXIX. There is ſome probability, that the reaſon and end for which nations had eſtabliſhed this cuſtom of making ſlaves in war, was principally to induce the captors to abſtain from ſlaughter, from a view of the advantages they reaped from their ſlaves. Thus hiſtorians obſerve, that civil wars were more cruel than others, the general practice in that case being to put the prisoners to the sword, because they could not make slaves of them.

XXX. But Christian nations have generally agreed among themselves, to abolish the custom of making their prisoners yield perpetual service to the conqueror. At present it is thought sufficient to keep those that are taken in war, till their ransom is paid, the estimation of which depends on the will of the conqueror, unless there is a cartel, or agreement, by which it is fixed.

CHAP. VII.

Of the rights of war over the goods of an enemy.

I. AS to the goods of an enemy, it is certain that the state of war permits us to carry them off, to ravage, to spoil, or even intirely to destroy them; for as *Cicero* very well observes, * *It is not contrary to the law of nature, to plunder a person whom we may lawfully kill:* and all these mischiefs, which the law of nations allows us to do to the enemy, by ravaging and wasting his lands and goods, are called spoil or plunder.

II. This right of spoil, or plunder, extends in general to all things belonging to the enemy; and the law of nations, properly so called, does not exempt even sacred things; that is, things consecrated

* Cic. de Off. lib. III. cap. vi.

either to the true God, or to falſe deities, and deſigned for the uſe of religion.

III. It is true, the practices and cuſtoms of nations do not agree in this reſpect; ſome having permitted the plunder of things ſacred and religious, and others having looked upon it as a criminal profanation. But whatever the uſes and cuſtoms of different people are, they can never conſtitute the primitive rule of right. In order, therefore, to be aſſured of the right of war in regard to this article, we muſt have recourſe to the law of nature and nations.

IV. I obſerve then, that things ſacred are not in themſelves different from thoſe we call profane. The former differ from the latter, only by the religious uſe to which they were intended. But this application or uſe does not give the things the quality of holy and ſacred, as an intrinſic and indelible character, of which they cannot be deprived.

V. The things, thus conſecrated, always belong either to the ſtate, or to the ſovereign; and there is no reaſon why the prince, who has devoted them to religious purpoſes, may not afterwards apply them to the uſes of life; for they, as well as all other public things, are at his diſpoſal.

VI. It is therefore a groſs ſuperſtition to believe, that by the conſecration, or deſtination of theſe things to the ſervice of God, they, as it were, change maſter, and belong no more to men; that they are entirely withdrawn from commerce, and that the property of them paſſes from man to God. This is a dangerous ſuperſtition, owing to the ambition of the clergy.

VII. We muſt therefore conſider ſacred things as public goods, which belong to the ſtate or ſovereign. All the liberty which the right of war gives over the goods belonging to the ſtate, it alſo gives with reſpect to things called ſacred. They may therefore be ſpoiled or waſted by the enemy, at leaſt as far as is neceſſary and conducive to the deſign of the war; a limitation which is no way peculiar to the plunder of ſacred or religious things.

VIII. For, in general, it is evident that it is not lawful to plunder for plunder's ſake, and that it is juſt and innocent only, when it has ſome relation to the deſign of the war; that is, when ſome advantage accrues directly from it to ourſelves, by appropriating thoſe goods, or at leaſt, when by ravaging and deſtroying them, we in ſome meaſure weaken the enemy. It would be a madneſs, equally brutal and criminal, to do evil to another without a proſpect of doing ſome good, either directly or indirectly, to ourſelves. It very ſeldom happens, for inſtance, that after the taking of towns, there is any neceſſity for ruining temples, ſtatues, or other public or private ſtructures: we ſhould therefore generally ſpare all theſe, as well as the tombs and ſepulchers.

IX. It may however be obſerved, with reſpect to things ſacred, that thoſe who believe they contain

contain something divine, and inviolable, are really in the wrong to meddle with them at all; but this is only, because they act against their own conscience. And here, by the way, we may take notice of a reason given to clear the Pagans of the imputation of sacrilege, even when they pillaged the temples of the gods whom they acknowledged as such; which is, they imagined that when a city was taken, the guardian deities of that place quitted, at the same time, their temples and altars, especially after those deities, with every thing else that was sacred, had been *invited out* with certain ceremonies. This is excellently described by *Cocceius*, in his dissertation *De Evocatione Sacrorum*.

X. Let us on this subject add the wise reflections which *Grotius* makes, to persuade generals to behave with moderation in regard to plunder, from the advantages which may accrue to themselves from such a conduct. And first he says, "by this means "we take from the enemy one of the most power-"ful weapons, desperation. Besides, by sparing "the enemy's country, we give room to believe "that we are pretty confident of victory: and cle-"mency is of itself proper to soften and engage the "minds of men. All which may be proved by "several illustrious examples."

XI. Besides the power which war gives to spoil and destroy the goods of an enemy, it likewise confers a right of acquiring, appropriating, and justly retaining the goods we have taken from him, till the sum due to us is paid, including the expences of of the war, in which his refusal of payment engaged us; and whatever else we think necessary to secure to ourselves, by way of caution from the enemy.

XII. By the law of nations, not only he that makes war for a just reason, but also every man, in a just war, acquires a property in what he takes from the enemy, and that without rule or measure, at least as to the external effects, with which the right of property is accompanied; that is to say, neutral nations ought to regard the two parties at war, as lawful proprietors of what they can take from each other by force of arms; the state of neutrality not permitting them to espouse either side, or to treat either of the contending powers as an usurper, pursuant to the principles already established.

XIII. This is generally true, as well with respect to moveables as immoveables, so long as they are in the possession of him who has acquired them by the right of war. But if from the hands of the conqueror they have passed into the power of a third, there is no reason, if they are immoveables, why the antient owner should not try to recover them from that third, who holds them of the enemy, by what title soever; for he has as good a right against the new possessor, as against the enemy himself.

XIV. I said, *if they are immoveables*; for with respect to moveable effects, as they may easily be transferred by commerce into the hands of the subjects of a neutral state, often without their know-

ing

ing that they were taken in war; the tranquillity of nations, the good of commerce, and even the ſtate of neutrality, require that they ſhould always be reputed lawful prize, and the property of the perſon of whom we hold them. But the caſe is otherwiſe with reſpect to immoveables, they are immoveable in their nature; and thoſe to whom a ſtate, which has taken them from an enemy, would reſign them, cannot be ignorant of the manner in which it poſſeſſes them.

XV. Here a queſtion is moved, when is it that things are ſaid to be taken by the right of war, and are juſtly deemed to belong to him who is in poſſeſſion of them? *Grotius* anſwers as a civilian, that a man is deemed to have taken moveable things by the right of war, as ſoon as they are ſecured from the purſuit of the enemy; or when he has made himſelf maſter of them in ſuch a manner, that the firſt owner has loſt all probable hopes of recovering them. Thus, ſays he, at ſea, ſhips and other things are not ſaid to be taken, till they are brought into ſome port or harbour belonging to us, or to ſome part of the ſea where our fleet rides; for it is only then that the enemy begins to deſpair of recovering them.

XVI. But, in my opinion, this manner of anſwering the queſtion is altogether arbitrary, and has no foundation in nature. I ſee no reaſon why the prizes, taken from the enemy, ſhould not become our property as ſoon as they are taken. For when two nations are at war, both of them have all the requisites for the acquisition of property, at the very moment they take a prize. They have an intention to acquire a title of just property, namely, the right of war; and they are actually in possession of the thing. But if the principle, which *Grotius* supposes, was to be allowed, and the prizes taken from the enemy were not deemed a lawful acquisition, till they are transported to a place of safety, it would follow, that the booty which a small number of soldiers has taken from an enemy, may be retaken from them by a stronger body of troops of the same party, as still belonging to the enemy, if this second body of troops has attacked the first before they had conveyed their booty to a place of safety.

XVII. This last circumstance is therefore altogether indifferent, with respect to the present question. The greater or smaller difficulty the enemy may find, in recovering what has been taken from him, does not hinder the capture from actually belonging to the conqueror. Every enemy as such, and so long as he continues such, always retains the will to recover what the other has taken from him; and his present inability only reduces him to the necessity of waiting for a more favourable opportunity, which he still seeks and desires. Hence, with respect to him, the thing ought no more to be deemed taken, when in a place of safety, than when he is still in a condition of pursuing it. All that can be said, is, that in the latter case, the possession of the conqueror is not so secure as in the former. The truth is, this distinction has been invented

vented only to eſtabliſh the rules of the right of poſtliminy, or the manner in which the ſubjects of the ſtate, from whom ſomething has been taken in war, re-enter upon their rights; rather than to determine the time of the acquiſition of things taken by one enemy from another.

XVIII. This to me ſeems to be what the law of nature determines in this point. *Grotius* obſerves alſo, that by the cuſtoms eſtabliſhed in his time among the ſtates of *Europe*, it is ſufficient that the prize has been twenty four hours in the enemy's poſſeſſion, to account it loſt. *Thuanus*, in his hiſtory on the year 1595, gives us an example, that this cuſtom was obſerved alſo by land. The town of *Liere* in *Brabant* having been taken and re-taken the ſame day, the plunder was returned to the inhabitants, becauſe it had not been twenty-four hours in the hands of the enemy. But this rule was afterwards changed, with reſpect to the *United Provinces*; and in general we may obſerve, that every ſovereign has a right to eſtabliſh ſuch rules, in regard to this point, as he thinks proper, and to make what agreements he pleaſes with other powers. There have been ſeveral made, at different times, between the *Dutch* and *Spaniards*, the *Portugueze* and the northern ſtates.

XIX. *Grotius* applies theſe principles alſo to lands; they are not to be reputed loſt as ſoon as they are ſeized on, but for this effect they are to be ſo ſecured with durable fortifications, that, without being forced, they cannot be repoſſeſs'd by the firſt owner.

owner. But to this caſe we may alſo apply the reflections already made. A territory belongs to an enemy as ſoon as he is maſter of it, and as long as he continues in poſſeſſion of it. The greater, or leſſer precautions he may take to ſecure it, are nothing to the purpoſe.

XX. But be this as it may, it is to be obſerved, that during the whole time of the war, the right we acquire over the things we have taken from the enemy, is of force only with reſpect to a third diſintereſted party; for the enemy himſelf may retake what he has loſt, whenever he finds an opportunity, till by a treaty of peace he has renounced all his pretenſions.

XXI. It is alſo certain, that in order to appropriate a thing by the right of war, it muſt belong to the enemy; for things belonging to people who are neither his ſubjects, nor animated with the ſame ſpirit as he againſt us, cannot be taken by the right of war, even tho' they are found in the enemy's country. But if neutral ſtrangers furniſh our enemy with any thing, and that with a deſign to put him into a condition of hurting us, they may be looked upon as taking part with our enemy, and their effects may conſequently be taken by the right of war.

XXII. It is however to be obſerved, that in dubious caſes it is always to be preſumed, that what we find in the enemy's country, or in their ſhips, is deemed to belong to them; for beſides that this pre-

presumption is very natural, if the contrary maxim was to take place, it would lay a foundation for an infinite number of frauds. But this presumption, however reasonable in itself, may be destroyed by contrary proofs.

XXIII. Neither do the ships of friends become lawful prizes, tho' some of the enemy's effects are found in them, unless it is done by the consent of the owners; who by that means seem to violate the neutrality, or friendship, and give us a just right to treat them as an enemy.

XXIV. But in general we must observe, with respect to all these questions, that prudence and good policy require, that sovereigns should come to some agreement among themselves in regard to these different cases, in order to avoid the disputes which may arise from them.

XXV. Let us also take notice of a consequence of the principles here established; which is, that when we have taken things from the enemy, which he himself had taken from another by the right of war, the former possessor cannot claim them.

XXVI. Another question is, whether things, taken in a public and solemn war, belong to the state, or to the individuals who are members of it, or to those who made the first seizure? I answer, that as the right of war is lodged in the sovereign alone, and is undertaken by his authority, all that is taken is originally and

pri

primarily acquired to him, whatever hands it firſt falls into.

XXVII. However, as the war is burdenſome to the ſubjects, both equity and humanity require that the ſovereign ſhould make them partake of the advantages which may accrue from it. This may be done, either by aſſigning to thoſe who take the field a certain pay from the public, or by ſharing the booty among them. As to foreign troops, the ſovereign is obliged to give them no more than their pay; what he gives them above that, is pure liberality.

XXVIII. *Grotius*, who examines this queſtion at large, diſtinguiſhes between acts of hoſtility truly public, and private acts that are done upon the occaſion of a public war. By the latter, according to him, private perſons acquire to themſelves principally, and directly, what they take from the enemy; whereas, by the former, every thing taken belongs to the whole body of the people, or to the ſovereign. But this deciſion has been juſtly criticiſed upon. As all public war is made by the authority of the people, or of their chief, it is from this ſource we muſt originally derive whatever right individuals may have to things taken from the enemy. In this caſe there muſt always be an expreſs or tacit conſent of the ſovereign.

XXIX. It is alſo to be obſerved, that in treating this point *Grotius* has confounded different things. The queſtion does not relate to the law of nations, properly

properly ſo called; for in whatever manner that law is underſtood, and whatever it be founded on, it ought to relate to the affairs in diſpute between two different ſtates: Now whether the booty belongs to the ſovereign who makes war, or to the generals, or to the ſoldiers, or to other perſons, who take any thing from the enemy; that is nothing to the enemy, nor to other ſtates. If what is taken be a good prize, it is of ſmall conſequence to the enemy in whoſe hands it remains. As to neutral people, it is ſufficient that ſuch of them as have purchaſed, or any other way acquired a moveable thing taken in war, cannot be moleſted, or proſecuted upon that account. The truth is, the regulations and cuſtoms, relating to this ſubject, are not of public right; and their conformity, in many countries, implies no more than a civil right, common to ſeveral nations ſeparately.

XXX. As for what in particular relates to the acquiſition of *incorporeal things* by the right of war; it is to be obſerved, that they do not become our property, except we are in poſſeſſion of the ſubject in which they inhere. Now the ſubjects they inhere in, are either things or perſons. We often annex, for inſtance, to certain lands, rivers, ports and towns, particular rights, which always follow them, whatever poſſeſſors they come to; or rather, thoſe who poſſeſs them, are thereby inveſted with certain rights over other things and perſons.

XXXI. The rights which belong directly and immediately to perſons, regard either other perſons, or

only

only certain things. Thoſe which are annexed to perſons over other perſons, are not obtained but with the conſent of the perſons themſelves; who are ſuppoſed not to have given a power over them to any man promiſcuouſly, but to ſome certain perſon. Thus, for inſtance, tho' a king happen to be made priſoner of war, his enemies have not therefore acquired his kingdom with him.

XXXII. But with reſpect to perſonal rights over things, the bare ſeizure of the perſon of the enemy, is not a ſufficient title to the property of all his effects, unleſs we really take poſſeſſion of theſe effects at the ſame time. This may be illuſtrated by the example, given by *Grotius* and *Puffendorf*, of the preſent which *Alexander the Great* made to the *Theſſalians*, after having deſtroyed the city of *Thebes*, of an inſtrument, in which the *Theſſalians* acknowledged that they owed the *Thebans* a hundred talents.

XXXIII. Theſe are the rights which war gives us over the effects of the enemy. But *Grotius* pretends, that the right by which we acquire things taken from the enemy, is ſo proper and peculiar to a ſolemn war, declared in form, that it has no force in others, as in civil wars, *&c.* and that in civil wars, in particular, there is no change of property, but in virtue of the ſentence of a judge.

XXXIV. We may obſerve, however, upon this point, that in moſt civil wars no common judge is acknowledged. If the ſtate is monarchical, the diſpute turns either upon the ſucceſſion to the crown, or or upon a conſiderable part of the ſtate's pretending that the king has abuſed his power, in a manner which authoriſes the ſubject to take up arms againſt him.

XXXV. In the firſt caſe, the very nature of the cauſe, for which the war is undertaken, occaſions the two parties of the ſtate to form, as it were, two diſtinct bodies, till they come to agree upon a chief by ſome treaty. Thus, with reſpect to the two parties which were at war, it is on ſuch a treaty that the right depends, which perſons may have to that which has been taken on either ſide; and nothing hinders, but this right may be left on the ſame footing, and admitted to take place in the ſame manner, as in public wars between two ſtates always diſtinct.

XXXVI. As to other nations, who were not concerned in the war, they have no more authority to examine the validity of the acquiſitions, than they have to be judges of a war made between two different ſtates.

XXXVII. The other caſe, I mean an inſurrection of a conſiderable part of the ſtate againſt the reigning prince, can rarely happen, except when that prince has given room for it, either by tyranny, or by the violation of the fundamental laws of the kingdom. Thus the government is then diſſolved, and the ſtate is actually divided into two diſtinct and independent bodies; ſo that we are to form here the ſame judgment as in the firſt caſe.

XXXVIII.

XXXVIII. For much ſtronger reaſons does this take place in the civil wars of a republican ſtate; in which the war, immediately of itſelf, deſtroys the ſovereignty, which ſubſiſts ſolely in the union of its members.

XXXIX. *Grotius* ſeems to have taken his ideas on this ſubject from the *Roman* laws; for theſe decreed, that priſoners taken in a civil war could not be reduced to ſlavery. This was, as *Ulpian* the civilian * remarks, becauſe they looked upon a civil war not properly as a war, but as a *civil diſſenſion*; for, adds he, a real war is made between thoſe who are enemies, and animated with a hoſtile ſpirit, which prompts them to endeavour the ruin of each other's ſtate. Whereas, in a civil war, however hurtful it often proves to the nation, the one wants to ſave itſelf in one manner, and the other in another. Thus they are not enemies, and every perſon of the two parties remains always a citizen of the ſtate ſo divided.

XL. But all this is a ſuppoſition, or *fiction of right*, which does not hinder what I have been ſaying from being true, and from taking place in general. And if, among the *Romans*, a perſon could not appropriate to himſelf the priſoners taken in a civil war, as real ſlaves, this was in virtue of a particular law received among them, and not on account of any defect of the conditions, or formalities, which, according to *Grotius*, are required by the law of nations, in a public or ſolemn war.

* Lib. XXI. ſect. 1. ff. de capt. & reverſ.

XLI. Laſtly, as for the wars of robbers and pirates, if they do not produce the effects we have mentioned; if they do not give to theſe pirates a right of appropriating what they have taken, it is becauſe theſe people are robbers, and enemies to mankind, and conſequently perſons whoſe acts of hoſtility are manifeſtly unjuſt, which authoriſes all nations to treat them as enemies. Whereas, in other kinds of war, it is often difficult to judge on which ſide the right lies; ſo that the diſpute continues, and ought to continue, undecided, with reſpect to thoſe who are unconcerned in the war.

CHAP. VIII.

Of the right of ſovereignty acquired over the conquered.

I. BEſides the effects of war, hitherto mentioned, there remains one more, the moſt important of all, and which we ſhall here conſider; I mean the right of ſovereignty acquired over the conquered. We have already remarked, when explaining the different ways of acquiring ſovereignty, that in general it may be acquired either in a violent manner, and by the right of conqueſt, *&c.*

II. We muſt however obſerve, that war or conqueſt, conſidered in itſelf, is not properly the cauſe of this acquiſition; that is, it is not the ſource, or immediate origin of ſovereignty. This is always founded on the tacit or expreſs conſent of the people, without which the ſtate of war ſtill ſubſiſts; for we cannot conceive how there can be an obligation to obey a perſon, to whom we have promiſed no ſubjection. War then is, properly ſpeaking, no more than the occaſion of obtaining the ſovereignty; as the conquered chuſe rather to ſubmit to the victor's ſway, than to expoſe themſelves to total deſtruction.

III. Beſides, the acquiſition of ſovereignty by the right of conqueſt cannot, ſtrictly ſpeaking, paſs for lawful, unleſs the war be juſt in itſelf; and unleſs the lawful end propoſed, authoriſes the conqueror to puſh the acts of hoſtility ſo far, as to acquire the ſovereignty over the vanquiſhed: that is to ſay, either our enemy muſt have no other means of paying what he owes us, and of indemnifying us for the damages he has committed; or our own ſafety muſt abſolutely oblige us to make him dependent on us. In theſe circumſtances, it is certain that the reſiſtance of a vanquiſhed enemy, authoriſes us to puſh the acts of hoſtility againſt him ſo far, as to reduce him entirely under our power; and we may, without injuſtice, take advantage of the ſuperiority of our arms, to extort from him the conſent which he ought to give us voluntarily, and of his own accord.

IV. Theſe are the true principles on which ſovereignty, by the right of conqueſt, is grounded. Hence we may conclude, that if, upon theſe foundations, we were to judge of the different acquiſitions of this nature, few of them would be found well

well eſtabliſhed; for it rarely happens, that the vanquiſhed are really reduced to ſuch an extremity, as not to be able to ſatisfy the juſt pretenſions of the conqueror, otherwiſe than by ſurrendering, and ſubmitting themſelves to his dominion.

V. Let us however obſerve, that the intereſt and tranquillity of nations require, that we ſhould deviate a little from the rigour of the principles now eſtabliſhed. Indeed, if he who has conſtrained another, by the ſuperiority of his arms, to ſubmit to his ſway, had undertaken a war manifeſtly unjuſt, or if the pretext, on which it is founded, is viſibly frivolous in the judgment of every reaſonable perſon, I confeſs that a ſovereignty, acquired in theſe circumſtances, would to me appear viſibly unjuſt; and I ſee no reaſon, why the vanquiſhed people ſhould be more obliged to keep ſuch a treaty, than a man, who had fallen into the hands of robbers, would be obliged to pay, at their demand, the money he had promiſed them for the ranſom of his life and liberty.

VI. But if the conqueror had undertaken a war for ſome ſpecious reaſon, tho' perhaps at the bottom not ſtrictly juſt, the common intereſt of mankind requires, that we ſhould exactly obſerve the engagements we have entered into with him, tho' extorted by a terror in itſelf unjuſt; ſo long, at leaſt, as no new reaſon ſupervenes, which may lawfully exempt us from keeping our promiſe. For as the law of nature directs that ſocieties, as well as individuals, ſhould labour for their preſervation, it obliges us, for this reaſon, not indeed to conſider the acts of hoſtility committed by an unjuſt conqueror as properly juſt, but to look upon the engagement of an expreſs, or tacit treaty, as nevertheleſs valid. So that the vanquiſhed cannot be releaſed from keeping it, under the pretext of its being cauſed by an unjuſt fear, as he might otherwiſe do, had he no regard to the advantages accruing from it to mankind.

VII. Theſe conſiderations will have ſtill a greater weight, if we ſuppoſe that the conqueror, or his poſterity, peaceably enjoy the ſovereignty which he has acquired by right of conqueſt; and beſides, that he govern the vanquiſhed like a humane and generous conqueror. In theſe circumſtances, a long poſſeſſion, accompanied with an equitable government, may legitimate a conqueſt, in its beginning and principle the moſt unjuſt.

VIII. There are modern civilians, who explain the thing ſomewhat differently. Theſe maintain, that in a juſt war the victor acquires a full right of ſovereignty over the vanquiſhed, by the ſingle right of conqueſt, independently of any convention; and even though the victor has otherwiſe obtained all the ſatisfaction, and indemnification, he could require.

IX. The principal reaſon theſe doctors make uſe of to prove their opinion, is, that otherwiſe the conqueror could not be certain of the peaceable poſſeſſion of what he has taken, or forced the conquered

to

to give him, for his juſt pretenſions; ſince they might retake it from him, by the ſame right of war.

X. But this reaſon proves only that the conqueror, who has taken poſſeſſion of the enemy's country, may command in it while he holds it, and not reſign it, 'till he has good ſecurity that he ſhall obtain or poſſeſs, without hazard, what is neceſſary for the ſatisfaction and indemnity, which he has a right to exact by force. But the end of a juſt war does not always demand, of itſelf, that the conqueror ſhould acquire an abſolute and perpetual right of ſovereignty over the conquered. It is only a favourable occaſion of obtaining it; and for that purpoſe, there muſt always be an expreſs or tacit conſent of the vanquiſhed. Otherwiſe, the ſtate of war ſtill ſubſiſting, the ſovereignty of the conqueror has no other title than that of force, and laſts no longer than the vanquiſhed are unable to throw off the yoke.

XI. All that can be ſaid, is, that the neutral powers, purely becauſe they are ſuch, may, and ought to look upon the conqueror as the lawful poſſeſſor of the ſovereignty, even tho' they ſhould believe the war unjuſt on his ſide.

XII. The ſovereignty thus acquired by the right of war, is generally of the abſolute kind. But ſometimes the vanquiſhed enter into certain conditions with the conqueror, which put ſome limitations to the power he acquires over them. Be this as it may, it is certain that no conqueſt ever au-

 thoriſes

thorises a prince to govern a people tyrannically; since, as we have before shewn, the most absolute sovereignty gives no right to oppress those who have surrendered; for even the thing itself, and the laws of nature, equally conspire to lay the conqueror under an obligation, to govern those whom he has subdued, with moderation and equity.

XIII. There are, therefore, several precautions to be used in the exercise of the sovereignty acquired over the vanquished; such, for instance, was that prudent moderation of the antient *Romans*, who confounded, in some measure, the vanquished with the victors, by hasting to incorporate them with themselves, and to make them sharers of their liberty and advantages. A piece of policy doubly salutary; which, at the same time that it render'd the condition of the vanquish'd more agreeable, considerably strengthened the power and empire of the *Romans*. "What would our empire now have been," says *Seneca*, "if the vanquish'd had not been intermixed with "the victors, by the effect of a sound policy?" "*Romulus*, our founder," says *Claudius* in *Tacitus*, "was very wise with respect to most of the peo-"ple he subdued, by making those, who were his "enemies, the same day citizens."

XIV. Another moderation in victory, consists in leaving to the conquered, either kings or people, the sovereignty which they enjoyed, and not to change the form of their government. No better method can be taken to secure a conquest; and of this we have several examples in antient

antient hiſtory, eſpecially in that of the *Romans*.

XV. But if the conqueror cannot, without danger to himſelf, grant all theſe advantages to the conquered; yet things may be ſo moderated, that ſome part of the ſovereignty ſhall be left to them, or to their kings. Even when we ſtrip the vanquiſh'd intirely of their ſovereignty, we may ſtill leave them their own laws, cuſtoms, and magiſtrates, in regard to their private and public affairs, of ſmall importance.

XVI. We muſt not, above all things, deprive the vanquiſh'd of the exerciſe of their religion, unleſs they happen to be convinced of the truth of that which the conqueror profeſſes. This complaiſance is not only of itſelf very agreeable to the vanquiſh'd, but the conqueror is abſolutely obliged to it; and he cannot, without tyranny, oppreſs them in this reſpect. Not that he ought not to try to bring the vanquiſh'd to the true religion; but he ought only to uſe ſuch means, as are proportioned to the nature of the thing, and to the end he has in view; and ſuch as have in themſelves nothing violent, or contrary to humanity.

XVII. Let us obſerve, laſtly, that not only humanity, but prudence alſo, and even the intereſt of the conqueror, require that what we have been ſaying, with reſpect to a vanquiſh'd people, ſhould be ſtrictly practiſed. It is an important maxim in politics, that it is more difficult to keep, than to conquer provinces.

vinces. Conquefts demand no more than force, but juftice muft preferve them. Thefe are the principal things to be obferved, in refpect to the different effects of war, and to the moft effential queftions relative thereto. But as we have already had occafion to fpeak of neutrality, it will not be improper to fay fomething more particular about it.

Of Neutrality.

I. There is a *general*, and a *particular neutrality.* The general is, when without being allied to either of the two enemies at war, we are difpofed to render to each the good offices which every nation is naturally obliged to render to others.

II. The particular neutrality is, when we are particularly engaged to be neuter by fome compact, either tacit or exprefs.

III. The laft fpecies of neutrality is either full and intire, when we act equally in all refpects towards both parties; or limited, as when we favour one fide more than the other, with refpect to certain things or actions.

IV. We cannot lawfully conftrain any perfon to enter into a particular neutrality; becaufe every one is at liberty to make, or not make particular treaties, or alliances, and becaufe, at leaft, they are not bound to do it but by virtue of an imperfect obligation. But he, who has undertaken a juft war, may oblige other

other nations to observe an exact and general neutrality; that is to say, not to favour his enemy more than himself.

V. We shall give here an abstract, as it were, of the duties of neutral nations. They are obliged equally to put in practise, towards both parties at war, the laws of nature, as well absolute as conditional, whether they impose a perfect, or only an imperfect obligation.

VI. If they do the one any office of humanity, they ought not to refuse the like to the other, unless there is some manifest reason which engages them to do something in favour of the one, which the other had otherwise no right to demand.

VII. But they are not obliged to do offices of humanity to one party, when they expose themselves to great dangers, by refusing them to the other, who has as good a right to demand them.

VIII. They ought not to furnish either party with things which serve to exercise acts of hostility, unless they are authorised to do it by some particular engagement; and as for those which are of no use in war, if they supply one side with them, they must also the other.

IX. They ought to use all their endeavours to bring matters to an accommodation, that the injured party may obtain satisfaction, and that the war may be brought to a speedy conclusion.

X.

X. But if they are under any particular engagement, they ought to fulfill it punctually.

XI. On the other ſide, thoſe who are at war muſt exactly obſerve, towards neutral nations, the laws of ſociability, and not exerciſe any acts of hoſtility againſt them, nor ſuffer their country to be ravaged or plundered.

XII. They may however, in a caſe of neceſſity, take poſſeſſion of a place ſituated in a neutral country; provided, that as ſoon as the danger is over, they reſtore it to the right owner, and make him ſatisfaction for the damages he has received.

CHAP. IX.

Of public treaties in general.

I. THE ſubject of public treaties conſtitutes a conſiderable part of the law of nations, and deſerves to have its principles and rules explained with ſome exactneſs. By public treaties, we mean ſuch agreements as can be made only by public authority, or thoſe which ſovereigns, conſidered as ſuch, make with each other, concerning things which directly concern the good of the ſtate. This is what diſtinguiſhes theſe agreements, not only from thoſe which individuals make with each other, but alſo from the contracts of kings, in regard to their private affairs.

II.

II. What we have before obſerved, concerning the neceſſity of introducing conventions betwixt private men, and the advantages ariſing from them, may be applied to nations and different ſtates. Nations may, by means of treaties, unite themſelves more particularly into a ſociety, which ſhall reciprocally aſſure them of ſeaſonable aſſiſtance, either for the neceſſaries and conveniences of life, or to provide for their greater ſecurity upon the breaking out of a war.

III. As this is the caſe, ſovereigns are no leſs obliged, than individuals, inviolably to keep their word, and be faithful to their engagements. The law of nations makes this an indiſpenſable duty; for it is evident, that were it otherwiſe, not only public treaties would be uſeleſs to nations, but moreover, that the violation of theſe would throw them into a ſtate of diffidence and continual war; that is to ſay, into the moſt terrible ſituation. The obligation therefore of ſovereigns, in this reſpect, is ſo much the ſtronger, as the violation of this duty has more dangerous conſequences, which intereſt the happineſs of numbers of individuals. The ſanctity of an oath, which generally accompanies public treaties, is an additional motive to engage princes to obſerve them with the utmoſt fidelity; and certainly nothing is more ſhameful for ſovereigns, who ſo rigorouſly puniſh ſuch of their ſubjects as fail in their engagements, than to ſport with treaties and public faith, and to look upon them only as the means of deceiving each other.

The royal word ought therefore to be inviolable, and ſacred. But there is reaſon to fear, that if princes

princes are not more attentive to this point, this expression will ſoon degenerate into an oppoſite ſenſe, in the ſame manner as formerly *Carthaginian faith* * was taken for perfidy.

IV. We muſt alſo obſerve, that all the principles we have heretofore eſtabliſhed concerning the validity, or invalidity of conventions in general, agree to public treaties, as well as to the contracts of inviduals. In both, therefore, there muſt be a ſerious conſent, properly declared, and exempt from *error*, *fraud*, and *violence*.

V. If treaties, made in theſe circumſtances, are obligatory between the reſpective ſtates or ſovereigns, they are alſo obligatory, with regard to the ſubjects of each prince in particular. They oblige, as compacts between the contracting powers; but they have the force of laws, with reſpect to the ſubjects conſidered as ſuch; for it is evident that two ſovereigns, who conclude a treaty, lay their ſubjects thereby under an obligation of doing nothing contrary to it.

VI. There are ſeveral diſtinctions of public treaties; and 1°. ſome turn ſimply on things, to which we were obliged by the law of nature before; and others ſuperadd ſome particulars to the duties of natural law.

VII. Under the firſt head we may rank all thoſe treaties, by which we are purely and ſimply en-

* Punica fides.

gaged to do no harm to others, but, on the contrary, to perform all the duties of humanity towards them. Among civilifed nations, who profefs to follow the laws of nature, fuch treaties are not neceffary. Duty alone is fufficient, without a formal engagement. But among the antients thefe treaties were thought expedient, the common opinion being, that they were obliged to obferve the laws of humanity only to fellow-fubjects, and that they might confider all ftrangers as enemies, and treat them as fuch, unlefs they had entered into fome engagement to the contrary: and of this we have many inftances in hiftory. The profeffion of free-booter, or pirate, was no way fhameful among feveral nations; and the word *hoftis*, which the *Romans* ufed to exprefs an enemy, originally fignified no more than a ftranger.

VIII. Under the fecond kind I comprehend all thofe compacts, by which two nations enter into fome new, or more particular obligation, with refpect to each other; as when they formally engage to things to which they were not obliged, but in virtue of an imperfect obligation, or even to which they were no ways before obliged.

IX. 2°. Treaties, by which we engage to fomething more than what we were obliged to, in virtue of the law of nature, are alfo of two kinds; fome *equal*, others *unequal*.

3°. Both are made either in time of war, or in full peace.

X.

X. Equal treaties, are thoſe contracted with an entire equality on both ſides; that is to ſay, when not only the engagements and promiſes are equal on both ſides, either purely and ſimply, or in proportion to the ſtrength of each contracting party; but alſo, when they engage on the ſame footing; ſo that neither of the parties is in any reſpect inferior to the other.

XI. Theſe treaties are made, either with a view to *commerce*, or to community of war, or, in ſhort, to any other matter. With reſpect to commerce, for example, by ſtipulating that the ſubjects, on either ſide, ſhall be free from all cuſtom or toll, or that no more ſhall be demanded of them, than of the natives of the country, *&c.* Equal treaties, or leagues relating to war, are, when we ſtipulate, for example, that each ſhall furniſh the other an equal number of troops, ſhips, and other things; and this in all kinds of war, defenſive as well as offenſive, or in defenſive only, *&c.* Laſtly, treaties of equality may alſo turn upon any other matter; as when it is agreed, that one ſhall have no forts on the other's frontiers; that one ſhall not grant protection to the other's ſubjects, in ſome criminal caſes, but order them to be ſeized and ſent back; that one ſhall not give the other's enemies paſſage thro' his country, and the like.

XII. What we have been ſaying, ſufficiently ſhews the meaning of unequal treaties. And theſe are, when the promiſes are either unequal, or ſuch as lay harder conditions on one of the parties, than on the other. The inequality of the things ſtipulated, is ſometimes on the ſide of the moſt powerful confederate, as when he promiſes his aſſiſtance to the other, without requiring the like; and ſometimes, on the ſide of the inferior confederate, as when he engages to do more for the ſtronger, than the latter promiſes in return.

XIII. All the conditions of unequal treaties are not of the ſame nature; ſome there are, which tho' burdenſome to the inferior ally, yet leave the ſovereignty entire; others, on the contrary, include a diminution of the independance, and ſovereignty of the inferior ally.

Thus, in the treaties between the *Romans* and the *Carthaginians*, at the end of the ſecond *Punic war*, it was ſtipulated, that the *Carthaginians* ſhould not begin any war, without the conſent of the *Roman* people; an article which evidently diminiſhed the ſovereignty of *Carthage*, and made her dependant on *Rome*.

But the ſovereignty of the inferior ally continues entire, tho' he engages, for example, to pay the other's army, to defray the expences of the war, to diſmantle ſome towns, to give hoſtages, to look upon all thoſe as friends or enemies, who are friends or enemies to the other, to have no forts, or ſtrong holds in certain parts, to avoid ſailing in particular ſeas, to acknowledge the pre-eminence of the other, and, upon occaſion, to ſhew reverence and honour to his power and majeſty, *&c.*

XIV. However, tho' theſe, and other ſimilar conditions,

ditions, do not diminish the sovereignty, it is certain that such treaties of inequality are often of so delicate a nature, as to require the greatest circumspection in managing them; and that if the prince, who is superior to the other in dignity, surpasses him also considerably in strength and power, it is to be feared that the former will gradually acquire an absolute sovereignty over him, especially if the confederacy be perpetual.

XV. 4°. Public treaties are also divided into *real* and *personal.* The latter are those made with a prince, purely in regard to his person, and expire with him. The former are such, as are made rather with the whole body of the state, than with the king or government, and which consequently outlive those who made them, and oblige their successors.

XVI. To know which of these two classes every treaty belongs to, the following rules may be laid down.

1°. We must first attend to the form and phrase of the treaty, to its clauses, and the views proposed by the contracting parties. *Utrum autem in rem, an in personam factum est, non minus ex verbis, quam ex mente convenientium æstimandum est* *. Thus, if there is an express clause that the treaty is perpetual, or for a certain number of years, or for the good of the state, or with the king for him and his successors, we may conclude that the treaty is real.

* Leg. VII. sect. VIII. ff. de Pactis.

2°. Every

2°. Every treaty made with a republic, is in its own nature real, becauſe the ſubject, with whom we contract it, is a thing permanent.

3°. Tho' the government ſhould happen to be changed from a republic into a monarchy, the treaty is ſtill in force, becauſe the body is ſtill the ſame, and has only another chief.

4°. We muſt however make an exception here, which is, when it appears that the preſervation of the republican government was the true cauſe of the treaty; as when two republics enter into an alliance, by which they agree to aſſiſt one another, againſt ſuch as ſhall endeavour by force to alter their conſtitution, and deprive them of their liberties.

5°. In caſe of doubt, every public treaty made with a king ought to be deemed real, becauſe, in dubious caſes, the king is ſuppoſed to act as chief, and for the good of the ſtate.

6°. Hence it follows, that as after the change of a democracy into a monarchy, the treaty is ſtill in force, in regard to the new king; ſo if the government, from a monarchy, becomes a republic, the treaty made with the king does not expire, unleſs it was manifeſtly perſonal.

7°. Every treaty of peace is real in its own nature, and ought to be kept by the ſucceſſors; for as ſoon as the conditions of the treaty have been punctually fulfilled, the peace effectually effaces the injuries which excited the war, and reſtores the nations to their natural ſituation.

8°. If one of the confederates has performed what the treaty obliged him to, and the other ſhould die before he performs the engagements on his part, the ſucceſſor of the deceaſed king is obliged either intirely to indemnify the other party for what he has performed, or to fulfill his predeceſſor's engagement.

9°. But if nothing is executed on either part, or the performances on both ſides are equal, then if the treaty tends directly to the perſonal advantage of the king, or his family, it is evident, that as ſoon as he dies, or his family is extinct, the treaty muſt alſo expire.

10°. Laſtly, we muſt obſerve that it is grown into a cuſtom for ſucceſſors to renew, at leaſt in general terms, even the treaties manifeſtly acknowledged for real, that they may be the more ſtrongly bound to obſerve them, and may not think themſelves diſpenſed from that obligation, under a pretext that they have different ideas concerning the intereſts of the ſtate, from thoſe of their predeceſſors.

XVII. Concerning treaties, or alliances, it is often diſputed, whether they may be lawfully made with thoſe who do not profeſs the true religion? I anſwer, that by the law of nature there is no difficulty in this point. The right of making alliances is common to all men, and has nothing oppoſite to the principles of true religion; which is ſo far from condemning prudence and humanity, that it ſtrongly recommends both *.

XVIII. To judge rightly of the cauſes which put

* See Grotius on war and peace, lib. II. ch. xv. ſect. 8, 9, 10, 11, 12.

an end to public treaties, we muſt carefully attend to the rules of conventions in general.

1°. Thus a treaty, concluded for a certain time, expires at the end of the term agreed on.

2°. When a treaty is once expired, it muſt not be ſuppoſed to be tacitly renewed; for a new obligation is not eaſily preſumed.

3°. And therefore, if after the treaty expires, ſome acts are continued, which ſeem conformable to the terms of the preceding alliance, they ought rather to be looked upon as ſimple marks of friendſhip and benevolence, than as a tacit renovation of the treaty.

4°. We muſt however make this exception, unleſs ſuch acts intervene, as can bear no other conſtruction, than that of a tacit renovation of the preceding compact. Thus, for example, if one ally has engaged to pay another a certain ſum annually, and after the expiration of the term of the alliance, the ſame ſum is paid the following year, the alliance is tacitly renewed for that year.

5°. It is a conſequence of the nature of all compacts in general, that when one of the parties violates the engagements into which he had entered by treaty, the other is freed, and may refuſe to ſtand to the agreement; for generally each article of the treaty has the force of a condition, the want of which renders it void.

6°. This is generally the caſe, that is to ſay, when there is no agreement otherwiſe; for ſometimes this clauſe is inſerted, that the violation of any ſingle article of the treaty ſhall not break it intirely, to the end that neither party ſhould fly from their engagements for every ſlight offence. But he who, by the action of another, ſuffers any damage, ought to be indemnified in ſome ſhape or another.

XIX. None but the ſovereign can make alliances and treaties, either by himſelf, or by his officers and miniſters. Treaties concluded by miniſters, oblige the ſovereign and the ſtates, only when the miniſters have been duly authoriſed to make them, and have done nothing contrary to their orders and inſtructions. And here it may be obſerved, that among the *Romans* the word *fœdus*, *a public compact*, or *ſolemn agreement*, ſignified a treaty made by order of the ſovereign power, or that had been afterwards ratified; but when public perſons, or miniſters of ſtate, had promiſed ſomething relating to the ſovereign power, without advice and command from it, this was called *ſponſio*, or a ſimple promiſe and engagement.

XX. In general it is certain, that when miniſters, without the order of their ſovereign, conclude a treaty concerning public affairs, the ſovereign is not obliged to ſtand to it; and the miniſter, who has entered into the negotiation without inſtructions, may be puniſhed according to the exigence of the caſe. However, there may be circumſtances in which a ſovereign is obliged, either by the rules of prudence, or even thoſe of juſtice and equity, to ratify a treaty, tho' concluded without his orders.

XXI. When a ſovereign is informed of a treaty, made by one of his miniſters without his orders, his *silence* alone does not imply a *ratification*, unless it is accompanied with some act, or other circumstance, which cannot well bear another explication. And much more, if the agreement was made upon condition of its being ratified by the sovereign, it is of no force till the sovereign has ratified it in a formal and express manner.

CHAP. X.

Of compacts made with an enemy.

I. AMONG public compacts, those which suppose *a state of war*, and are made with an enemy, deserve a particular attention. There are two kinds of these; some which do not put an end to the war, but only moderate or suspend the acts of hostility; and others, which end the war intirely. But before we consider these compacts in particular, let us first inquire into the validity of them in general.

Whether we ought to keep our faith given to an enemy?

II. This question is certainly one of the most beautiful and important belonging to the law of nations. *Grotius* and *Puffendorf* are not agreed in this point. The former maintains generally, that all compacts made with an enemy ought to be kept with an inviolable fidelity. But *Puffendorf* is somewhat dubious with respect to these compacts, which leave us in a state of war, without a design to remove it. Let us therefore endeavour to establish some principles, by means of which we may determine with respect to these two opinions.

III. I observe, 1°. That tho' war of itself destroys the state of society between two nations, we must not thence conclude that it is subjected to no law, and that all right and obligation are absolutely at an end between two enemies.

2°. On the contrary, every body grants that there is a right of war, obligatory of itself, between enemies, and which they cannot break thro', without being defective in their duty. This is what we have proved before, by shewing that there are just and unjust wars; and that even in the justest, it is not allowable to push acts of hostility to the utmost extremity, but that we ought to keep within certain bounds; and consequently, that there are things *unjust* and *unlawful*, even with respect to an enemy. Since therefore war does not, of itself, subvert all the laws of society, we cannot from this alone conclude, that because two nations are at war with each other, they are dispensed from keeping their word, and from fulfilling the engagements they have made with each other, during the course of the war.

3°. As war is in itself a very great evil, it is the common interest of nations, not to deprive themselves voluntarily of the means which prudence suggests to moderate the rigour, and to suspend the effects of it. On the contrary, it is their duty to endeavour to procure these means, and to make use of them upon occasion; so far at least, as the attainment of the lawful end of war will permit. Now there is nothing but *public faith* that can procure, to the parties engaged in war, the liberty to take breath; nothing but this can ſecure to towns, that have ſurrendered, the ſeveral rights which they have reſerved by capitulation. What advantage would a nation gain, or rather, what is it they would not loſe, if they were to have no regard to their faith given to an enemy, and if they looked upon compacts, made in ſuch circumſtances, only as the means of circumventing one another? Surely it is not to be ſuppoſed, that the law of nature approves of maxims ſo manifeſtly oppoſite to the common good of mankind. Beſides, we ought never to wage war, purely for the ſake of it, but only thro' neceſſity, in order to obtain a juſt and reaſonable ſatisfaction and a ſolid peace; from whence it evidently follows, that the right of war between enemies cannot extend ſo far, as to render hoſtilities perpetual, and to create an invincible obſtacle to the re-eſtabliſhment of the public tranquillity.

4°. And yet this would certainly be the conſequence, if the law of nature did not lay us under an indiſpenſable obligation of performing whatever agreement we have voluntarily made with the enemy during the war; whether theſe agreements tend only to ſuſpend, or moderate acts of hoſtility, or whether they are deſigned to make them ceaſe intirely, and to re-eſtabliſh peace.

For, in ſhort, there are only two ways of obtaining peace. The firſt is, the total and entire deſtruction of our enemy; and the ſecond is, the entering into articles of treaty with him. If therefore treaties and compacts, made between enemies, were not in themſelves ſacred and inviolable, there would

 be

be no other means of procuring a ſolid peace, than carrying on the war to the utmoſt extremity, and to the total ruin of our enemies. But who does not ſee that a principle, which tends neceſſarily to the deſtruction of mankind and ſocieties, is directly contrary to the law of nature and nations, whoſe principal end is the preſervation and happineſs of human ſociety in general, and of civil ſocieties in particular?

5°. We can make no diſtinction, in this reſpect, between the different treaties that we may enter into with an enemy; for the obligation which the laws of nature lay upon us, to obſerve them inviolably, relates as well to thoſe which do not put an end to the war, as to thoſe which tend to re-eſtabliſh peace. There is no medium, and we muſt lay it down as a general rule, that all compacts with an enemy are obligatory, or that none of them are really ſuch.

And, indeed, if it was lawful, for inſtance, to break on purpoſe a ſolemn truce, and to detain, without any reaſon for it, people, to whom we had given paſs-ports, *&c.* what harm would there be in circumventing an enemy, under a pretext of treating of peace? When we enter into a negotiation of this kind, we are ſtill enemies; and 'tis properly but a kind of truce, which we agree to, in order to ſee if there are any means of coming to an accommodation. If the negotiations prove unſucceſsful, it is not then a new war which we begin, ſince the differences, that occaſioned our taking up arms, are not yet adjuſted; we only continue the acts of hoſtility which had been ſuſpended for ſome time: ſo that we could no more rely on the enemy's ſincerity, with reſpect

respect to compacts which tend to re-establish peace, than to those whose end is only to suspend, or moderate acts of hostility. Thus distrusts would be continual, wars eternal, and a solid peace unattainable.

6°. The more frequent unnecessary wars are become, thro' the avarice and ambition of sovereigns, the more a steady adherence to the principles, here established, is indispensably necessary for the interest of mankind. *Cicero* therefore justly affirms, that there is a right of war, which ought to be observed between the contending parties, and that the enemy retains certain rights, notwithstanding the war *.

Nor is it sufficient to say, as *Puffendorf* does, that it is a custom which, among others, has obtained among civilized nations, out of particular respect to military bravery, that all compacts made with an enemy ought to be looked upon as valid. He should also have added, that this is an indispensable duty, that justice requires it, that it is not in the power of nations to establish things on another footing, and that they cannot innocently deviate from the rules which the law of nature prescribes, in this case, for their common advantage.

IV. It will not be difficult, by means of the principles here established, to answer the reasonings by which *Puffendorf* pretends to shew, that all compacts made with an enemy, are not of themselves obligatory. We shall be content with observing, 1°. that the arguments he uses prove nothing,

* *Est etiam jus bellicum; fidesque jurisjurandi sæpe cum hoste servanda.* Off. lib. IV. cap. 29.

nothing, becauſe they prove too much, *&c.* and 2°. that all that can be concluded from them is, that we ought to act prudently, and take proper precautions before we paſs our word, or enter into any engagement with an enemy; becauſe mankind are apt to break their promiſes for their own intereſt, eſpecially when they have to deal with people whom they hate, or by whom they are hated.

V. But it will be ſaid, is it not an inconteſtable principle of the law of nature, that all conventions and treaties, extorted by injuſtice and violence, are void of themſelves; and conſequently, that he who has been forced to make them againſt his will, may innocently break his word, if he thinks he can do it with ſafety.

Violence and force are the characteriſtics of war; and it is generally the conqueror that obliges the vanquiſh'd to treat with him, and by the ſuperiority of his arms, conſtrains them to accept the conditions he propoſes to them, whether the war he has undertaken be juſt or not. How then is it poſſible, that the law of nature and nations ſhould declare treaties, made in theſe circumſtances, to be ſacred and inviolable?

I anſwer, that however true the principle on which this objection is founded, may be in itſelf, yet we cannot apply it, in all its extent, to the preſent queſtion.

The common intereſt of mankind requires, that we ſhould make ſome difference between promiſes extorted by fear, among private perſons, and thoſe to which a ſovereign prince or people is conſtrained, by the ſuperiority of the arms of a conqueror, whoſe pre-

pretensions were unjust. The law of nations then makes an exception here to the general rule of the law of nature, which disannuls conventions extorted by unjust fear; or, in other words, the law of nations holds for just on both sides, that fear which induces enemies to treat with each other, during the course of a war; for otherwise, there would be no method, either of moderating its fury, or of putting a final period to it, as we have already shewn.

VI. But that nothing may be omitted, relating to this question, we shall add something for the further illustration of what we have been saying.

First then, it is necessary, I think, to distinguish here, whether he, who by the superiority of his arms has compelled his enemy to treat with him, had undertaken the war without reason; or whether he could alledge some specious pretext for it. If the conqueror had undertaken the war for some plausible reason, tho' perhaps unjust at bottom, then it is certainly the interest of mankind, that the law of nations should make us regard the treaties, concluded in such circumstances, as valid and obligatory; so that the conquered cannot refuse to observe them, under a pretext that they were extorted by an unjust fear.

But if we suppose that the war was undertaken without reason, or if the motive alledged is manifestly frivolous, or unjust, as *Alexander's* going to subdue remote nations, who had never heard of him, *&c.* As such a war is a downright robbery, I confess I do not think the vanquished more obliged to observe the treaty to which they were compelled, than

than a man, fallen into the hands of thieves, is obliged to pay a ſum of money, which he had promiſed them, as a ranſom for his life or liberty.

VII. We muſt alſo add, as a very neceſſary remark, that even ſuppoſing the war was undertaken for ſome apparent and reaſonable cauſe, if the treaty, which the conqueror impoſes on the vanquiſhed, includes ſome condition manifeſtly barbarous, and intirely contrary to humanity; we cannot, in theſe circumſtances, deny the vanquiſhed a right of receding from their engagements, and of beginning the war afreſh, in order to free themſelves, if they can, from the hard and inhuman conditions to which they were ſubjected, by the abuſe their enemy made of his victory, contrary to the laws of humanity. The juſteſt war does not authoriſe the conqueror to keep no meaſures, or to uſe all liberties with reſpect to the vanquiſhed; and he cannot reaſonably complain of the breaking of a treaty, the conditions of which are both unjuſt in themſelves, and full of barbarity and cruelty.

VIII. The *Roman* hiſtory furniſhes us with an example to this purpoſe, which deſerves our notice.

The *Privernates* had been ſeveral times ſubdued by the *Romans*, and had as often revolted; but their city was at laſt retaken by the conſul *Plautius*. In theſe diſtreſſed circumſtances, they ſent ambaſſadors to *Rome* to ſue for peace. Upon a ſenator's aſking them what puniſhment they thought they deſerved; one of them anſwered, *that which is due to men who think themſelves worthy of liberty*. Then the conſul aſked

asked them, whether there was any room to hope, that they would observe the peace, if their fault was pardoned? "The peace shall be perpetual between "us, replied the ambassador, and we shall faith-"fully observe it, if the conditions you lay upon "us are just and reasonable; but if they are hard "and dishonourable, the peace will not be of long "continuance, and we shall very soon break it."

Tho' some of the senators were offended at this answer, yet most of them approved of it, and said that it was worthy of a man, and of a man who was born free: acknowledging therefore the force of the rights of human nature, they cried out, that those alone deserved to be citizens of *Rome*, who esteemed nothing in comparison of liberty. Thus the very persons, who were at first threatened with punishment, were admitted to the rights of citizens, and obtained the conditions they wanted; and the generous refusal of the *Privernates* to comply with the terms of a dishonourable treaty, gained them the privilege of being incorporated into a state, which at that time could boast of the bravest, and most virtuous subjects in the universe *.

Let us therefore conclude, that a due medium is to be observed, that we ought inviolably to observe treaties made with an enemy, and that no exception of an unjust fear should authorise us to break our promise, unless the war was a downright robbery, or the conditions imposed on us were highly unjust, and full of barbarity and cruelty.

IX. There is still another case, in fine, in which we

* Livy, lib. VIII. cap. xx, xxi.

we may avoid the crime of perfidiousness, and yet not perform what we have promised to an enemy; which is, when a certain condition, supposed to be the basis of the engagement, is wanting. This is a consequence of the very nature of compacts; by this principle, the infidelity of one of the contracting parties sets the other at liberty: for according to the common rule, all the articles of one and the same agreement are included one in the other, in the manner of a condition, as if a person was expressly to say, *I will do such or such a thing, provided you do so or so* *.

CHAP. XI.

Of compacts with an enemy, which do not put an end to the war.

I. AMONG those compacts which leave us in a state of war, one of the principal is a *truce*.

A truce is an agreement, by which we engage to forbear all acts of hostility for some time, the war still continuing.

II. A truce is not therefore a peace, for the war continues. But if we agree, for instance, on certain contributions during the war, as these are granted only to prevent acts of hostility, they ought to cease during the truce; since, at that time, such acts are not lawful. And, on the contrary, if it is agreed

* See above.

that

that any particular thing is to take place in time of peace, the time of truce is not included.

III. As every truce leaves us in a ſtate of war, it follows, that after the term is expired, there is no neceſſity that war ſhould be declared again; becauſe we do not begin a new war, but only continue that in which we were formerly engaged.

IV. This principle, that the war renewed after a truce is not a new war, may be applied to ſeveral other caſes. In a treaty of peace, concluded between the Biſhop of *Trent* and the *Venetians*, it was agreed, *that each party ſhould be put in poſſeſſion of what they enjoyed before the laſt war.*

In the beginning of this war the biſhop had taken a caſtle from the *Venetians*, which they afterwards retook. The biſhop refuſed to give it up, under a pretext that it had been retaken after ſeveral truces, which had been made during the courſe of that war. The diſpute was evidently to be decided in favour of the *Venetians*.

V. There are truces of ſeveral kinds.

1°. Sometimes, during the truce, the armies on both ſides are in the field, and in motion; and theſe are generally limited to a few days. Sometimes the parties lay down their arms, and retire to their own countries; and in this caſe the truces are of longer duration.

2°. There is a *general truce* for all the territories and dominions of both parties; and a *particular truce* reſtrained to particular places; as for example, by ſea, and not by land, *&c.*

3°.

3°. Laſtly, there is an abſolute, indeterminate, and general truce, and a truce limited and determined to certain things; for example, to bury the dead, or if a beſieged town has obtained a truce, only to be ſheltered from certain attacks, or from particular acts of hoſtility, ſuch as ravaging the country.

VI. We muſt alſo obſerve, that, ſtrictly ſpeaking, a truce can be made only by an expreſs agreement; and that it is very difficult to eſtabliſh a treaty of this kind on the footing of a tacit convention, unleſs the facts are ſuch in themſelves, and in their circumſtances, that they can be referred to no other principle, than to a ſincere deſign of ſuſpending acts of hoſtility for a time.

Thus, tho' for a time we abſtain from acts of hoſtility, the enemy cannot from that alone conclude, that we have conſented to a truce.

VII. The nature of a truce ſufficiently ſhews what the effects of it are.

1°. If the truce is general and abſolute, all acts of hoſtility ought, generally ſpeaking, to ceaſe, both with reſpect to perſons and things; but this ſhould not hinder us, during the truce, to raiſe new troops, erect magazines, repair fortifications, *&c.* unleſs there is ſome formal convention to the contrary; for theſe are not in themſelves acts of hoſtility, but defenſive precautions, which may be taken in time of peace.

2°. It is a violation of the truce, to ſeize on any place poſſeſſed by the enemy, by corrupting the garriſon.

rison. It is also evident, that we cannot justly, during a truce, take possession of places deserted by the enemy, but really belonging to him, whether the garrison were withdrawn before or after the truce.

3°. In consequence hereof, we must restore those things belonging to the enemy, which during the truce have accidentally fallen into our hands, even tho' they had been formerly our property.

4°. During a truce, it is allowed to pass and repass from one place to another, but without any train or attendance that may give umbrage.

VIII. And here it may be asked, whether they who, by any unexpected and inevitable accident, are found unfortunately in the enemy's country, at the expiration of a truce, can be detained prisoners, or whether they ought to have the liberty of retiring? *Grotius* and *Puffendorf* maintain, that by the right of war we may detain them as prisoners; but *Grotius* adds, that it is certainly more humane and generous, not to insist on such a right. As for my own part, I am of opinion that it is a consequence of a treaty of truce, that we should set such persons at liberty: for since, in virtue of that engagement, we are obliged to grant them free egress and regress, during the time of the truce; we ought also to grant them the same permission after the truce is expired, if it appears manifestly that a superior force, or an unexpected accident has hindered them from making use of it during the time agreed upon. Otherwise, as these accidents may happen every day, such a permission would often become a ſnare to make a great many people fall into the hands of the enemy. Such are the principal effects of an abſolute and general truce.

IX. As for a particular truce, determined to certain things, its effects are limited by the particular nature of the agreement.

1°. Thus if a truce is granted only for burying the dead, we ought not to undertake any thing new, which may alter our ſituation; for inſtance, we cannot, during that time, retire into a more ſecure poſt, nor intrench ourſelves, *&c.* for he, who has granted a ſhort truce for the interment of the dead, has granted it for that purpoſe only, and there is no reaſon to extend it beyond the caſe agreed on. Hence it follows, that if he, to whom ſuch a truce has been granted, ſhould take advantage of it to intrench himſelf, for example, or for ſome other uſe, the other party would have a right to prevent him by force. The former could not complain; for it never could be reaſonably pretended, that a truce, which was granted for the interment of the dead, and reſtrained to that ſingle act, gives a right to undertake, and carry on any other thing undiſturbed. The only obligation it impoſes on the perſon who has granted it, is, not forcibly to oppoſe the interment of the dead; tho' *Puffendorf*, indeed, is of a contrary opinion *.

2°. It is in conſequence of the ſame principles, that if we ſuppoſe that by the truce perſons only, and not things, are protected from acts of hoſtility; in this caſe, if in order to defend our goods we

* See the Law of Nature and Nations, l. VIII. c. vii. ſect. 9.

wound

wound any perſon, it is not a breach of the truce; for when the ſecurity of perſons on both ſides is agreed on, the right of defending againſt pillage is alſo reſerved. And hence the ſecurity of perſons is not general, but only for thoſe who go and come without deſign to take any thing from the enemy, with whom ſuch limited truce is made.

X. Every truce obliges the contracting parties, from the moment the agreement is concluded. But as for the ſubjects on both ſides, they are under no obligation in this reſpect, till the truce has been ſolemnly notified. Hence it follows, that if before this notification the ſubjects commit ſome acts of hoſtility, or do ſomething contrary to the truce, they are liable to no puniſhment. The powers, however, who have concluded the truce, ought to indemnify thoſe that have ſuffered, and to reſtore things, as much as poſſible, to their former ſtate.

XI. Laſtly, if the truce ſhould happen to be violated on one ſide, the other is certainly at liberty to proceed to acts of hoſtility, without any new declaration. But when it is agreed, that he who firſt breaks the truce ſhall pay a certain fine; if he pays the fine, or ſuffers the penalty, the other has not a right to begin acts of hoſtility, before the expiration of the term: but beſides the penalty ſtipulated, the injured party has a right to demand an indemnification of what he has ſuffered by the violation of the truce. It is to be obſerved however, that the actions of private perſons do not break a truce, unleſs the ſovereign has ſome hand in them, either by an order, or by an approbation; and he is ſuppoſed to approve what has been done, if he will neither puniſh, nor deliver up the offender, or if he refuſes to reſtore the things taken during the ceſſation of arms.

XII. Safe conducts are alſo compacts made between enemies, and deſerve to be conſidered. By a ſafe conduct, we underſtand a privilege granted to ſome perſon of the enemy's party, without a ceſſation of arms; by which he has free paſſage and return, and is in no danger of being moleſted.

XIII. All the queſtions relating to ſafe conducts may be decided, either by the nature of the privilege granted, or by the general rules of right interpretation.

1°. A ſafe conduct granted to ſoldiers, extends not only to inferior officers, but alſo to thoſe who command in chief; becauſe the natural and ordinary uſe of the word has determined it ſo.

2°. If leave is given to go to a certain part, it implies one alſo to return, otherwiſe the firſt permiſſion would be often uſeleſs. There may, however, be caſes, in which the one does not imply the other.

3°. He that has had leave to come, has not, generally ſpeaking, liberty to ſend another in his place. And, on the contrary, he who has had a permiſſion to ſend another perſon, cannot come himſelf; becauſe theſe are two different things, and the permiſſion ought to be naturally reſtrained to the perſon himſelf, to whom it was granted; for perhaps it would not have been given to another.

4°. A

4°. A father who has obtained a paſs-port, cannot take his ſon with him, nor a huſband his wife.

5°. As for ſervants, tho' not mentioned, it ſhall be preſumed to be allowed to take one or two, or even more, according to the quality of the perſon.

6°. In a dubious caſe, and generally ſpeaking, licence to paſs freely, does not ceaſe by the death of him who has granted it; it may, however, for good reaſons, be revoked by the ſucceſſor: but in ſuch a caſe the perſon, to whom the paſs-port has been granted, ought to have notice given him, and the neceſſary time allowed him for betaking himſelf to a place of ſafety.

7°. A ſafe conduct, granted during pleaſure, imports of itſelf a continuation of ſafe conduct, till it is expreſsly revoked; for otherwiſe, the will is ſuppoſed to ſubſiſt ſtill the ſame, whatever time may be elapſed: but ſuch a ſafe conduct expires, if the perſon who has given it, is no longer in the employment, in virtue of which he was impowered to grant ſuch ſecurity.

XIV. The redemption of captives is alſo a compact which is often made, without putting an end to the war. The antient *Romans* were very backward in the ranſoming of priſoners. Their practice was to examine whether thoſe, who were taken by the enemy, had obſerved the laws of military diſcipline, and conſequently, whether they deſerved to be ranſomed. But the ſide of rigour generally prevailed, as moſt advantageous to the republic.

XV. But in general, it is certainly more agreeable,

both to the good of the ſtate, and to humanity, to ranſom priſoners; unleſs experience convinces us, that it is neceſſary to uſe that ſeverity towards them, in order to prevent, or redreſs greater evils, which would otherwiſe be unavoidable.

XVI. An agreement made for the ranſom of a priſoner cannot be revoked, under a pretext that he is found to be much richer than we imagined: for this circumſtance, of the priſoner's being more or leſs rich, has no relation to the engagement; ſo that if his ranſom was to be ſettled by his worth, that condition ſhould have been ſpecified in the contract.

XVII. As priſoners of war are not now made ſlaves, the captor has a right to nothing but what he actually takes: hence money, or other things, which a priſoner has found means to conceal, certainly remain his property, and he may conſequently make uſe of them to pay his ranſom. The enemy cannot take poſſeſſion of what they know nothing of; and the priſoner lies under no obligation to make a diſcovery of all his effects to the enemy.

XVIII. There is alſo another queſtion, whether the heir of a priſoner of war is obliged to pay the ranſom, which the deceaſed had agreed upon? The anſwer is eaſy, in my opinion. If the priſoner died in captivity, the heir owes nothing, for the promiſe of the deceaſed was made upon condition, that he ſhould be ſet at liberty: but if he was ſet at liberty before he died, the heir is certainly chargeable with the ranſom.

XIX.

XIX. One queſtion more, is, whether a priſoner, who was releaſed on condition of releaſing another, is obliged to return to priſon, if the other dies before he has obtained his releaſement? I anſwer, that the releaſed priſoner is not obliged to return into cuſtody, for that was not ſtipulated in the agreement; neither is it juſt that he ſhould enjoy his liberty for nothing. He muſt therefore give an indemnification, or pay the full value of what he could not perform.

CHAP. XII.

Of compacts made, during the war, by ſubordinate powers, as generals of armies, or other commanders.

I. ALL that we have hitherto ſaid, concerning compacts between enemies, relates to thoſe made by ſovereign powers. But ſince princes do not always conclude ſuch agreements themſelves, we muſt now enquire what we ought to think of treaties made by generals, or other inferior commanders.

II. In order to know whether theſe engagements oblige the ſovereign, the following principles will direct us.

1°. Since every perſon may enter into an engagement, either by himſelf or by another, it is plain that the ſovereign is bound by the compacts made by his miniſters or officers, in con-

 ſequence

ſequence of the full powers and orders expreſsly given them.

2°. He that gives a man a certain power, is reaſonably ſuppoſed to have given him whatever is a neceſſary conſequence and appendage of that power, and without which it cannot be exerciſed. But he is not ſuppoſed to have granted him any thing further.

3°. If he, who has had a commiſſion to treat, has kept within the bounds of the power annexed to his office, tho' he act contrary to his private inſtructions, yet the ſovereign is to abide by what he has done; otherwiſe we could never depend on engagements contracted by proxy.

4°. A prince is alſo obliged by the act of his miniſters and officers, tho' done without his orders, if he has ratified the engagements they have made, either by an expreſs conſent, and then there is no difficulty, or in a tacit manner; that is to ſay, if being informed of what has paſſed, he yet permits things to be done, or does them himſelf, which cannot reaſonably be referred to any other cauſe, than the intention of executing the engagements of his miniſter, tho' contracted without his participation.

5°. The ſovereign may alſo be obliged to execute the engagements contracted by his miniſters without his orders, by the thing itſelf; that is, by the law of nature, which forbids us to enrich ourſelves at another's expence. Equity requires, that in theſe circumſtances we ſhould exactly obſerve the conditions of the contract, tho' concluded by miniſters who had not full powers.

6°. Theſe

6°. These are the general principles of natural equity, in virtue of which sovereigns may be more or less obliged to stand to the agreements of their generals. But to what has been said, we must add this general exception: unless the laws and customs of the country have regulated it otherways, and these be sufficiently known to the persons with whom the agreement is made.

7°. Lastly, if a public minister exceeds his commission, so that he cannot perform what he has promised, and his master is not obliged to it, he himself is certainly bound to indemnify the person with whom he has treated. But if there should be any deceit on his part, he may be punished for it, and his person, or his goods, or both, are liable to be seized, in order to make a recompence.

III. Let us illustrate these general principles, by applying them to some particular examples.

1°. A commander in chief cannot enter into a treaty, that regards the causes and consequences of the war; for the power of making war, in whatever extent it has been given, does not imply the power of finishing it.

2°. Neither does it belong to generals to grant truces for a considerable space of time; for 1°. that does not necessarily depend on their commission. 2°. The thing is of too great consequence to be left entirely to their discretion. 3°. And lastly, circumstances are not generally so pressing, as not to admit of time to consult the sovereign; which a general ought to do, both in duty and prudence, as much as possible, even with respect to things which he has power to transact of himself. Much

Much less, therefore, can generals conclude these kinds of truces, which withdraw all the appearance of war, and come very near a real peace.

3°. With respect to truces of a short duration, it is certainly in the power of a general to make them; for example, to bury the dead, &c.

IV. Lieutenant-Generals, or even inferior commanders, may also make particular truces, during the attack, for instance, of a body of the enemy intrenched, or in the siege of a town; for this being often very necessary, it is reasonably presumed, that such a power must needs be included in the extent of their commission.

V. But a question here arises, whether these particular truces oblige only the officers who granted them, and the troops under their command, or whether they bind the other officers, and even the commander in chief? *Grotius* declares for the first opinion, tho' the second appears to me the best founded; for 1°. since we suppose that it is in consequence of the tacit consent of the sovereign, that such a truce has been granted by an inferior officer, no other officer, whether equal or superior, can break the agreement, without indirectly wounding the authority of the sovereign.

2°. Besides, this would lay a foundation for fraud and distrusts, which might tend to render the use of truces, so necessary on several occasions, useless and impracticable.

VI. It does not belong to a general to release perſons taken in war, nor to diſpoſe of conquered ſovereignties and lands.

VII. But it is certainly in the power of generals to grant, or leave things, which are not as yet actually poſſeſſed: becauſe in war many cities, for example, and often men, ſurrender themſelves, upon condition of preſerving their lives and liberties, or ſometimes their goods; concerning which the preſent circumſtances do not commonly allow time ſufficient to conſult the ſovereign. Inferior commanders ought alſo to have this right, concerning things within the extent of their commiſſion.

VIII. In fine, by the principles here eſtabliſhed, we may eaſily judge of the conduct of the *Roman* people, with reſpect to *Bituitus* king of the *Arverni*, and to the affair of the *Caudine Forks*.

CHAP. XIII.

Of compacts made with an enemy by private perſons.

I. IT ſometimes happens in war, that private perſons, whether ſoldiers or others, make compacts with an enemy. *Cicero* juſtly remarks, that if a private perſon, conſtrained by neceſſity, has promiſed any thing to the enemy, he ought religiouſly to keep his word *.

* De Offic. lib. I. cap. xiii.

II.

II. And, indeed, all the principles we have hitherto eſtabliſhed, manifeſtly prove the juſtice and neceſſity of this duty. Beſides, unleſs this be allowed, frequent obſtacles would be put to liberty, and an occaſion given for maſſacres, *&c.*

III. But tho' theſe compacts are valid in themſelves, yet it is evident that no private perſon has a right to alienate what belongs to the public; for this is not allowed even to generals of armies.

IV. With reſpect to the actions and effects of each individual, tho' the covenants made with the enemy on theſe affairs may ſometimes be prejudicial to the ſtate, they are nevertheleſs obligatory. Whatever tends to avoid a greater evil, tho' detrimental in itſelf, ought to be conſidered as a public good; as for example, when we promiſe to pay certain contributions to prevent pillage, or the burning of places, *&c.* Even the laws of the ſtate cannot, without injuſtice, deprive individuals of the right of providing for their own ſafety, by impoſing too burdenſome an obligation on the ſubjects, which is entirely repugnant to nature and reaſon.

V. It is in conſequence of theſe principles that we juſtly tolerate the promiſe of a captive to return to priſon. Without this he would not be ſuffered to go home; and it is certainly better for him, and for the ſtate, that he ſhould have this permiſſion for a time, than that he ſhould remain always in priſon. It was, therefore, to fulfill his duty, that *Regulus* returned

returned to *Carthage*, and ſurrendered himſelf into the hands of the enemy *.

VI. We muſt judge, in like manner, of the promiſe by which a priſoner engages *not to bear arms againſt the releaſer*. In vain would it be objected, that ſuch an engagement is contrary to the duty we owe to our country. It is no way contrary to the duty of a good citizen, to procure our liberty by promiſing to forbear a thing which it is in the enemy's power to hinder. Our country loſes nothing by that, but rather gains; ſince a priſoner, ſo long as he is not releaſed, is as uſeleſs to it, as if he was really dead.

VII. If a priſoner has promiſed not to make his eſcape, he ought certainly to keep his word; even tho' he was in fetters when he made it. But if a perſon has given his word, on condition that he ſhould not be confined in that manner, he may break it, if he be laid in irons.

VIII. But here ſome will aſk, whether private men, upon refuſing to perform what they have promiſed to the enemy, may be compelled to it by the ſovereign? I anſwer, certainly: otherwiſe it would be to no purpoſe, that they were bound by a promiſe, if there was no one who could compel them to perform it.

* Cicer. de Offic. lib. III. cap. xxix.

CHAP.

CHAP. XIV.

Of public compacts which put an end to war.

I. COmpacts which put an end to war, are either *principals* or *accessories*. Principals are those which terminate the war, either by themselves, as a treaty of peace, or by a consequence of what has been agreed upon; as when the end of the war is referred to the decision of lot, to the success of a combat, or to the judgment of an arbitrator. Accessories are such, as are sometimes joined to the principal compacts, in order to confirm them, and to render the execution of them more certain. Such are hostages, pledges, and guaranties.

II. We have already treated of single combats agreed on by both parties, and of arbitrators, considered as means of hindering or terminating a war; it now only remains that we speak of treaties of peace.

III. The first question which presents itself on this subject, is whether compacts, which terminate a war, can be disannulled by the exception of an unjust fear which has extorted them.

After the principles which we have heretofore established, to shew that we ought to keep our faith given to an enemy, it is not necessary to prove this point again. Of all public conventions, treaties of peace are those which a nation ought to look upon as most sacred and inviolable, since nothing is of greater

greater importance to the repofe and tranquillity of mankind. As princes and nations have no common judge, to take cognizance of their differences, and to decide concerning the juftice of a war, we could never depend on a treaty of peace, if the exception of an unjuft fear was in this cafe to be generally admitted.' I fay *generally*, for when the injuftice of the conditions of the peace is highly evident, and the unjuft conqueror abufes his victory fo far, as to impofe the hardeft, cruelleft, and moft intolerable conditions on the vanquifhed, the law of nations cannot authorife fuch treaties, nor lay an obligation on the vanquifhed tamely to fubmit to them. Let us alfo add, that tho' the law of nations ordains, that, except in the cafe here mentioned, treaties of peace are to be faithfully obferved, and cannot be difannulled, under a pretext of an unjuft conftraint; it is neverthelefs certain, that the conqueror cannot in confcience take the advantage of fuch a treaty, and that he is obliged, by internal juftice, to reftore all that he has taken in an unjuft war.

IV. Another queftion is, to know whether a fovereign, or a ftate, is obliged to obferve treaties of peace which they have made with their rebellious fubjects? I anfwer, 1°. that when a fovereign has reduced rebellious fubjects by force of arms, he may deal with them as he fees beft. 2°. But if he has entered into any accommodation with them, he is thereby fuppofed to have pardoned them what is paft; fo that he cannot lawfully refufe to keep his word, under a pretext that he had given it to rebellious fubjects.

jects. This obligation is so much the more inviolable, as princes are apt to give the name of rebellion to a resistance, by which the subject only maintains his just rights, and opposes the violation of the most essential engagements of sovereigns. History furnishes but too many examples of this kind.

V. None but he who has a right of making war, has a right to terminate it by a treaty of peace. In a word, this is an essential part of sovereignty. But can a king, who is a prisoner, make a treaty of peace, which shall be valid, and shall bind a nation? I think not, for there is no probability, neither can it be reasonably presumed, that the people would have conferred the sovereignty upon one, with a power to exercise it, even in matters of the greatest importance, at a time when he is not master of his own person. But with respect to contracts which a king, tho' a prisoner, has made concerning what belongs to him in private, they are certainly valid, according to the principles we have established in the preceding chapter. But what shall we say of a king who is in exile? If he has no dependance upon any person, it is certainly in his power to make peace.

VI. To know for certainty what things a king can dispose of by a treaty of peace, we need only consider the nature of the sovereignty, and the manner in which he possesses it.

1°. In patrimonial kingdoms, considered in themselves, nothing hinders but that the king may alienate the sovereignty, or a part of it.

2°. But princes, who hold the sovereignty only

in an usufructuary manner, cannot by any treaty alienate it, either in whole or in part. To render such alienations valid, the consent of the body of the people, or of the states of the kingdom, is necessary.

3°. With respect to the crown domains, or the goods of the kingdom, it is not generally in the power of the sovereign to alienate them.

4°. As for the effects of private subjects, the sovereign, as such, has a transcendental or superеminent right over the goods and fortunes of private men; consequently he may give them up, as often as the public advantage, or necessity requires it; but with this consideration, that the state ought to indemnify the subject for the loss he has sustained beyond his own proportion.

VII. For the better interpretation of the articles of a treaty of peace, we need only attend to the general rules of interpretation, and the intention of the contracting parties.

1°. In all treaties of peace, if there is no clause to the contrary, it is presumed that the parties hold themselves reciprocally discharged from all damages occasioned by the war. Hence the clauses of general amnesty are only for the greater precaution.

2°. But the debts between individuals, contracted before the war, and the payment of which could not be exacted during the war, are not to be accounted forgiven by the treaty of peace.

3°. Unknown injuries, whether committed before, or during the war, are supposed to be comprehended

prehended in the general terms, by which we forgive the enemy the evil he has done us.

4°. Whatever has been taken ſince the concluſion of the peace, muſt certainly be reſtored.

5°. If the time be limited, in which the conditions of peace are to be performed, it muſt be interpreted in the ſtricteſt ſenſe; ſo that when it is expired, the leaſt delay is inexcuſable, unleſs it proceeds from a ſuperior force, or it manifeſtly appears that it is owing to no bad deſign.

6°. It is laſtly to be obſerved, that every treaty of peace is of itſelf perpetual, and, as it were, eternal in its nature; that is to ſay, the parties are deemed to be agreed never to take up arms on account of the differences which occaſioned the war, and for the future to look upon them as entirely at an end.

VIII. It is alſo an important queſtion to know, when a peace may be looked upon as broken.

1°. Some diſtinguiſh between *breaking a peace*, and *giving a new occaſion of war*. To break a peace, is to violate ſome articles of the treaty; but to give a new occaſion of war, is to take up arms for ſome new reaſon not mentioned in the treaty.

2°. But when we give a new occaſion of war in this manner, the treaty is by that means indirectly broken, if we refuſe to make ſatisfaction for the offence: for then the offended having a right to take up arms, and to treat the offender as an enemy, againſt whom every thing is lawful, he muſt alſo certainly diſpenſe with obſerving the conditions of the peace, tho' the treaty has not been formally broken with reſpect

respect to its tenor. Besides, this distinction cannot be much used at present; because treaties of peace are conceived in such a manner, as to include an engagement to live for the future in good friendship, in all respects. We must therefore conclude, that every new act of unjust hostility is an infringement of the peace.

3°. As for those who only repel force by force, they by no means break the peace.

4°. When a peace is concluded with several allies of him with whom the treaty has been made, the peace is not broken if one of those allies takes up arms, unless it has been concluded on that footing. But this is what cannot be presumed, and certainly they who thus invade us without the assistance of others, shall be considered as the breakers of the peace.

5°. Acts of violence or hostility, which some subjects may commit of their own accord, cannot break the peace, except we suppose that the sovereign approves them; and this is presum'd, if he knows the fact, has power to punish it, and neglects to do so.

6°. The peace is supposed to be broken, when, without a lawful reason, acts of hostility are committed, not only against the whole body of a state, but also against private persons; for the end of a treaty of peace is, that every subject of the government should, for the future, live in perfect security.

7°. The peace is certainly broken by a contravention to the clear and express articles of the treaty. Some civilians, however, distinguish between the articles which are *of great importance*, and thoſe of *ſmall importance*. But this diſtinction is not only uncertain in itſelf, but alſo very difficult and delicate in its application. In general, all the articles of a treaty ought to be looked upon as important enough to be obſerved. We muſt, however, pay ſome regard to what is required by humanity, and rather pardon ſlight faults, than purſue the reparation of them by arms.

8°. If one of the parties is, by an abſolute neceſſity, reduced to an impoſſibility of performing his engagements, we are not for that to look upon the peace as broken: but the other party ought either to wait ſome time for the performance of what has been promiſed, if there is ſtill any hope of it, or he may demand a reaſonable equivalent.

9°. Even when there is treachery on one ſide, it is certainly at the choice of the innocent party to let the peace ſubſiſt; and it would be ridiculous to pretend, that he who firſt infringes the peace can diſengage himſelf from the obligation which he lay under, by acting contrary to that very obligation.

IX. To treaties of peace, for the ſecurity of their execution, are ſometimes joined hoſtages, pledges, and guarantees. Hoſtages are of ſeveral ſorts; for they either give themſelves voluntarily, or are given by order of the ſovereign, or they are forcibly taken by the enemy. Nothing, for inſtance, is at preſent more common, than to carry off hoſtages for the ſecurity of contributions.

X. The ſovereign may, in virtue of his authority,

rity, oblige ſome of his ſubjects to put themſelves into the hands of the enemy as hoſtages; for if he has a right, when neceſſity requires it, to expoſe them to the danger of their lives, much more may he engage their corporal liberty. But on the other hand, the ſtate ought certainly to indemnify the hoſtages for the loſſes they may have ſuſtained for the good of the ſociety.

XI. Hoſtages are demanded, and given, for the ſecurity of the execution of ſome engagement; therefore it is neceſſary that they ſhould be retained, in ſuch manner as ſhall be judged proper, till the performance of what has been agreed on. Hence it follows that an hoſtage, who has made himſelf ſuch voluntarily, or he who has been given by the ſovereign, cannot make his eſcape. *Grotius*, however, grants this liberty to the latter; but his opinion does not ſeem to be well founded: for either it was the intention of the ſtate, that the hoſtage ſhould not remain in the hands of the enemy; or the ſtate had not the power of obliging the hoſtage to remain. The firſt is manifeſtly falſe, for otherwiſe the hoſtage could be no ſecurity, and the convention would be illuſive. Nor is the other more true; for if the ſovereign, in virtue of his tranſcendental property, can expoſe the lives of the citizens, why may he not engage their liberty? Thus *Grotius* himſelf agrees, that the *Romans* were obliged to return *Clelia* to *Porſenna*. But the caſe is not preciſely the ſame, with reſpect to hoſtages taken by the enemy; for theſe have a right to make their eſcape, ſo long as they have not given their word to the contrary.

XII. It is a queſtion often controverted, whether he, to whom hoſtages are given, can put them to death, in caſe the enemy do not perform their engagements? I anſwer, that hoſtages themſelves cannot give the enemy any power over their lives, of which they are not maſters. As for the ſtate, it has certainly the power of expoſing the lives of the ſubjects, when the public good requires it. But in this caſe, all that the public good requires, is to engage the corporal liberty of the hoſtages; and they can no more be rendered reſponſible, at the peril of their lives, for the infidelity of the ſovereign, than an innocent perſon can be treated as a criminal. Thus the ſtate by no means engages the lives of hoſtages. He, to whom they are given, is ſuppoſed to receive them on theſe conditions; and tho' by the violation of the treaty they are at his mercy, it does not follow that he has a right, in conſcience, to put them to death; he can only retain them as priſoners of war.

XIII. Hoſtages, given for a certain purpoſe, are free as ſoon as that purpoſe is anſwered, and conſequently cannot be detained upon any other account, for which no hoſtages were promiſed. But if we have broke our faith in any other caſe, or contracted ſome new debt, the hoſtages then may be detained, not as hoſtages, but in conſequence of this rule of the law of nations, which authoriſes us to detain the perſons of ſubjects for the deeds of their ſovereigns.

XIV The query is, whether an hoſtage is at liberty

berty by the death of the ſovereign, who made the covenant? This depends on the nature of the treaty, for the ſecurity of which the hoſtage was given; that is to ſay, we muſt examine whether it is *perſonal*, or *real*.

But if the hoſtage becomes ſucceſſor to the prince who gave him up, he is no longer obliged to be detained as an hoſtage, though the treaty be real; he ought only to put another in his place, whenever it is demanded. This caſe is ſuppoſed to be tacitly excepted; for it cannot be preſumed that a prince, for example, who has given his own ſon and preſumptive heir as an hoſtage, could have imagined he ever intended, that in caſe he ſhould die, the ſtate ſhould be without its chief.

XV. Sometimes pledges are alſo given for the ſecurity of a treaty of peace; and as we have ſaid that hoſtages may be detained for other debts, this may alſo be applied to pledges.

XVI. Another way, in fine, of ſecuring peace, is, when princes or ſtates, eſpecially thoſe who have been mediators of the peace, become guarantees, and engage their faith, that the articles ſhall be obſerved on both ſides; which engagement of theirs implies an obligation of interpoſing their good offices, to obtain a reaſonable ſatisfaction to the party injured contrary to treaty, and even of aſſiſting him againſt the injurious aggreſſor.

CHAP. XV.

Of the right of ambaſſadors.

I. NOTHING now remains but to ſay ſomething of ambaſſadors, and of the privileges which the law of nations grants them. It is natural to treat of this ſubject here, ſince it is by means of theſe miniſters that treaties are generally negotiated and concluded.

II. Nothing is more common than the maxim, which eſtabliſhes that the perſons of ambaſſadors are ſacred and inviolable, and that they are under the protection of the law of nations. We cannot doubt but that it is of the utmoſt importance to mankind in general, and to nations in particular, not only to put an end to wars and diſputes, but alſo to eſtabliſh and maintain commerce and friendſhip between each other. Now as ambaſſadors are neceſſary to procure theſe advantages, it follows that God, who certainly commands every thing that contributes to the preſervation and happineſs of human ſociety, cannot but forbid, by the law of nature, the doing any injury to theſe perſons; but on the contrary, that he orders we ſhould grant them all the ſecurity and privileges, which the deſign and nature of their employment requires.

III. Before we enter into the application of the privileges which the law of nations grants to ambaſſadors, we muſt firſt obſerve with *Grotius*, that they

they belong only to ambaſſadors ſent by ſovereign powers to each other. For as to deputies ſent by cities or provinces to their own ſovereigns, it is not by the law of nations that we muſt judge of their privileges, but by the civil law of the country. In a word, the privileges of ambaſſadors regard only foreigners; that is to ſay, ſuch as have no dependance on us.

Nothing then hinders an inferior ally from having a right to ſend ambaſſadors to a ſuperior ally; for in the caſe of an unequal alliance, the inferior does not ceaſe to be independent.

It is a queſtion, whether a king, vanquiſh'd in war, and ſtript of his kingdom, has a right of ſending ambaſſadors? But indeed this queſtion is uſeleſs, with reſpect to the conqueror, who will not even ſo much as think whether he ought to receive ambaſſadors from a perſon whom he has deprived of his kingdom. As for other powers, if the conqueror has entered into the war for ſome reaſons manifeſtly unjuſt, they ought ſtill to acknowledge him for the true king, who really is ſo, as long as they can do it without ſome great inconveniency; conſequently they cannot refuſe to receive his ambaſſadors.

But in civil wars the caſe is extraordinary; for then neceſſity ſometimes makes way for this right, ſo as to receive ambaſſadors on both ſides. The ſame nation, in that caſe, is for a time accounted two diſtinct bodies of people. But pirates and robbers, that do not conſtitute a ſettled government, can have no right of nations belonging to them, nor conſequently that of ſending ambaſſadors, unleſs

leſs they have obtained it by a treaty, which has ſometimes happened.

IV. The antients did not diſtinguiſh different ſorts of perſons ſent by one power to another; the *Romans* called them all *legati*, or *oratores*. At preſent there are various titles given to theſe public miniſters, but the employment is at bottom the ſame; and all the diſtinctions that are made, are founded rather on the greater or leſſer ſplendor with which they ſupport their dignity, and on the greatneſs or ſmallneſs of their ſalary, than on any other reaſon relating to their character.

V. The moſt common diſtinction of ambaſſadors, at preſent, is into *extraordinary* and *ordinary*. This difference was entirely unknown to the antients. All the ambaſſadors they ſent were extraordinary, that is to ſay, charged with only one particular negotiation; whereas the ordinary ambaſſadors are thoſe who reſide in the courts of allied nations, to manage all kinds of buſineſs, and even to obſerve what paſſes there.

The change of the ſituation of things in *Europe*, ſince the deſtruction of the *Roman* empire, the different ſovereignties and republics that have been erected, together with the increaſe of trade, have rendered theſe ordinary ambaſſadors neceſſary, and introduced the uſe of them. Hence ſeveral hiſtorians juſtly obſerve, that the *Turks*, who keep no miniſters in foreign countries, act very impoliticly in this particular; for as they receive their news only by *Jewiſh* or *Armenian* merchants, they do not generally

generally hear of things till very late, or their informations are bad, which often makes them take falſe meaſures, becauſe they have had falſe advices.

VI. *Grotius* obſerves, that there are two principal maxims of the law of nations, concerning ambaſſadors. The firſt, *that we ought to admit them*; the ſecond, *that we ſhould offer no violence to them, and that their perſons are ſacred and inviolable.*

VII. With regard to the firſt of theſe maxims, we muſt obſerve that the obligation of admitting ambaſſadors, is founded in general on the principles of ſociety and humanity: for as all nations form a kind of ſociety among themſelves, and conſequently ought to aſſiſt each other by a mutual commerce of good offices, the uſe of ambaſſadors becomes neceſſary between them for that very reaſon. It is therefore a rule of the law of nations, that we ought to admit ambaſſadors, and to reject none without a juſt cauſe.

VIII. But tho' we are obliged to admit ambaſſadors, it is only a bare duty of humanity, which produces but an imperfect, and not a ſtrict obligation. So that a ſimple refuſal cannot be regarded as an injuſtice, properly ſpeaking, ſufficient to lay a juſt foundation for a war. Beſides the obligation to admit ambaſſadors, regards as well thoſe ſent to us by an enemy, as thoſe who come from an allied power. It is the duty of princes, who are at war, to ſeek the means of re-eſtabliſhing a juſt and reaſonable peace; and they cannot obtain it, unleſs they

they are diſpoſed to liſten to the propoſals which may be made on each ſide; which cannot be ſo well negotiated, as by employing ambaſſadors or miniſters. The ſame duty of humanity alſo obliges neutral, or indifferent princes, to afford a paſſage thro' their territories to ambaſſadors ſent by other powers.

IX. I mentioned that we ought not, without a juſt cauſe, to refuſe admittance to an ambaſſador; for it is poſſible that we may have very good reaſons to reject him: for example, if his maſter has already impoſed upon us under pretext of an embaſſy, and we have juſt reaſon to ſuſpect the like fraud; if the prince, by whom the ambaſſador is ſent, has been guilty of treachery, or of ſome other heinous crime againſt us; or, in fine, if we are ſure that, under pretext of ſome negotiations, the ambaſſador is ſent only in the character of a ſpy, to pry into our affairs, and to ſow the ſeeds of ſedition.

Thus, in the retreat of the ten thouſand of which *Xenophon* has left us the hiſtory, the generals reſolved, that as long as they were in the enemy's country they would receive no heralds; and what moved them to this reſolution, was their having found that the perſons who had been ſent among them, under pretence of embaſſies, came really to ſpy, and to corrupt the ſoldiers.

It may alſo be a juſt reaſon for refuſing admittance to an ambaſſador, or envoy from an allied power, when by admitting him we are likely to give diſtruſt to ſome other power, with whom it is proper we ſhould have a good underſtanding. Laſtly, the perſon or character of the ambaſſador himſelf may furniſh juſt reaſons for our not admitting him. This is ſufficient concerning the maxim relating to the admittance of ambaſſadors.

X. As for the other rule of the law of nations, which directs that no violence be offered to ambaſſadors, and that their perſons ought to be looked upon as ſacred and inviolable, it is a little more difficult to decide the ſeveral queſtions relating to it.

1°. When we ſay that the law of nations forbids any violence to ambaſſadors, either by words or actions, we do not by this give any particular privilege to ambaſſadors; for this is no more than what every man has a right to by the law of nature, a right that his life, his honour, and his property, ſhould be perfectly ſecure.

2°. But when we add, that the perſons of ambaſſadors are ſacred and inviolable by the law of nations, we attribute ſome prerogatives and privileges to them, which are not due to private perſons, *&c.*

3°. When we ſay that the perſon of an ambaſſador is ſacred, this ſignifies no more than that we inflict a ſeverer puniſhment on thoſe who have offered violence to an ambaſſador, than on thoſe who have done ſome injury or inſult to private perſons; and that the character, which renders ambaſſadors ſacred, is the reaſon of our inflicting ſo different a puniſhment for the ſame kind of offence.

4°. Laſtly, the reaſon why we call the perſons of ambaſſadors ſacred, is becauſe they are not ſubject

ject to the civil or criminal jurisdiction of the sovereign to whom they are sent, either with respect to their persons, retinue, or effects; so that we cannot act against them, according to the ordinary ways of justice; and it is in this that their privileges principally consist.

XI. The foundation of these privileges, which the law of nations grants to ambassadors, is, that as an ambassador represents the person of his master, he ought of course to enjoy all the privileges and rights which his master himself, as a sovereign would have, was he to come into the states of another prince to transact his own affairs, to negotiate, for instance, or conclude a treaty, or an alliance, to regulate some branch of commerce, and other things of a similar nature, *&c.* Now, for whatever reason a sovereign goes from his own into a foreign country, surely we cannot imagine that he loses his character and independence, and that he becomes subject to the prince in whose territories he is: on the contrary, he ought to be thought to continue as he was before, equal and independent of the civil or criminal jurisdiction of the prince, into whose territories he goes; and the latter receives him on that footing as he would choose to be received himself, if he went into the other's dominions. We must grant the ambassador the same prerogative and immunities, in consequence of his representative character.

The very end and design of embassies render these privileges of ambassadors necessary; for it is certain, that if an ambassador can treat with the prince

to

to whom he is ſent, with a full independence, he will be much better qualified to perform his duty, and ſerve his maſter effectually, than if he was ſubject to the juriſdiction of the prince with whom he is to negotiate, or if he and his retinue could be conſigned over to juſtice, and his goods arreſted and ſeized, *&c.* It is not, therefore, without reaſon, that all nations have, in favour of ambaſſadors, made an exception to the general cuſtom, by which it is eſtabliſhed, that people who reſide in a foreign prince's dominions, ſhall be ſubject to that prince's laws.

XII. Theſe principles being ſuppoſed, I ſay

1°. That there is no difficulty with reſpect to ambaſſadors, who come to a power with whom their maſter is at peace, and who have injured no man. The moſt common and moſt evident maxims of the law of nature, require they ſhould be perfectly ſecure. So that if we affront or inſult ſuch an ambaſſador, in any manner whatſoever, we give his maſter juſt reaſon for declaring war. Of this king *David* furniſhes us with an example *.

2°. As to ambaſſadors who come from an enemy, and who have done no harm before they are admitted, their ſafety depends entirely on the laws of humanity; for an enemy, as ſuch, has a right to annoy his enemy. Thus, ſo long as there is no particular agreement upon this article, we are obliged to ſpare the ambaſſador of an enemy, only in virtue of the ſentiments of humanity, which we ought always to retain, and which oblige us to have a

* 2 Sam. ch. x.

regard

regard for every thing which tends to the preservation of peace.

3°. But when we have promised to admit, or have actually admitted the ambassador of an enemy, we have thereby manifestly engaged to procure him entire security, so long as he behave himself well. We must not even except heralds, who are sent to declare war, provided they do it in an inoffensive manner. So much for innocent ambassadors.

4°. As to ambassadors, who have rendered themselves culpable, they have done the injury either of their own head, or by their master's order.

If they have done it of their own head, they forfeit their right to security, and to the enjoyment of their privileges, when their crime is manifest and heinous: for no ambassador whatever can pretend to more privilege than his master would have in the same case; now such a crime would not be pardoned in the master.

By *heinous crimes*, we here mean such as tend to disturb the state, or to destroy the lives of the subjects of the prince to whom the ambassador is sent, or to do them some considerable prejudice in their honour or fortunes.

When the crime directly affects the state, or the head of it, whether the ambassador has actually used violence or not, that is to say, whether he has stirred up the subjects to sedition, or conspired himself against the government, or favoured the plot; or whether he has taken arms with the rebels or the enemy, or engaged his attendants so to do, *&c.* we may be revenged on him, even by killing him, not

not as a ſubject, but as an enemy; for his maſter himſelf would have no reaſon to expect better treatment. And the end of embaſſies, eſtabliſhed for the general good of nations, does not require that we ſhould grant to an ambaſſador, who firſt violates the moſt ſacred rules of the law of nations, the privileges which that law allows to ambaſſadors. If ſuch an ambaſſador makes his eſcape, his maſter is obliged to deliver him up when he is demanded.

But if the crime, however heinous or manifeſt, affects only a private perſon, the ambaſſador is not for that alone to be reputed an enemy to the prince or ſtate. Suppoſe his maſter had committed a crime of the ſame nature, we ought to demand ſatisfaction of him, and not take up arms againſt him till he had refuſed it; ſo the ſame reaſon of equity directs, that the prince, at whoſe court the ambaſſador has committed ſuch a crime, ſhould ſend him back to his maſter, deſiring him either to deliver him up, or to puniſh him: for to keep him in priſon till his maſter ſhall recall him, in order to puniſh him, or declare that he has abandoned him, would be to teſtify ſome diſtruſt of the juſtice of his maſter, and by that means affront him in ſome meaſure, becauſe the ambaſſador ſtill repreſents him.

5°. But if the crime is committed by the maſter's order, it would certainly be imprudence to ſend the ambaſſador back; ſince there is juſt reaſon to believe, that the prince who ordered the commiſſion of the crime, will hardly ſurrender, or puniſh the criminal. We may, therefore, in this caſe, ſecure the perſon of the ambaſſador, till the maſter ſhall repair the injury done both by his ambaſſador and himſelf. As for thoſe who do not repreſent the perſon of the prince, ſuch as common meſſengers, trumpets, *&c.* we may kill them on the ſpot, if they come to inſult a prince by order of their maſter.

But nothing is more abſurd than what ſome maintain, namely, that all the evil done by ambaſſadors, by order of their maſter, ought to be imputed intirely to the maſter. Were it ſo, ambaſſadors would have more privilege in the territories of another prince, than their maſter himſelf, ſhould he appear there: and, on the other hand, the ſovereign of the country would have leſs power in his own dominions, than a maſter of a family has in his own houſe.

In a word, the ſecurity of ambaſſadors ought to be underſtood in ſuch a manner, as to imply nothing contrary to the ſecurity of the powers to whom they are ſent, and who neither would, nor could receive them upon other terms. Now it is plain, that ambaſſadors will be leſs bold in undertaking any thing againſt the ſovereign, or members of a foreign ſtate, if they are apprehenſive, that in caſe of treaſon, or ſome other heinous crimes, the ſovereign of the country can call them to an account for it, than if they had nothing to fear but correction from their maſter.

6°. When the ambaſſador himſelf has committed no crime, it is not lawful to uſe him ill, or to kill him by the law of *retaliation*, or *repriſals*; for as ſoon as we have admitted him under that character, we have renounced the right we had to any ſuch revenge.

In

In vain would it be to object a great many instances of revenge taken after this manner, which are to be met with in history; for historians not only relate just and lawful actions, but also a great many things done contrary to justice in the heat of anger, by the influence of some irregular and tumultuous passion.

7°. What has been hitherto said of the rights of ambassadors, ought to be applied to their domestics, and all their retinue. If any of the ambassador's domestics has done an injury, we may desire his master to deliver him up. If he does not comply, he makes himself accessary to his crime, and in this case we have a right to proceed against him in the same manner, as if he had committed the crime himself.

An ambassador, however, cannot punish his own domestics; for as this is not conducive to the end of his employment, there is no reason to presume that his master has given it him.

8°. With respect to the effects of ambassadors, we can neither seize them for payment, nor for security, in the way of justice; for this would suppose, that he was subject to the jurisdiction of the sovereign at whose court he resides. But if he refuses to pay his debts, we ought, after giving him notice, to apply to his master, and if his master refuses to do us justice, we may seize the effects of the ambassador.

9°. Lastly, as for the right of azylums and protections, it is by no means a consequence of the nature and end of embassies. However, if it is once granted to the ambassadors of a certain power, nothing

nothing authoriſes us to revoke it, unleſs the good of the ſtate require it.

Neither ought we, without good reaſons, to refuſe ambaſſadors the other ſorts of rights and honours, which are eſtabliſhed by the common conſent of ſovereigns; for this would be a kind of an affront to them.

The End of the Fourth and laſt Part.

ERRATA.

Page 239. l. ult. for *authorize*, read *does not authorize*.
—— 291. l. 8. for *uſes*, read *uſages*.

www.ingramcontent.com/pod-product-compliance
Lightning Source LLC
Chambersburg PA
CBHW031544260326
41914CB00002B/267

* 9 7 8 1 5 8 4 7 7 3 8 0 1 *